Celebrating the Eucharist Music Accompaniment

for Keyboard, Guitar, Cantor, and Choir

FIRST SUNDAY OF ADVENT – CHRIST THE KING

YEAR C

DECEMBER 3, 2000 – DECEMBER 1, 2001

THE LITURGICAL PRESS
Collegeville, Minnesota

ISBN 0-8146-2718-8

RESPONSORIAL PSALMS

Jay F. Hunstiger

(unless otherwise noted)

FIRST SUNDAY OF ADVENT
December 3, 2000

To you, O Lord, I lift my soul.

Psalm 25:4-5, 8-9, 10, 14

1. Your ways, O LORD, make known to me; teach me your paths,
2. Good and upright is the LORD;
3. All the paths of the LORD are kindness and constancy

guide me in your truth and teach me,
thus he shows sin - - - - ners the way.
toward those who keep his covenant and his de - crees.

for you are God my sav - ior, and for you I wait all the day.
He guides the hum - - - ble to jus - tice, and teaches the hum - ble his way.
The friendship of the LORD is with those who fear him, and his covenant, for their in - struc-tion.

IMMACULATE CONCEPTION

December 8, 2000

Sing to the Lord a new song, for he has done marv-'lous deeds.

Psalm 98:1, 2-3, 3-4

1. Sing to the LORD a new song, for he has done won - drous deeds;
2. The LORD has made his sal - va - tion known: in the sight of the nations he has re - vealed his jus - tice.
3. All the ends of the earth have seen the salvation by our God.

his right hand has won victory for him, his ho - ly arm.
He has remembered his kindness and his faith - ful - ness toward the house of Israel.
Sing joyfully to the LORD, all you lands; break into song; sing praise.

SECOND SUNDAY OF ADVENT
December 10, 2000

The Lord has done great things for us; we are filled with joy, we are filled with joy.

Psalm 126:1-2, 2-3, 4-5, 6

1. When the LORD brought back the captives of Zi - on,
2. Then they said a - - - - - mong the na - tions,
3. Restore our fortunes, O LORD,
4. Although they go forth weep - ing,

we were like men dream - ing.
"The LORD has done great things for them."
like the torrents in the south - ern des - ert.
carrying the seed to be sown,

Then our mouth was filled with laugh - - - ter, and our tongue with re - joic - - ing,
The LORD has done great things for us; we are glad in - deed.
Those that sow in tears shall reap re - joic - ing.
they shall come back re - joic - - - ing, carrying their sheaves.

5

THIRD SUNDAY OF ADVENT
December 17, 2000

Isaiah 12:2-3, 4, 5-6

Cry out with joy and glad-ness: for a-mong you is the great and Ho-ly One of Is - ra - el.

1. God indeed is my sav - ior; I am confident and
2. Give thanks to the LORD, ac - claim
3. Sing praise to the LORD for his glori - ous a - chieve - ment; let this be known through -

un - a - fraid. My strength and my courage is the
his name; among the nations make
out all the earth. Shout with exultation, O city of Zion, for

LORD, and he has been my savior. With joy you will draw water at the fountain of sal -
known his deeds, pro - claim how ex - - - - - alt - ed
great in your midst is the Holy One of

va - tion.
is his name.
Is - ra - el!

FOURTH SUNDAY OF ADVENT

December 24, 2000

Psalm 80:2-3, 15-16, 18-19

Lord, make us turn to you, let us see your face and we shall be saved.

1. O shepherd of Israel, heark - en,
2. Once again, O LORD of hosts,
3. May your help be with the man of your right hand,

from your throne upon the cheru - bim, shine forth. Rouse your
look down from heaven, and see; take care of this
with the son of man whom you your - self made strong. Then we will no more with - draw from

pow - er, and come to save us.
vine, and protect what your right hand has plant - ed.
you; give us new life, and we will call upon your name.

The Vigil of Christmas

December 24, 2000

Psalm 89:4-5, 16-17, 27, 29

For-ev-er I will sing the good-ness of the Lord.

1. I have made a covenant with my chosen one, I have sworn to David my ser-vant:
2. Blessed the people who know the joyful shout; in the light of your countenance, O Lord, they walk.
3. He shall say of me, "You are my father, my God, the Rock, my sav-ior."

forever will I confirm your posteri - ty and establish your throne for all gen - er - ations.
At your name they rejoice all the day, and through your justice they are ex - alted.
Forever I will maintain my kindness toward him, and my covenant with him stands firm.

CHRISTMAS
December 25, 2000
MASS AT MIDNIGHT

To-day is born our Sav - ior, Christ the Lord. Lord.

Psalm 96:1-2, 2-3, 11-12, 13

1. Sing to the LORD a new song; sing to the LORD, all you lands.
2. Announce his salvation, day after day. Tell his glory a - mong the na - tions;
3. Let the heavens be glad and the earth re - joice; let the sea and what fills it re - sound;
4. They shall exult before the LORD, for he comes; for he comes to rule the earth.

Sing to the LORD; bless his name.
among all peo - ples, his won - drous deeds.
let the plains be joyful and all that is in them! Then shall all the trees of the forest ex - ult.
He shall rule the world with jus - tice and the peoples with his con - stan - cy.

CHRISTMAS

December 25, 2000

MASS AT DAWN

Psalm 97:1, 6, 11-12

1. The LORD is king; let the earth re - joice; let the many islands be glad.
2. Light dawns for the just; and gladness, for the upright of heart.

The heavens proclaim his jus - tice, and all peoples see his glo - ry.
Be glad in the LORD, you just, and give thanks to his ho - ly name.

CHRISTMAS
December 25, 2000
MASS DURING THE DAY

Organ introduction

Final ending

REFRAIN

All the ends of the earth have seen the sav - ing pow'r of God.

All the ends of the earth have seen the sav - ing pow'r of God.

Psalm 98:1, 2-3, 3-4, 5-6

VERSES

1.   Sing to the LORD a new song, for he has done
2. The LORD has made his sal - va - tion known: has shown his jus - tice
3.   All the ends of the earth have seen the sal - va - tion
4. Sing praise to the LORD with the harp, with the sound of

won - drous deeds;   His right hand has won vic - t'ry for him,
to the na - tions.   He has re - mem - bered his faith - ful - ness
by our God.   Sing joy - ful - ly to the LORD all you lands; break
mu - - - sic.   With trum-pets and the sound of the horn, sing

Organ interlude to antiphon

his   ho - ly arm.
toward the house of Is - rael.
in - to song; sing praise.
joy - ful - ly to God.

HOLY FAMILY
December 31, 2000
SUNDAY IN THE OCTAVE OF CHRISTMAS

Bless-ed are those who fear the Lord and walk in his ways.

Psalm 128:1-2, 3, 4-5

1. Blessed is everyone who fears the LORD, who walks in his ways!
2. Your wife shall be like a fruit - ful vine in the recesses of your home;
3. Behold, thus is the man blessed who fears the LORD.

For you shall eat the fruit of your hand - i - work;
your children like ol - ive plants
The LORD bless you from Zion:

blessed shall you be, and fav - ored.
a - - - - - - - round your ta - ble.
may you see the prosperity of Jerusalem all the days of your life.

SOLEMNITY OF MARY, MOTHER OF GOD

January 1, 2001

OCTAVE OF CHRISTMAS

May God bless us in his mer - cy.

Psalm 67:2-3, 5, 6, 8

1. May God have pity on us and bless us; may he let his face shine up - on us.
2. May the nations be glad and ex - ult because you rule the peoples in equity;
3. May the peoples praise you, O God; may all the peoples praise you!

So may your way be known upon earth; among all nations, your sal - va - tion.
the na - tions on the earth you guide.
May God bless us, and may all the ends of the earth fear him!

Epiphany

January 7, 2001

Lord, eve-ry na-tion on earth will a-dore you.

Psalm 72:1-2, 7-8, 10-11, 12-13

1. O God, with your judgment endow the king,
2. Justice shall flower in his days,
3. The kings of Tarshish and the Isles shall offer gifts;
4. For he shall rescue the poor man when he cries out,

and with your justice, the king's son;
and profound peace, till the moon be no more.
the kings of Arabia and Seba shall bring trib-ute.
and the afflicted when he has no one to help him.

he shall govern your peo-ple with jus-tice and your af-flict-ed ones with judg-ment.
May he rule from sea to sea, and from the Riv-er to the ends of the earth.
All kings shall pay him hom-age, all na-tions shall serve him.
He shall have pity for the low-ly and the poor; the lives of the poor he shall save.

BAPTISM OF THE LORD

January 8, 2001

Interlude from Verse to Refrain — REFRAIN — Gm — Dm — C — Gm — Dm

The Lord will bless his peo-ple with peace. The Lord will bless his peo-ple with

C — Gm — Dm — F — VERSES — Psalm 29:1-2, 3-4, 3, 9-10

peace, his peo - ple with peace.

1. Give to the LORD, you
2. The voice of the LORD is
3. The God of glo - ry

sons of God, give to the LORD glo - ry and praise, give to the
o - ver the wa - ters, the LORD, o - ver vast wa - ters, The voice of the
thun - ders, and in his tem - ple all say, "Glo - ry!" The LORD is en -

LORD the glo - ry due his name; a - dore the LORD in ho - ly at - tire.
LORD is might - y; the voice of the LORD is maj - es - tic.
throned a - bove the flood; the LORD is en - throned as king for - ever.

SECOND SUNDAY IN ORDINARY TIME

January 14, 2001

Proclaim his mar-ve-lous deeds to all the na-tions, to all the na-tions.

Psalm 96:1-2, 2-3, 7-8, 9-10

1. Sing to the LORD a new song; sing to the LORD, all you lands.
2. Announce his salvation, day af-ter day. Tell his glory a-mong the na-tions;
3. Give to the LORD, you families of na-tions, give to the LORD glo-ry and praise;
4. Worship the LORD in holy at-tire. Tremble before him, all the earth;

Sing to the LORD; bless his name.
Among all peo-ples, his won-drous deeds.
give to the LORD the glory due his name!
Say among the nations: The LORD is king. He governs the peoples with eq-ui-ty.

18

THIRD SUNDAY IN ORDINARY TIME
January 21, 2001

Your words, Lord, are spir-it and life, spir-it and life. Your

words, Lord, are spir-it and life, spir-it and life.

Psalm 19:8, 9, 10, 15

1. The law of the LORD is per - fect, refreshing the soul;
2. The precepts of the LORD are right, rejoicing the heart;
3. The fear of the LORD is pure, enduring for - ev - er;
4. Let the words of my mouth and the thought of my heart

The decree of the LORD is trustworthy, giving wisdom to the sim - ple.
The command of the LORD is clear, en - - light-en-ing the eye.
The ordinances of the LORD are true, all of them just.
find favor before you, O LORD, my rock and my re-deem - er.

FOURTH SUNDAY IN ORDINARY TIME

January 28, 2001

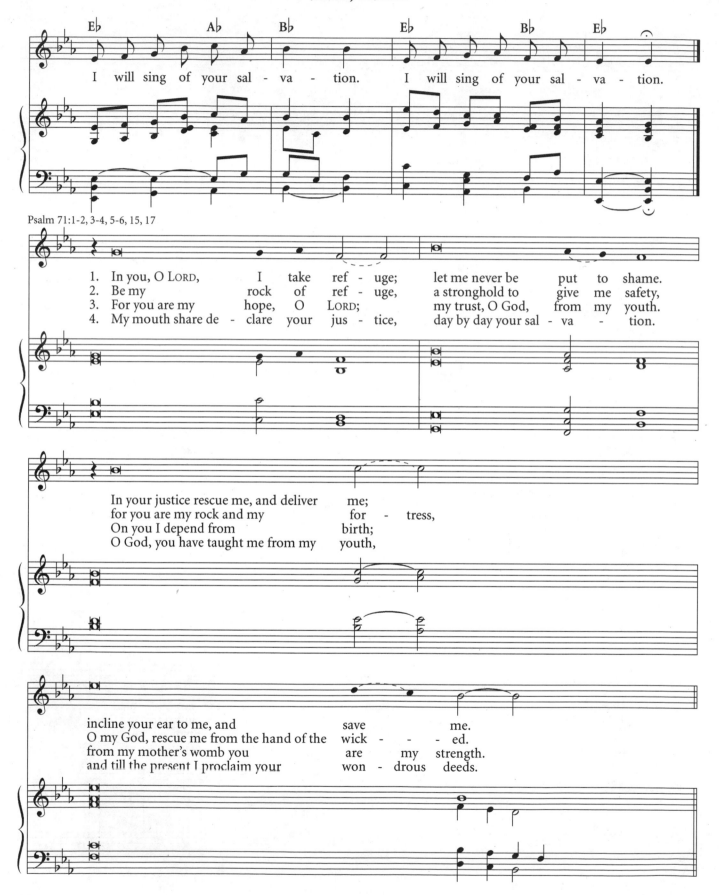

I will sing of your sal - va - tion. I will sing of your sal - va - tion.

Psalm 71:1-2, 3-4, 5-6, 15, 17

1. In you, O LORD, I take ref - uge; let me never be put to shame.
2. Be my rock of ref - uge, a stronghold to give me safety,
3. For you are my hope, O LORD; my trust, O God, from my youth.
4. My mouth share de - clare your jus - tice, day by day your sal - va - tion.

In your justice rescue me, and deliver me;
for you are my rock and my for - tress,
On you I depend from birth;
O God, you have taught me from my youth,

incline your ear to me, and save me.
O my God, rescue me from the hand of the wick - - - ed.
from my mother's womb you are my strength.
and till the present I proclaim your won - drous deeds.

PRESENTATION OF THE LORD

February 2, 2001

Who is this king of glo - ry? It is the Lord!

Psalm 24:7, 8, 9, 10

1. Lift up, O gates, your lin - tels; reach up, you an - cient portals,
2. Who is the king of glo - ry? The LORD, strong and mighty,
3. Lift up, O gates, your lin - tels; reach up, you an - cient portals,
4. Who is this king of glo - ry?

that the king of glory may come in!
the LORD, mighty in bat - tle.
that the king of glory may come in!
The LORD of hosts; he is the king of glo - ry.

21

FIFTH SUNDAY IN ORDINARY TIME
February 4, 2001

In the sight of the an-gels I will sing your prais-es, Lord.

In the sight of the an-gels I will sing your prais-es, Lord.

Psalm 138:1-2, 2-3, 4-5, 7-8

1. I will give thanks to you, O LORD, with all my heart,
2. Because of your kindness and your truth;
3. All the kings of the earth shall give thanks to you, O LORD,
4. Your right hand saves me.

you have heard the words of my mouth;
for you have made great above all things your name and your promise.
when they hear the words of your mouth;
The LORD will complete what he has done for me;

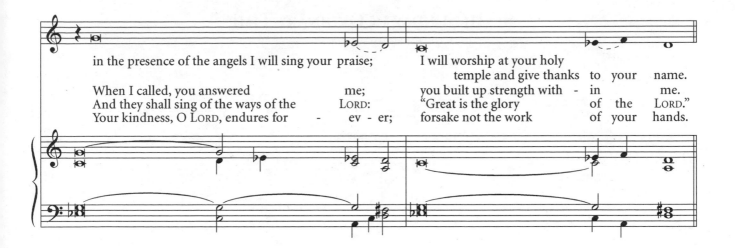

in the presence of the angels I will sing your praise;   I will worship at your holy
                                                                temple and give thanks to   your   name.

When I called, you answered   me;   you built up strength with - in   me.
And they shall sing of the ways of the   LORD: "Great is the glory   of   the   LORD."
Your kindness, O LORD, endures for   -   ev - er;   forsake not the work   of your hands.

SIXTH SUNDAY IN ORDINARY TIME
February 11, 2001

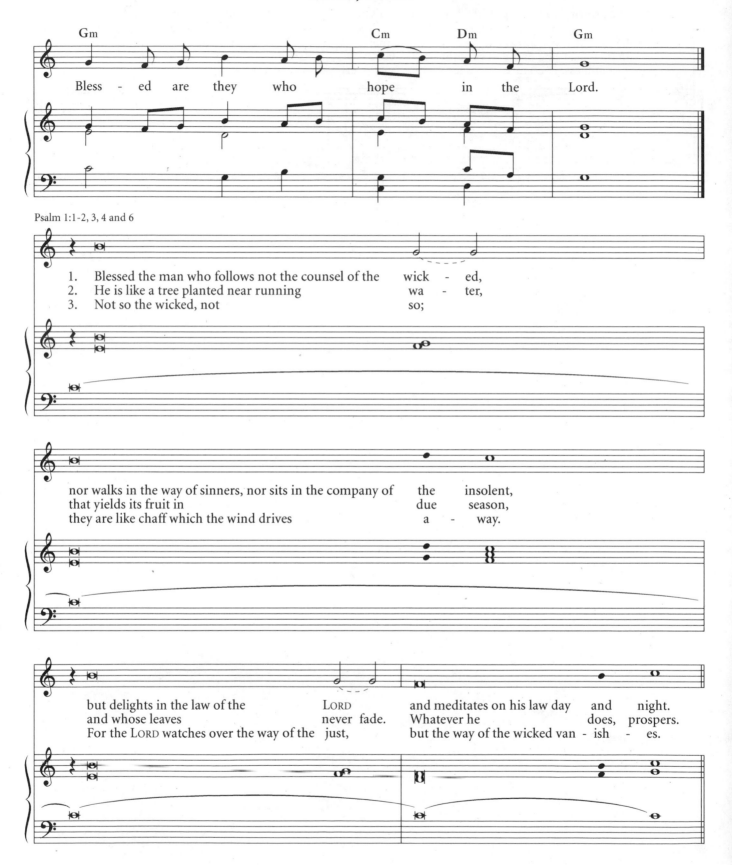

Bless - ed are they who hope in the Lord.

Psalm 1:1-2, 3, 4 and 6

1. Blessed the man who follows not the counsel of the wick - ed,
2. He is like a tree planted near running wa - ter,
3. Not so the wicked, not so;

nor walks in the way of sinners, nor sits in the company of the insolent,
that yields its fruit in due season,
they are like chaff which the wind drives a - way.

but delights in the law of the LORD and meditates on his law day and night.
and whose leaves never fade. Whatever he does, prospers.
For the LORD watches over the way of the just, but the way of the wicked van - ish - es.

SEVENTH SUNDAY IN ORDINARY TIME

February 18, 2001

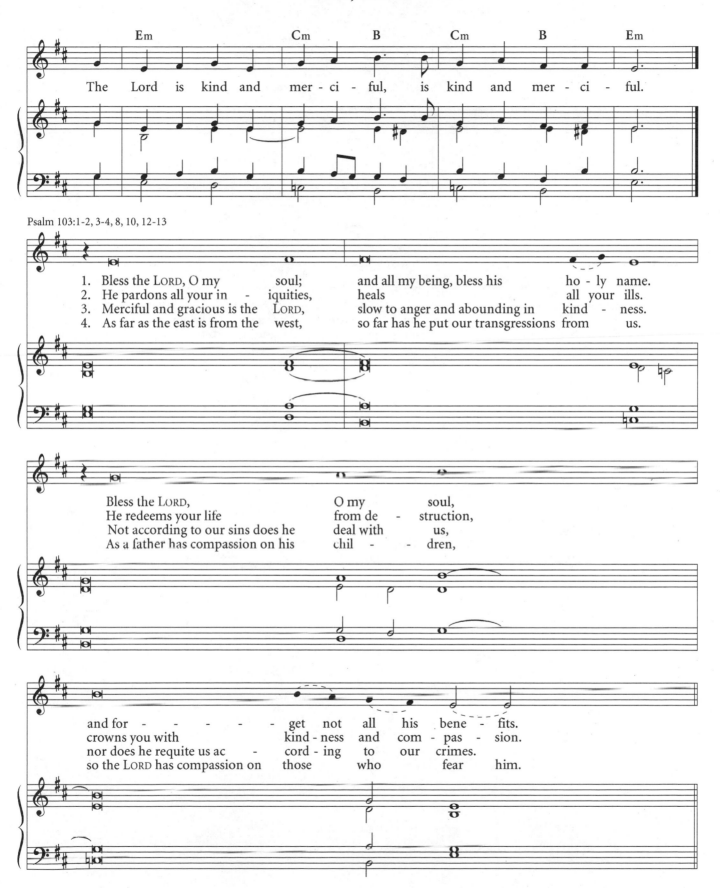

The Lord is kind and mer-ci-ful, is kind and mer-ci-ful.

Psalm 103:1-2, 3-4, 8, 10, 12-13

1. Bless the LORD, O my soul; and all my being, bless his ho - ly name.
2. He pardons all your in - iquities, heals all your ills.
3. Merciful and gracious is the LORD, slow to anger and abounding in kind - ness.
4. As far as the east is from the west, so far has he put our transgressions from us.

Bless the LORD, O my soul,
He redeems your life from de - struction,
Not according to our sins does he deal with us,
As a father has compassion on his chil - dren,

and for - get not all his bene - fits.
crowns you with kind - ness and com - pas - sion.
nor does he requite us ac - cord - ing to our crimes.
so the LORD has compassion on those who fear him.

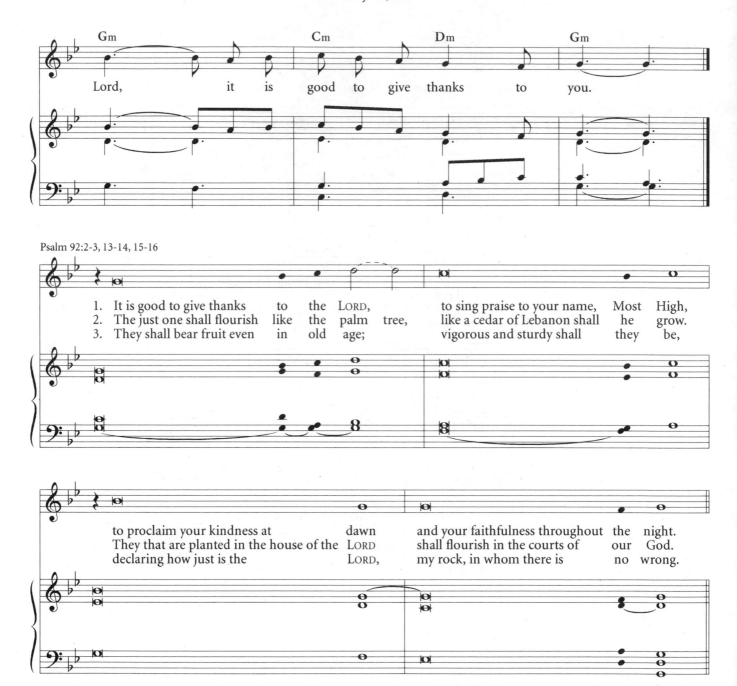

Psalm 92:2-3, 13-14, 15-16

1. It is good to give thanks to the LORD, to sing praise to your name, Most High,
2. The just one shall flourish like the palm tree, like a cedar of Lebanon shall he grow.
3. They shall bear fruit even in old age; vigorous and sturdy shall they be,

to proclaim your kindness at dawn and your faithfulness throughout the night.
They that are planted in the house of the LORD shall flourish in the courts of our God.
declaring how just is the LORD, my rock, in whom there is no wrong.

ASH WEDNESDAY

February 28, 2001

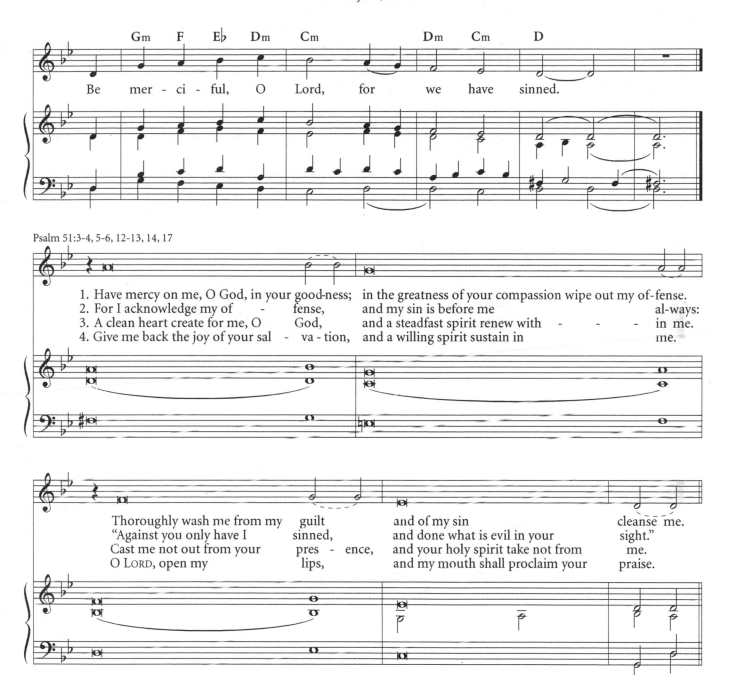

Be mer-ci-ful, O Lord, for we have sinned.

Psalm 51:3-4, 5-6, 12-13, 14, 17

1. Have mercy on me, O God, in your good-ness; in the greatness of your compassion wipe out my of-fense.
2. For I acknowledge my of - fense, and my sin is before me al-ways:
3. A clean heart create for me, O God, and a steadfast spirit renew with - - - in me.
4. Give me back the joy of your sal - va - tion, and a willing spirit sustain in me.

Thoroughly wash me from my guilt, and of my sin cleanse me.
"Against you only have I sinned, and done what is evil in your sight."
Cast me not out from your pres - ence, and your holy spirit take not from me.
O LORD, open my lips, and my mouth shall proclaim your praise.

First Sunday of Lent

March 4, 2001

Be with me, Lord, when I am in trou-ble. Be with me, Lord, when
I am in trou-ble. Be with me Lord. Be with me Lord.

Psalm 91:1-2, 10-11, 12-13, 14-15

1. You who dwell in the shelter of the Most High,
2. No evil shall be - - - fall you,
3. Upon their hands they shall bear you up,
4. Because he clings to me, I will de - liv - er him;

who abide in the shadow of the Al - might - y,
nor shall affliction come near your tent,
lest you dash your foot against a stone.
I will set him on high because he acknowledges my name.

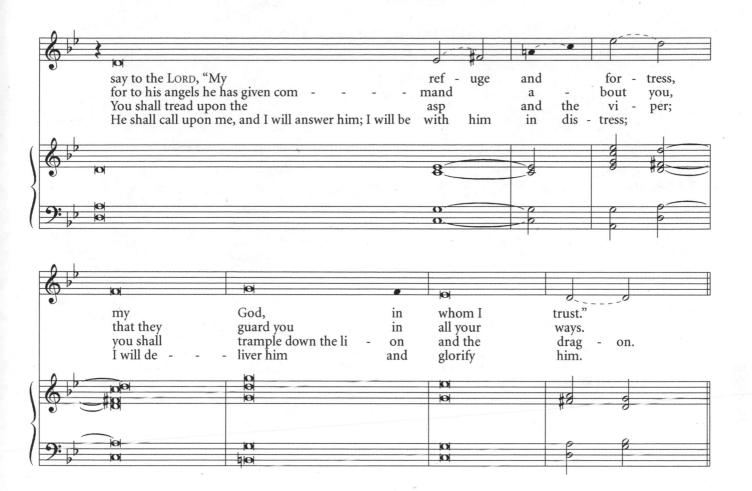

say to the Lord, "My ref - uge and for - tress,
for to his angels he has given com - - - - mand a - bout you,
You shall tread upon the asp and the vi - per;
He shall call upon me, and I will answer him; I will be with him in dis - tress;

my God, in whom I trust."
that they guard you in all your ways.
you shall trample down the li - on and the drag - on.
I will de - - - liver him and glorify him.

SECOND SUNDAY OF LENT

March 11, 2001

The Lord is my light and my sal-va-tion, the Lord is my light and my sal-va-tion.

Psalm 27:1, 7-8, 9, 13-14

1. The LORD is my light and my sal - - va - tion; whom should I fear?
2. Hear, O LORD, the sound of my call; have pity on me, and an - swer me.
3. Your presence, O LORD, I seek. Hide not your face from me;
4. I believe that I shall see the bounty of the LORD in the land of the liv - ing.

The LORD is my life's refuge; of whom should I be a - fraid?
Of you my heart speaks; you my glance seeks.
Do not in anger repel your servant. You are my helper cast me not off.
Wait for the LORD with courage; be stout hearted and wait for the LORD.

THIRD SUNDAY OF LENT

March 18, 2001

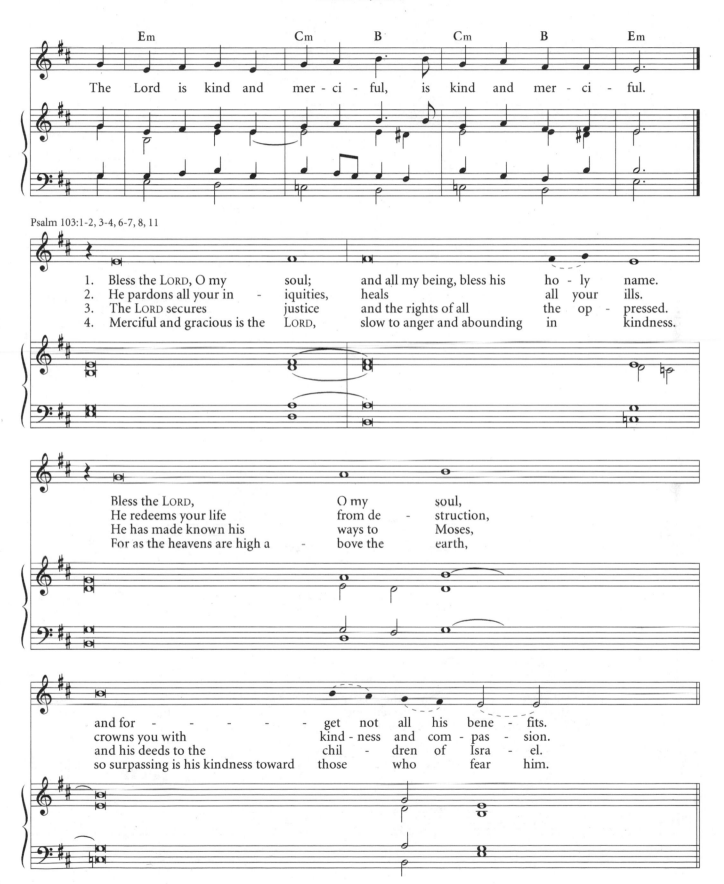

The Lord is kind and mer-ci-ful, is kind and mer-ci-ful.

Psalm 103:1-2, 3-4, 6-7, 8, 11

1. Bless the LORD, O my soul; and all my being, bless his ho - ly name.
2. He pardons all your in - iquities, heals all your ills.
3. The LORD secures justice and the rights of all the op - pressed.
4. Merciful and gracious is the LORD, slow to anger and abounding in kindness.

Bless the LORD, O my soul,
He redeems your life from de - struction,
He has made known his ways to Moses,
For as the heavens are high a - bove the earth,

and for - get not all his bene - fits.
crowns you with kind - ness and com - pas - sion.
and his deeds to the chil - dren of Isra - el.
so surpassing is his kindness toward those who fear him.

31

FOURTH SUNDAY OF LENT

March 25, 2001

Taste and see the good-ness of the Lord. Taste and see the good-ness of the Lord. Lord.

Psalm 34:2-3, 4-5, 6-7

1. I will bless the LORD at all times; his praise shall be ev-er in my mouth.
2. Glorify the LORD with me, let us together ex-tol his name.
3. Look to him that you may be radiant with joy, and your faces may not blush with shame.

Let my soul glory in the LORD; the lowly will hear me and be glad.
I sought the LORD, and he an-swered me and delivered me from all my fears.
When the poor one called out, the LORD heard, and from all his distress he saved him.

Fifth Sunday of Lent

April 1, 2001

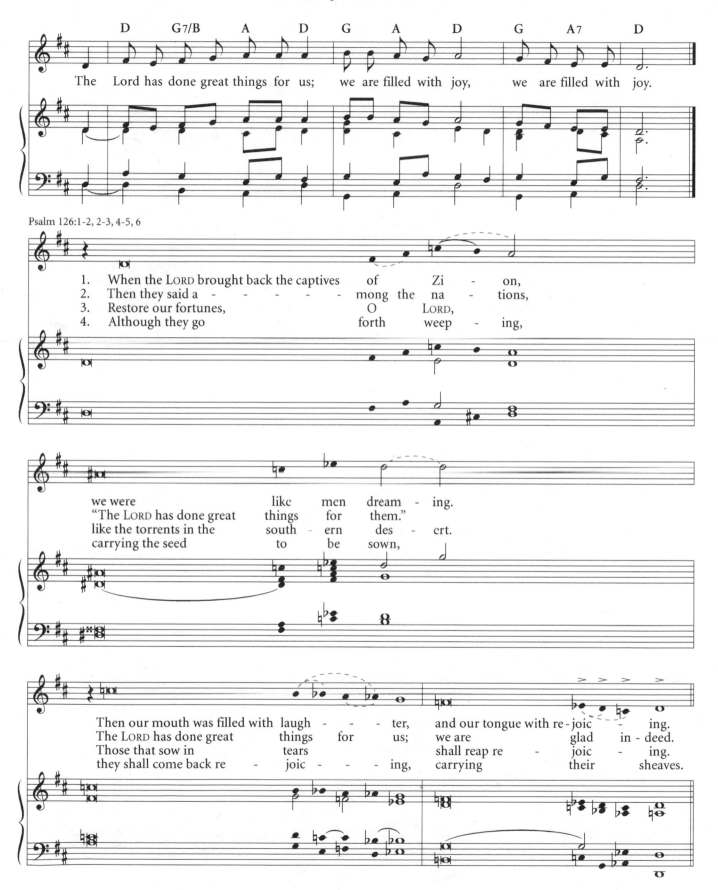

The Lord has done great things for us; we are filled with joy, we are filled with joy.

Psalm 126:1-2, 2-3, 4-5, 6

1. When the LORD brought back the captives of Zi - on,
2. Then they said a - - - - - - mong the na - tions,
3. Restore our fortunes, O LORD,
4. Although they go forth weep - ing,

we were like men dream - ing.
"The LORD has done great things for them."
like the torrents in the south - ern des - ert.
carrying the seed to be sown,

Then our mouth was filled with laugh - - - ter, and our tongue with re - joic - - ing.
The LORD has done great things for us; we are glad in - deed.
Those that sow in tears shall reap re - joic - ing.
they shall come back re - joic - - ing, carrying their sheaves.

33

PALM SUNDAY OF THE LORD'S PASSION

April 8, 2001

Psalm 22:8-9, 17-18, 19-20, 23-24

1. All who see me scoff at me; they mock me with parted lips, they
2. Indeed, many dogs surround me, a pack of evil doers closes in up-
3. They divide my garments among them, and for my vesture they cast
4. I will proclaim your name to my brethren; in the midst of the assembly I will

wag their heads: "He relied on the LORD; let him de-
on me; They have pierced my hands and my
lots. But you, O LORD, be not
praise you: "You who fear the LORD, praise him; all you descendants of Jacob,

liver him, let him rescue him, if he loves him."
feet; I can count all my bones.
far from me; O my help, hasten to aid me.
give glory to him; revere him, all you descendants of Israel!"

PALM SUNDAY OF THE LORD'S PASSION

April 8, 2001

My God, my God, why have you a-ban-doned me?

Psalm 22:8-9, 17-18, 19-20, 23-24

1. All who see me de-ride me, They curl their lips, they toss their heads. "He
2. Ma-ny dogs have sur-round-ed me, a wick-ed band be-sets me. They tear
3. They di-vide my clothes a-mong them. They cast lots for my robe._____ O
4. I will tell your name to my peo-ple and praise you where they ga-ther. All

trus-ted in the Lord, let God save him, and come to free him if this is God's friend."
holes in my hands and feet and lay me in the dust of death. I can count all my bones.
Lord, do not leave me a-lone,_____ — my strength, make haste to help me.
you who fear the Lord sing your prais-es, all tribes of Ja-cob,_____ give your glo-ry.

Music: Christopher Willcock ©

HOLY THURSDAY
April 12, 2001
EVENING MASS OF THE LORD'S SUPPER

Our bless - ing - cup   is   a com-mun-ion with the   Blood   of   Christ.

Psalm 116:12-13, 15-16, 17-18

1. How shall I make a return   to   the   LORD   for all the good he has   done   for   me?
2. Precious in the eyes   of   the   LORD   is the death of his   faith - ful   ones.
3. To you I will offer sacrifice of thanks - giving,   and I will call upon the name of   the   LORD.

The cup of salvation I will   take   up,   and I will call upon the name of   the   LORD.
I am your servant, the son of your hand - maid;   you have   loosed my   bonds.
My vows to the LORD   I   will   pay   in the presence of all his   peo - ple.

GOOD FRIDAY

April 13, 2001

CELEBRATION OF THE LORD'S PASSION

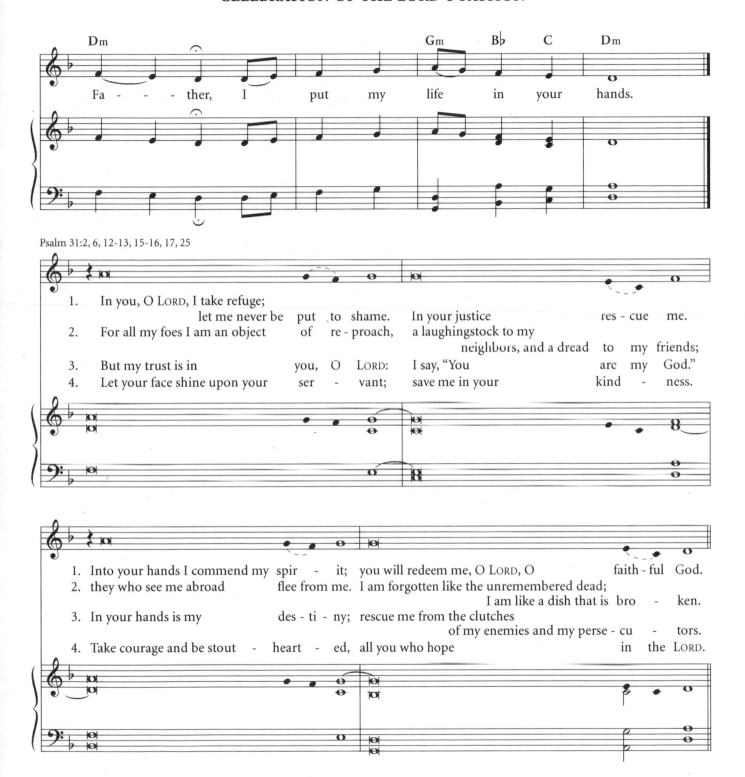

Fa - - - ther, I put my life in your hands.

Psalm 31:2, 6, 12-13, 15-16, 17, 25

1. In you, O LORD, I take refuge;
   let me never be put to shame. In your justice res - cue me.
2. For all my foes I am an object of re - proach, a laughingstock to my
   neighbors, and a dread to my friends;
3. But my trust is in you, O LORD: I say, "You are my God."
4. Let your face shine upon your ser - vant; save me in your kind - ness.

1. Into your hands I commend my spir - it; you will redeem me, O LORD, O faith - ful God.
2. they who see me abroad flee from me. I am forgotten like the unremembered dead;
   I am like a dish that is bro - ken.
3. In your hands is my des - ti - ny; rescue me from the clutches
   of my enemies and my perse - cu - tors.
4. Take courage and be stout - heart - ed, all you who hope in the LORD.

The Easter Vigil
April 14, 2001

A   After First Reading (Genesis 1:1–2:2)

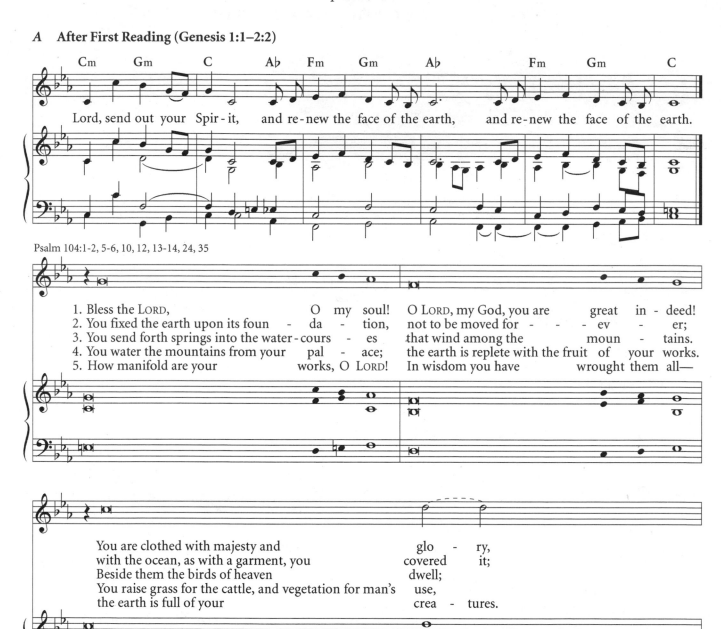

Cm   Gm   C   A♭   Fm   Gm   A♭   Fm   Gm   C

Lord, send out your Spir - it,   and re-new the face of the earth,   and re-new the face of the earth.

Psalm 104:1-2, 5-6, 10, 12, 13-14, 24, 35

1. Bless the LORD,   O my soul! O LORD, my God, you are   great in - deed!
2. You fixed the earth upon its foun - da - tion,   not to be moved for - - ev - er;
3. You send forth springs into the water - cours - es   that wind among the   moun - tains.
4. You water the mountains from your   pal - ace;   the earth is replete with the fruit of   your works.
5. How manifold are your   works, O LORD! In wisdom you have   wrought them all—

You are clothed with majesty and   glo - ry,
with the ocean, as with a garment, you   covered   it;
Beside them the birds of heaven   dwell;
You raise grass for the cattle, and vegetation for man's   use,
the earth is full of your   crea - tures.

38

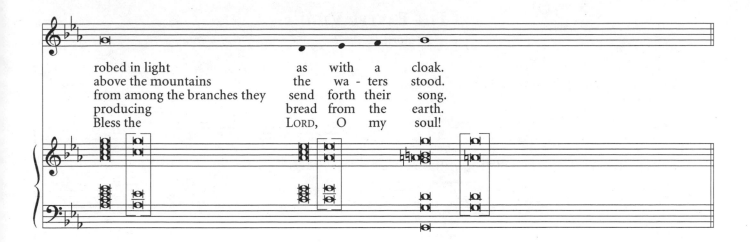

robed in light   as   with   a   cloak.
above the mountains   the   wa - ters   stood.
from among the branches they   send   forth   their   song.
producing   bread   from   the   earth.
Bless the   LORD,   O   my   soul!

THE EASTER VIGIL
April 14, 2001

B After First Reading (Genesis 1:1–2:2)

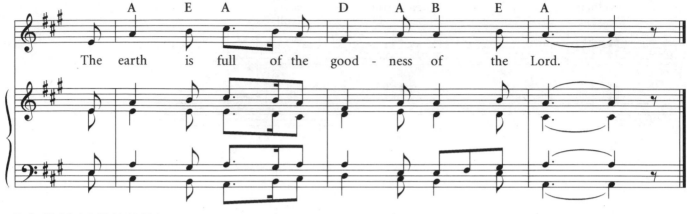

The earth is full of the good-ness of the Lord.

Psalm 33:4-5, 6-7, 12-13, 20-22

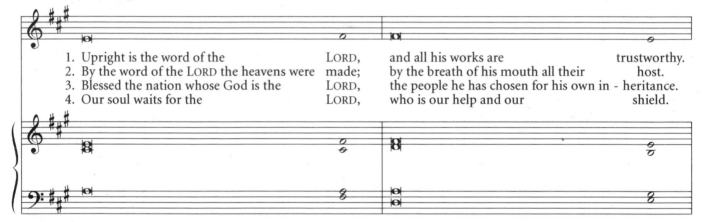

1. Upright is the word of the LORD, and all his works are trustworthy.
2. By the word of the LORD the heavens were made; by the breath of his mouth all their host.
3. Blessed the nation whose God is the LORD, the people he has chosen for his own in - heritance.
4. Our soul waits for the LORD, who is our help and our shield.

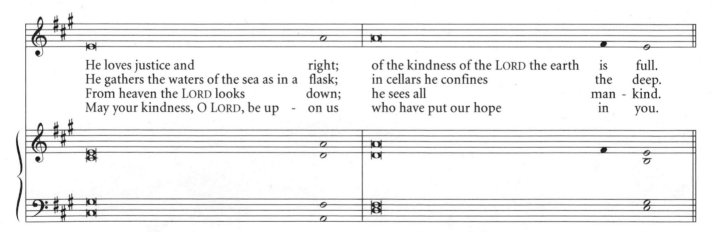

He loves justice and right; of the kindness of the LORD the earth is full.
He gathers the waters of the sea as in a flask; in cellars he confines the deep.
From heaven the LORD looks down; he sees all man - kind.
May your kindness, O LORD, be up - on us who have put our hope in you.

The Easter Vigil
April 14, 2001

After Second Reading (Genesis 22:1-18)

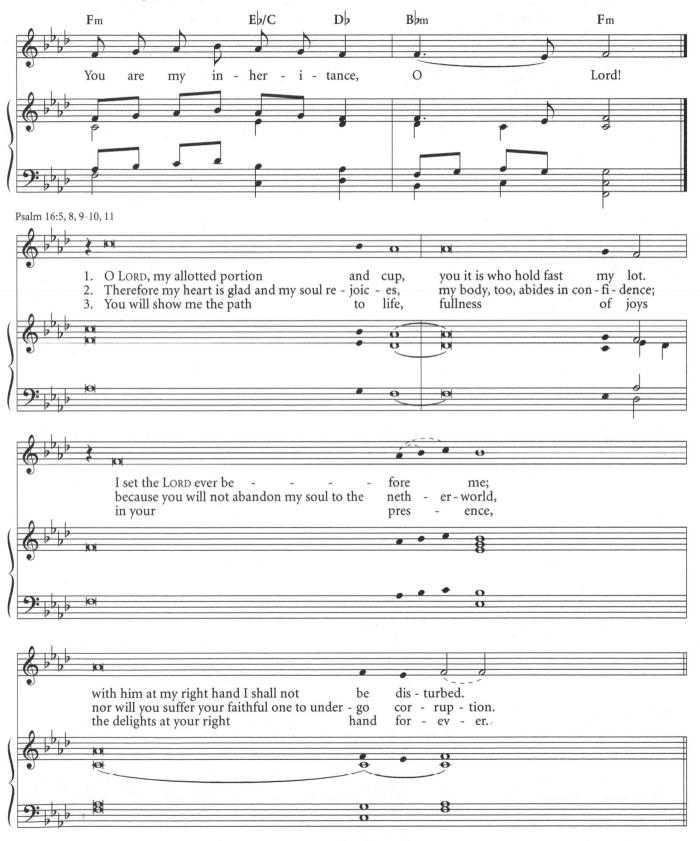

Psalm 16:5, 8, 9-10, 11

1. O LORD, my allotted portion and cup, you it is who hold fast my lot.
2. Therefore my heart is glad and my soul re - joic - es, my body, too, abides in con - fi - dence;
3. You will show me the path to life, fullness of joys

I set the LORD ever be - fore me;
because you will not abandon my soul to the neth - er - world,
in your pres - ence,

with him at my right hand I shall not be dis - turbed.
nor will you suffer your faithful one to under - go cor - rup - tion.
the delights at your right hand for - ev - er.

THE EASTER VIGIL

April 14, 2001

After Third Reading (Exodus 14:15–15:1)

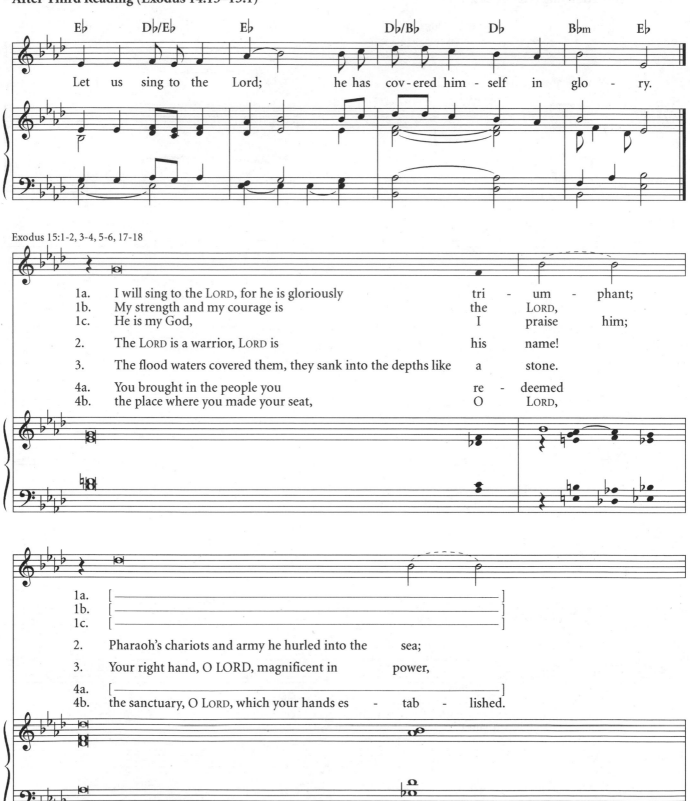

Let us sing to the Lord; he has cov-ered him-self in glo-ry.

Exodus 15:1-2, 3-4, 5-6, 17-18

1a. I will sing to the LORD, for he is gloriously tri - um - phant;
1b. My strength and my courage is the LORD,
1c. He is my God, I praise him;

2. The LORD is a warrior, LORD is his name!

3. The flood waters covered them, they sank into the depths like a stone.

4a. You brought in the people you re - deemed
4b. the place where you made your seat, O LORD,

1a. [_____]
1b. [_____]
1c. [_____]

2. Pharaoh's chariots and army he hurled into the sea;

3. Your right hand, O LORD, magnificent in power,

4a. [_____]
4b. the sanctuary, O LORD, which your hands es - tab - lished.

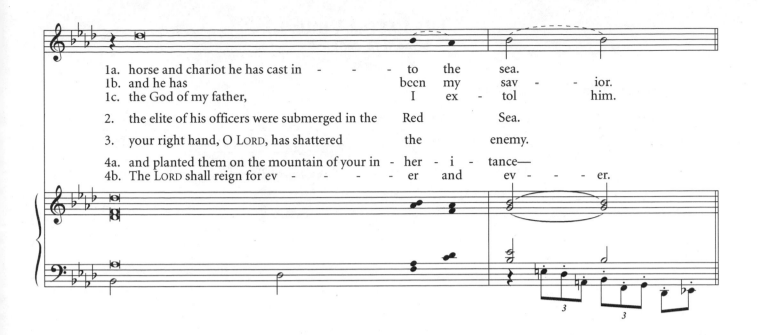

1a. horse and chariot he has cast in - - - to the sea.
1b. and he has been my sav - ior.
1c. the God of my father, I ex - tol him.

2. the elite of his officers were submerged in the Red Sea.

3. your right hand, O Lord, has shattered the enemy.

4a. and planted them on the mountain of your in - her - i - tance—
4b. The Lord shall reign for ev - - - - er and ev - - er.

THE EASTER VIGIL
April 14, 2001

After Fourth Reading (Isaiah 54:5-14)

I will praise you, Lord, for you have res - cued me.

Psalm 30:2, 4, 5-6, 11, 12, 13

1. I will extol you, O LORD, for you   drew me clear   and did not let my enemies rejoice   o - ver me.
2. Sing praise to the LORD, you his   faith - ful ones,   and give thanks to his   ho - ly name.
3. Hear, O LORD, and have pity   on   me;   O LORD, be my   help - er.

O LORD, you brought me up from the   neth - er - world;
For his anger lasts   but a mo - ment;
You changed my mourning   in - to danc - ing;

you preserved me from among those going down in - to the pit.
At nightfall, weeping enters in, but with the dawn re - joic - ing.
O LORD, my God, forever will I   give you thanks.

THE EASTER VIGIL

April 14, 2001

After Fifth Reading (Isaiah 55:1-11)

You will draw wa-ter joy-ful-ly from the springs of sal-va-tion.

Isaiah 12:2-3, 4, 5-6

1. God indeed is my savior; I am confident and un - a - fraid.
2. Give thanks to the LORD, ac - - - - claim his name;
3. Sing praise to the LORD for his glor - - - ious a - chievement;

My strength and my courage is the LORD, and he has been my savior.
among the nations make known his deeds, proclaim how ex - alted
let this be known throughout all the earth. Shout with exultation, O city of Zion,

With joy you will draw water at the fountain of sal - vation.
is his name.
for great in your midst is the Holy One of Is - ra - el!

THE EASTER VIGIL
April 14, 2001

After Sixth Reading (Baruch 3:9-15, 32—4:4)

Lord, you have the words of ev-er-last-ing life.

Psalm 19:8, 9, 10, 11

1. The law of the LORD is per - fect, refreshing the soul;
2. The precepts of the LORD are right, rejoicing the heart;
3. The fear of the LORD is pure, enduring for - ev - er;
4. They are more precious than gold, than a heap of pur - est gold;

the decree of the LORD is trustworthy, giving wisdom to the sim - ple.
the command of the LORD is clear, en - light-en - ing the eye.
the ordinances of the LORD are true, all of them just.
sweeter also than syrup or honey from the comb.

THE EASTER VIGIL
April 14, 2001

A **After Seventh Reading (Ezekiel 36:16-17, 18-28)**

Like a deer that longs for run-ning streams, my soul longs for you, my God.

Psalm 42:3, 5; 43:3, 4

1. Athirst is my soul for God, the liv - ing God.
2. I went with the throng and led them in procession to the house of God,
3. Send forth your light and your fi - delity; they shall lead me on
4. Then will I go in to the al - tar of God, the God of my glad - - - ness and joy;

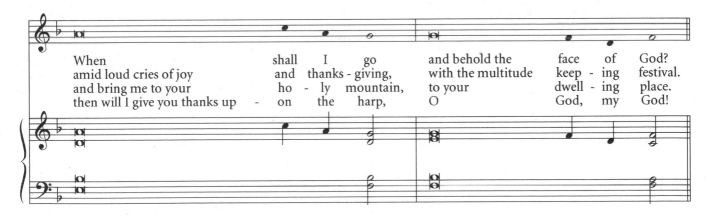

When shall I go and behold the face of God?
amid loud cries of joy and thanks - giving, with the multitude keep - ing festival.
and bring me to your ho - ly mountain, to your dwell - ing place.
then will I give you thanks up - on the harp, O God, my God!

Music: © The Order of St. Benedict, Inc.

47

B **After Seventh Reading (Ezekiel 36:16-17, 18-28)**

You will draw wa - ter joy - ful - ly from the springs of sal - va - tion.

Isaiah 12:2-3, 4, 5-6

1. God indeed is my savior; I am confident and un - a - fraid.
2. Give thanks to the LORD, ac - - - - claim his name;
3. Sing praise to the LORD for his glor - - - ious a - chievement;

My strength and my courage is the LORD, and he has been my savior.
among the nations make known his deeds, proclaim how ex - alted
let this be known throughout all the earth. Shout with exultation, O city of Zion,

With joy you will draw water at the fountain of sal - vation.
is his name.
for great in your midst is the Holy One of Is - ra - el!

THE EASTER VIGIL

April 14, 2001

C   After Seventh Reading (Ezekiel 36:16-17, 18-28)

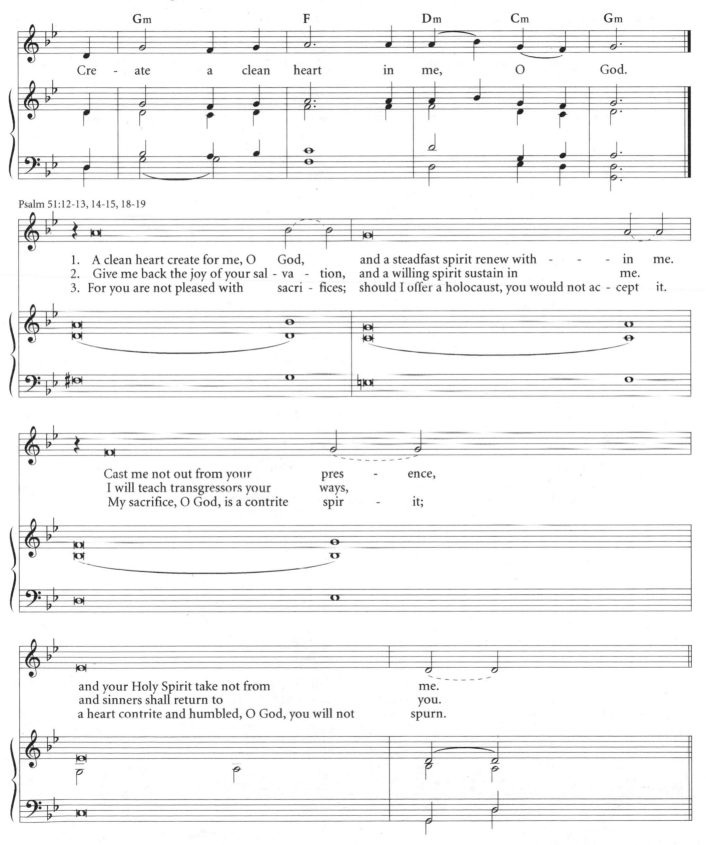

Create a clean heart in me, O God.

Psalm 51:12-13, 14-15, 18-19

1. A clean heart create for me, O God, and a steadfast spirit renew with - - - in me.
2. Give me back the joy of your sal - va - tion, and a willing spirit sustain in me.
3. For you are not pleased with sacri - fices; should I offer a holocaust, you would not ac - cept it.

Cast me not out from your pres - ence,
I will teach transgressors your ways,
My sacrifice, O God, is a contrite spir - it;

and your Holy Spirit take not from me.
and sinners shall return to you.
a heart contrite and humbled, O God, you will not spurn.

49

THE EASTER VIGIL
April 14, 2001

After Epistle (Romans 6:3-11)

Al - le - lu - ia, al - le - lu - ia, al - le - lu - ia, al - le - lu - ia. Al - le - lu - ia, al - le - lu - ia, al - le - lu - ia, al - le - lu - ia.

Psalm 118:1-2, 16-17, 22-23

1. Give thanks to the LORD, for he is good, for his mercy en - dures for - ev - er.
2. The right hand of the LORD has struck with pow - er; the right hand of the LORD is ex - alt - ed.
3. The stone which the builders re - ject - ed has become the cor - ner - stone.

Let the house of Isra - el say, "His mercy en - dures for - ev - er."
I shall not die, but live, and declare the works of the LORD.
By the LORD has this been done; It is wonderful in our eyes.

THE EASTER VIGIL

April 14, 2001

After Epistle (Romans 6:3-11)

Psalm 118:1-2, 16-17, 22-23

1. Give thanks to the Lord for he is good, for his mercy endures forever.
2. The right hand of the Lord has struck with power: the right hand of the Lord is exalted.
3. The stone which the builders rejected has become the cornerstone.

Let the house of Israel say, "His mercy endures forever."
I shall not die, but live and declare the works of the Lord.
By the Lord has this been done, it is wonderful in our eyes.

© John Lee

Easter Sunday

April 15, 2001

This is the day the Lord has made; let us re-joice, and be glad. This is the day the Lord has made; let us re-joice, and be glad.

Psalm 118:1-2, 16-17, 22-23

1. Give thanks to the Lord, for he is good, for his mercy en-dures for
2. The right hand of the Lord has struck with power; the right hand of the Lord is ex-
3. The stone which the builders re - ject - ed has be - - - come the cor - ner

ev - er. Let the house of Isra - el say: "His mercy en - dures for ev - er."
alted. I shall not die, but live, and de - clare the works of the Lord.
stone. By the Lord has this been done; it is wonderful in our eyes.

EASTER SUNDAY
April 15, 2001

Psalm 118:1-2, 16-17, 22-23

This is the day the Lord has made; let us re-joice and be glad!

1. Give thanks to the Lord, for he is good, his mer-cy en-dures for-ev-er, Let the
2. With pow-er the hand of the Lord has struck; the right hand of the Lord is ex-alt-ed.
3. The stone which the build-ers re-ject-ed has be-come the cor-ner-stone. By the

house of Is-ra-el say, "His mer-cy en-dures for-ev-er."
I shall not die, but live, live and de-clare the works of the Lord.
Lord has this been done; it is won-der-ful in our eyes.

Music: Jerome Coller, O.S.B., © The Order of St. Benedict, Inc.

53

Second Sunday of Easter

April 22, 2001

Psalm 118:2-4, 13-15, 22-24

Give thanks to the Lord for he is good, his love is ev-er-last - ing.

1. Let the house of Is - rael say, "His mercy en-dures for-
2. I was hard pressed and was fall - ing, but the LORD helped
3. The stone which the builders re - ject - ed has be - come the cor-ner-

ev - er." Let the house of Aar - on say, "His mercy en-dures for-
me. My strength and my courage is the LORD, and he has been my
stone. By the LORD has this been done; it is wonderful in our

ev - er." Let those who fear the LORD say, "His mercy en-dures for-ev-er."
sav - ior. The joyful shout of victory in the tents of the just.
eyes. This is the day the LORD has made; let us be glad and re-joice in it.

THIRD SUNDAY OF EASTER

April 29, 2001

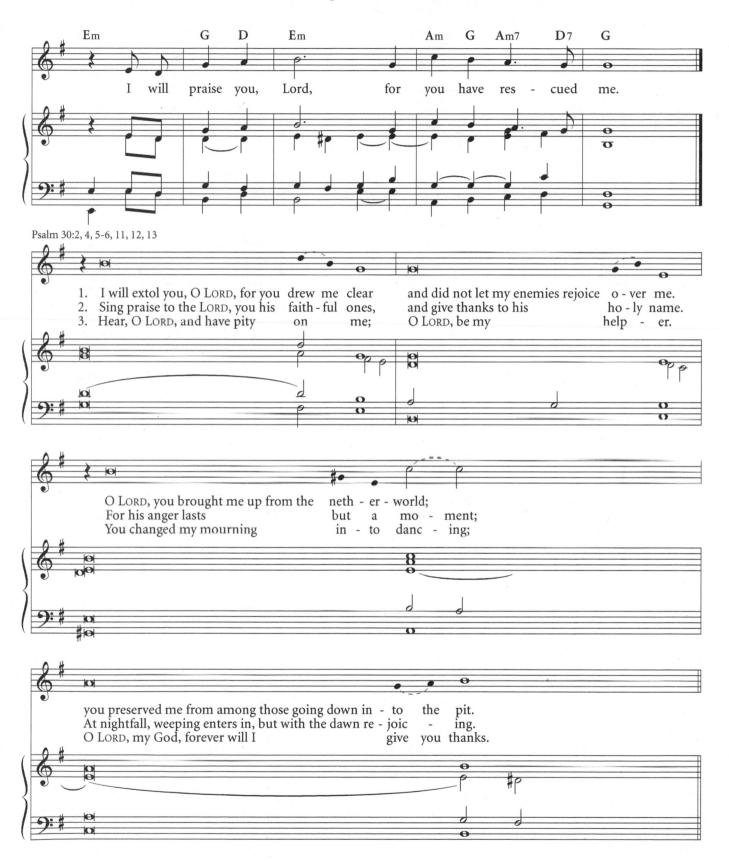

I will praise you, Lord, for you have res - cued me.

Psalm 30:2, 4, 5-6, 11, 12, 13

1. I will extol you, O LORD, for you drew me clear and did not let my enemies rejoice o - ver me.
2. Sing praise to the LORD, you his faith - ful ones, and give thanks to his ho - ly name.
3. Hear, O LORD, and have pity on me; O LORD, be my help - er.

O LORD, you brought me up from the neth - er - world;
For his anger lasts but a mo - ment;
You changed my mourning in - to danc - ing;

you preserved me from among those going down in - to the pit.
At nightfall, weeping enters in, but with the dawn re - joic - ing.
O LORD, my God, forever will I give you thanks.

FOURTH SUNDAY OF EASTER
May 6, 2001

Psalm 100:1-2, 3, 5

1. Sing joyfully to the LORD, all you lands; serve the LORD with gladness;
2. Know that the LORD is God; he made us, his we are;
3. The LORD is good: his kindness endures for - ever;

come before him with joy - ful song.
his people, the flock he tends.
and his faithfulness, to all gen - er - - - ations.

Fifth Sunday of Easter
May 13, 2001

I will praise your name for- ev - er, my king and my God.

Psalm 145:8-9, 10-11, 12-13

1. The LORD is gracious and mer - - - - ci - ful,
2. Let all your works give you thanks, O LORD,
3. Let them make known your might to the children of Adam,

slow to anger and of great kindness. The LORD is good to all
and let your faithful ones bless you. Let them discourse of the glory of your kingdom
and the glorious splendor of your kingdom. Your kingdom is a kingdom for all ages,

and compassionate toward all his works.
and speak of your might.
and your dominion endures through all gen - er - ations.

SIXTH SUNDAY OF EASTER

May 20, 2001

Psalm 67:2-3, 5, 6, 8

1. May God have pity on us and bless us; may he let his face shine up - on us.
2. May the nations be glad and ex - ult because you rule the peoples in equity;
3. May the peoples praise you, O God; may all the peoples praise you!

So may your way be known up - on earth; among all nations, your sal - va - tion.
the nations on the earth you guide.
May God bless us, and may all the ends of the earth fear him!

THE ASCENSION OF THE LORD

May 24, 2001

God mounts his throne to shouts of joy, to shouts of joy.

Psalm 47:2-3, 6-7, 8-9

1. All you peoples, clap your hands, shout to God with cries of gladness,
2. God mounts his throne amid shouts of joy; the LORD, amid trum - pet blasts.
3. For king of all the earth is God; sing hymns of praise.

for the LORD, the Most High, the awe - some, is the great king over all the earth.
Sing praise to God, sing praise; sing praise to our king, sing praise.
God reigns over the na - tions, God sits upon his ho - ly throne.

SEVENTH SUNDAY OF EASTER
May 27, 2001

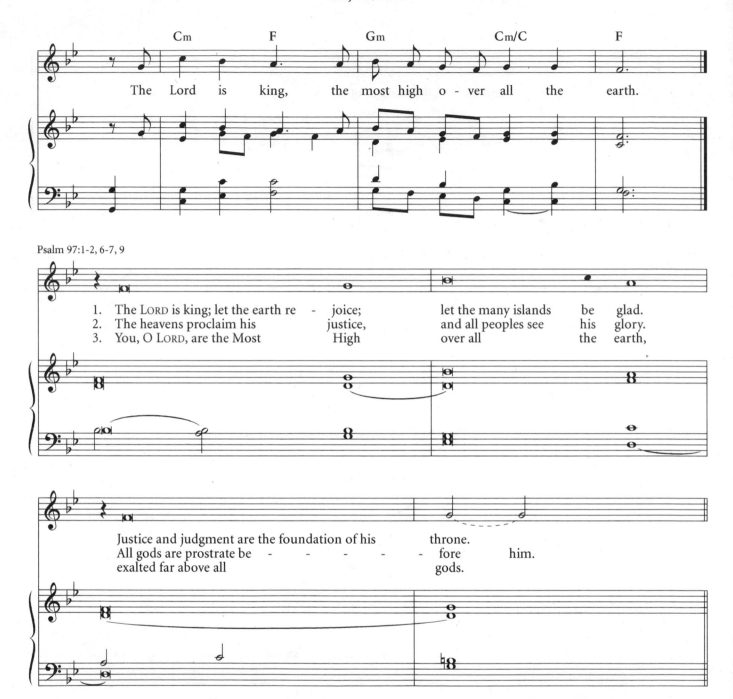

The Lord is king, the most high over all the earth.

Psalm 97:1-2, 6-7, 9

1. The LORD is king; let the earth re - joice; let the many islands be glad.
2. The heavens proclaim his justice, and all peoples see his glory.
3. You, O LORD, are the Most High over all the earth,

Justice and judgment are the foundation of his throne.
All gods are prostrate be - - - - - fore him.
exalted far above all gods.

THE VIGIL OF PENTECOST

June 2, 2001

Lord, send out your Spir-it, and re-new the face of the earth, and re-new the face of the earth.

Psalm 104:1-2, 24, 35, 27-28, 29, 30

1. Bless the LORD, O my soul! O LORD, my God, you are great in - deed!
2. How manifold are your works, O LORD! In wisdom you have wrought them all—
3. Creatures all look to you to give them food in due time.

You are clothed with majesty and glo - ry, robed in light as with a cloak.
the earth is full of your crea-tures; bless the LORD, O my soul! Al - le - lu - ia.
When you give it to them, they gather it; when you open your hand, they are filled with good things.

PENTECOST

June 3, 2001

MASS DURING THE DAY

Lord, send out your Spir-it, and re-new the face of the earth, and re-new the face of the earth.

Psalm 104:1, 24, 29-30, 31, 34

1. Bless the LORD, O my soul! O LORD, my God, you are great in-deed!
2. If you take a - - - way their breath, they perish and return to their dust.
3. May the glory of the LORD en-dure for - ev - er; may the LORD be glad in his works!

How manifold are your works, O LORD! the earth is full of your crea-tures.
When you send forth your spirit, they are cre - a - ted, and you renew the face of the earth.
Pleasing to him be my theme; I will be glad in the LORD.

TRINITY SUNDAY

June 10, 2001

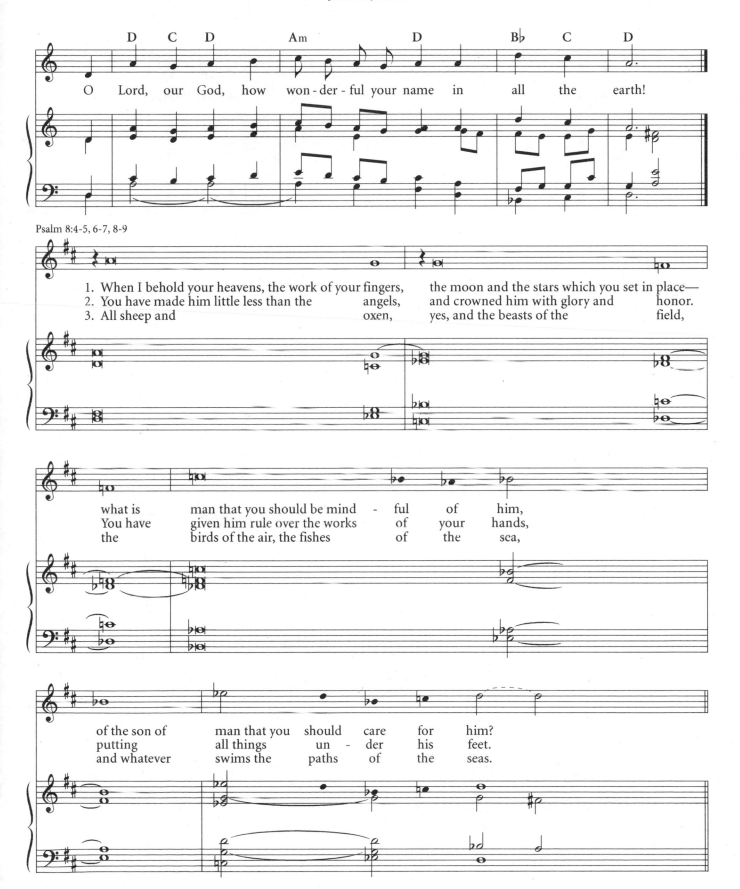

O Lord, our God, how won-der-ful your name in all the earth!

Psalm 8:4-5, 6-7, 8-9

1. When I behold your heavens, the work of your fingers, the moon and the stars which you set in place—
2. You have made him little less than the angels, and crowned him with glory and honor.
3. All sheep and oxen, yes, and the beasts of the field,

what is man that you should be mind - ful of him,
You have given him rule over the works of your hands,
the birds of the air, the fishes of the sea,

of the son of man that you should care for him?
putting all things un - der his feet.
and whatever swims the paths of the seas.

THE MOST HOLY BODY AND BLOOD OF CHRIST

June 17, 2001

You are a priest for - ev - er, in the line of Mel - chi - ze - dek.

Psalm 110:1, 2, 3, 4

1. The LORD said to my Lord: "Sit at my right hand
2. The scepter of your power the LORD will stretch forth from Zi - on:
3. "Yours is a princely power in the day of your birth, in ho - ly splen - dor;
4. The LORD has sworn, and he will not re - pent: "You are a priest for - ev - er,

till I make your enemies your foot - - - - stool."
"Rule in the midst of your en - e - - - mies."
before the daystar like the dew, I have be - got - ten you."
according to the order of Mel - chi - ze - - - dek."

THE NATIVITY OF JOHN THE BAPTIST

June 24, 2001

VIGIL MASS

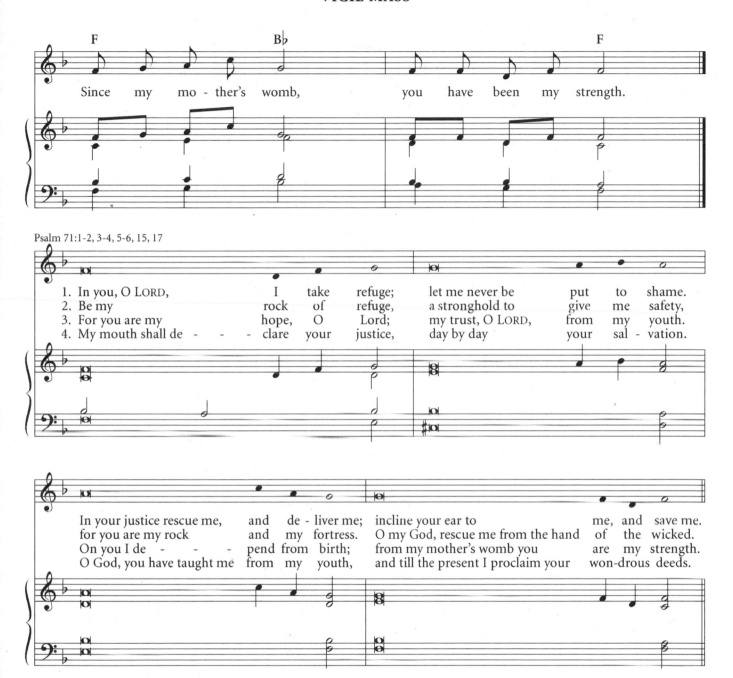

Since my mo-ther's womb, you have been my strength.

Psalm 71:1-2, 3-4, 5-6, 15, 17

1. In you, O LORD, I take refuge; let me never be put to shame.
2. Be my rock of refuge, a stronghold to give me safety,
3. For you are my hope, O Lord; my trust, O LORD, from my youth.
4. My mouth shall de - - - clare your justice, day by day your sal - vation.

In your justice rescue me, and de - liver me; incline your ear to me, and save me.
for you are my rock and my fortress. O my God, rescue me from the hand of the wicked.
On you I de - - - pend from birth; from my mother's womb you are my strength.
O God, you have taught me from my youth, and till the present I proclaim your won-drous deeds.

THE NATIVITY OF JOHN THE BAPTIST

June 24, 2001

MASS DURING THE DAY

I praise you for I am won-der-ful-ly made.

Psalm 139:1-3, 13-14, 14-15

1. O LORD you have probed me and
   you know me; you know when I sit and when I stand; you understand my thoughts from a - far.
2. Truly you have formed my in - most being; you knit me in my mo-ther's womb.
3. My soul you knew full well; nor was my frame un - known to you

My journeys and my rest you scru-ti-nize, with all my ways you are fa - miliar.
I give you thanks that I am fearfully, wonder-ful-ly made; wonderful are your works.
when I was made in secret, when I was fashioned in the depths of the earth.

THIRTEENTH SUNDAY IN ORDINARY TIME
July 1, 2001

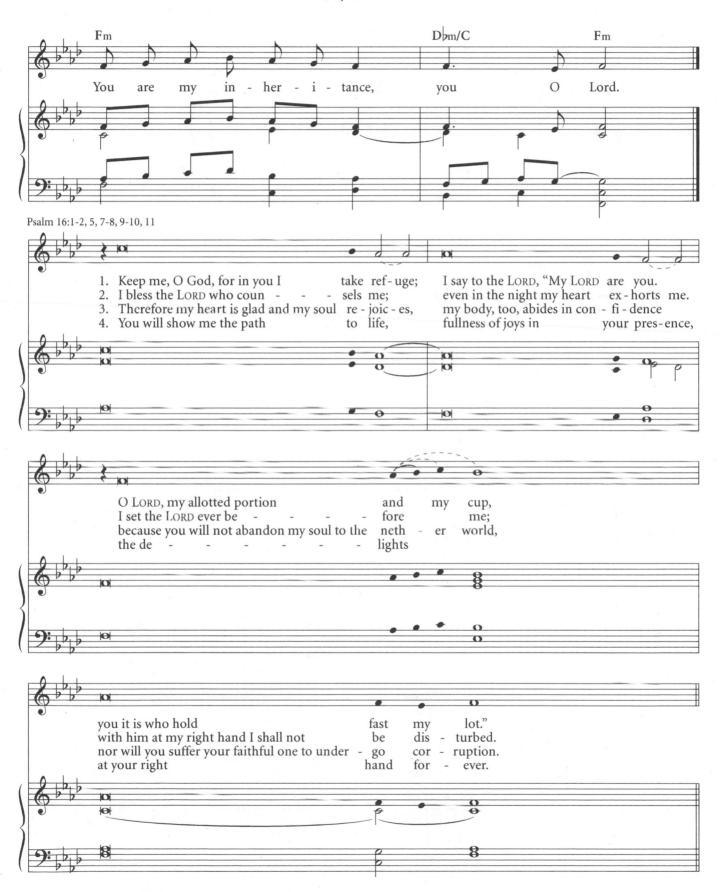

Psalm 16:1-2, 5, 7-8, 9-10, 11

You are my in-her-i-tance, you O Lord.

1. Keep me, O God, for in you I take ref-uge; I say to the LORD, "My LORD are you.
2. I bless the LORD who coun - - - sels me; even in the night my heart ex-horts me.
3. Therefore my heart is glad and my soul re-joic-es, my body, too, abides in con-fi-dence
4. You will show me the path to life, fullness of joys in your pres-ence,

O LORD, my allotted portion and my cup,
I set the LORD ever be - - - - fore me;
because you will not abandon my soul to the neth - er world,
the de - - - - - - lights

you it is who hold fast my lot."
with him at my right hand I shall not be dis - turbed.
nor will you suffer your faithful one to under - go cor - ruption.
at your right hand for - ever.

Fourteenth Sunday in Ordinary Time

July 8, 2001

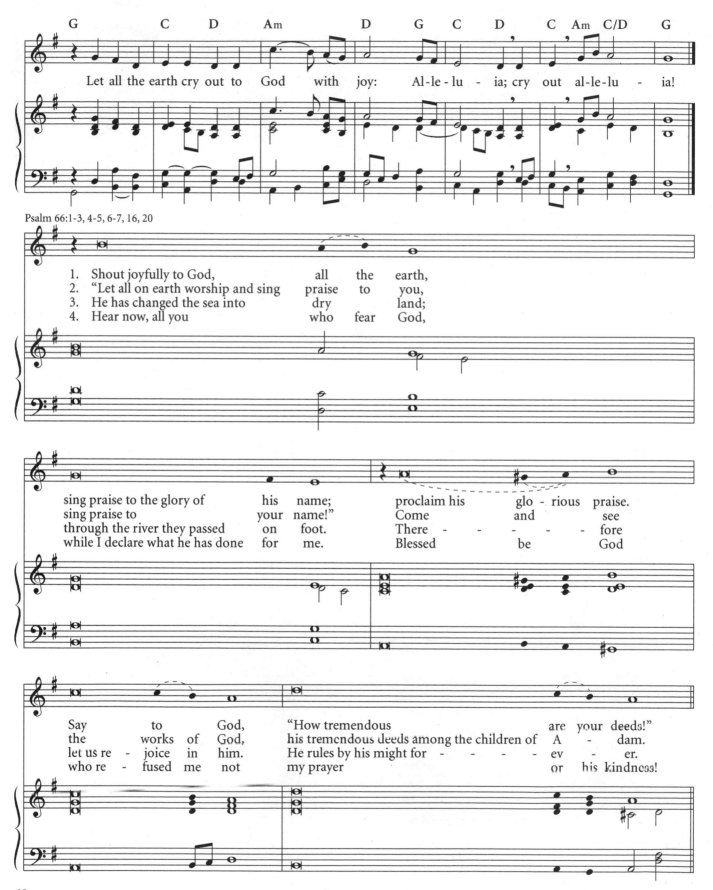

Let all the earth cry out to God with joy: Al-le-lu - ia; cry out al-le-lu - ia!

Psalm 66:1-3, 4-5, 6-7, 16, 20

1. Shout joyfully to God, all the earth,
2. "Let all on earth worship and sing praise to you,
3. He has changed the sea into dry land;
4. Hear now, all you who fear God,

sing praise to the glory of his name; proclaim his glo - rious praise.
sing praise to your name!" Come and see
through the river they passed on foot. There - - - - fore
while I declare what he has done for me. Blessed be God

Say to God, "How tremendous are your deeds!"
the works of God, his tremendous deeds among the children of A - dam.
let us re - joice in him. He rules by his might for - - - - ev - er.
who re - fused me not my prayer or his kindness!

FIFTEENTH SUNDAY IN ORDINARY TIME

July 15, 2001

Psalm 69:14, 17, 30-31, 33-34, 36, 37

Turn to the Lord in your need, and you will live.

I pray to you, O Lord, for the time of your favor, O God!
I am afflicted and in pain;
"See, you lowly ones, and be glad;
For God will save Zion

In your great kindness answer me with your con - stant help.
let your saving help, O God, pro - - tect me.
you who seek God, may your hearts re - vive!
and rebuild the cities of Ju - - dah.

Answer me, O Lord, for bounteous is your kindness: in your great mercy turn toward me.
I will praise the name of God in song, and I will glorify him with thanks-giving.
For the Lord hears the poor, and his own who are in bonds he spurns not."
The descendants of his servants shall inherit it, and those who love his name shall inhabit it.

SIXTEENTH SUNDAY IN ORDINARY TIME
July 22, 2001

He who does jus-tice will live in the pres-ence of the Lord.

Psalm 15:2-3, 3-4, 5

1. One who walks blamelessly and does jus-tice; who thinks the truth in his heart
2. Who harms not his fellow man, nor takes up a reproach a-gainst his neigh-bor;
3. Who lends not his money at usury and accepts no bribe a-gainst the inno-cent.

and slan-ders not with his tongue.
by whom the reprobate is de-spised, while he honors those who fear the LORD.
One who does these things shall never be dis-turbed.

SEVENTEENTH SUNDAY IN ORDINARY TIME
July 29, 2001

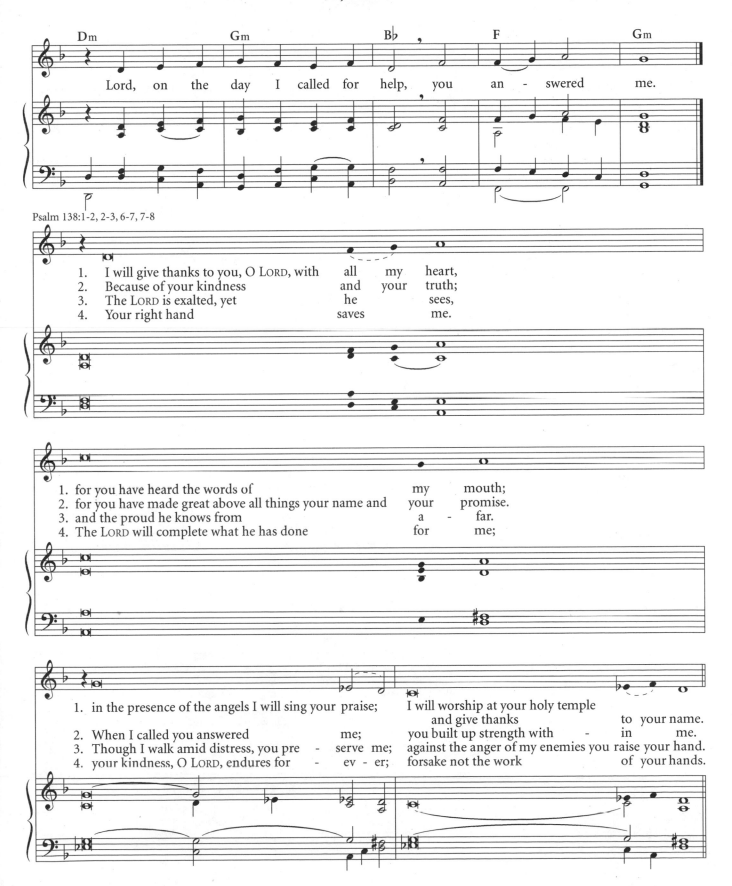

Lord, on the day I called for help, you an - swered me.

Psalm 138:1-2, 2-3, 6-7, 7-8

1. I will give thanks to you, O LORD, with all my heart,
2. Because of your kindness and your truth;
3. The LORD is exalted, yet he sees,
4. Your right hand saves me.

1. for you have heard the words of my mouth;
2. for you have made great above all things your name and your promise.
3. and the proud he knows from a - far.
4. The LORD will complete what he has done for me;

1. in the presence of the angels I will sing your praise; I will worship at your holy temple and give thanks to your name.
2. When I called you answered me; you built up strength with - in me.
3. Though I walk amid distress, you pre - serve me; against the anger of my enemies you raise your hand.
4. your kindness, O LORD, endures for - ev - er; forsake not the work of your hands.

EIGHTEENTH SUNDAY IN ORDINARY TIME

August 5, 2001

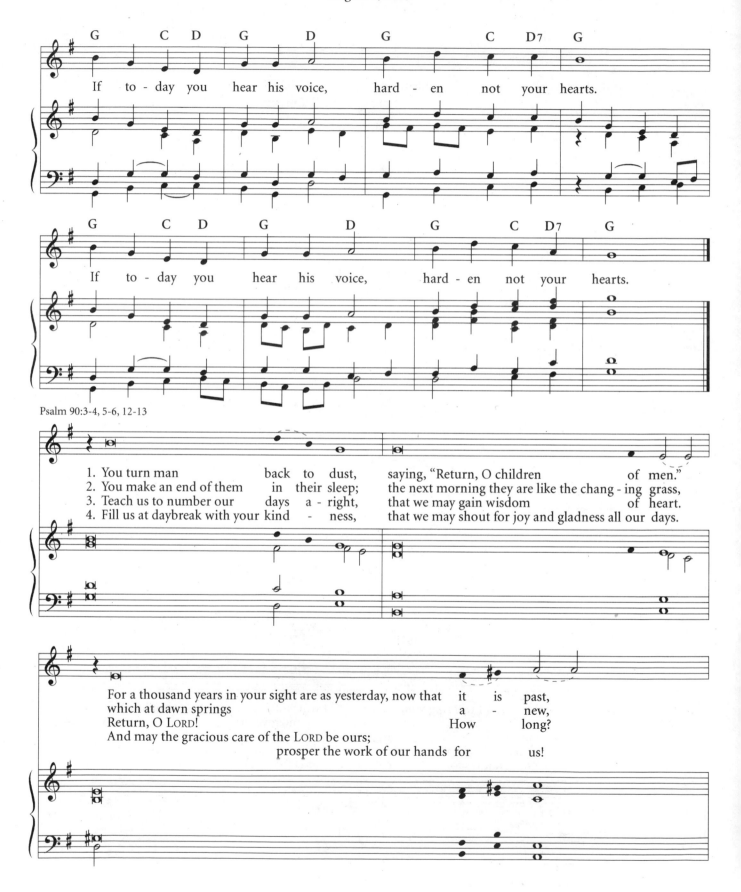

If to-day you hear his voice, hard-en not your hearts.

If to-day you hear his voice, hard-en not your hearts.

Psalm 90:3-4, 5-6, 12-13

1. You turn man back to dust, saying, "Return, O children of men."
2. You make an end of them in their sleep; the next morning they are like the chang-ing grass,
3. Teach us to number our days a-right, that we may gain wisdom of heart.
4. Fill us at daybreak with your kind - ness, that we may shout for joy and gladness all our days.

For a thousand years in your sight are as yesterday, now that it is past,
which at dawn springs a - new,
Return, O LORD! How long?
And may the gracious care of the LORD be ours;
prosper the work of our hands for us!

or as a watch   of   the   night.
but by evening   wilts   and   fades.
Have pity   on   your servants!
Prosper the work   of   our   hands!

NINETEENTH SUNDAY IN ORDINARY TIME

August 12, 2001

Psalm 33:1, 12, 18-19, 20-22

1. Exult, you just, in the LORD; praise from the upright is fit-ting.
2. See, the eyes of the LORD are upon those who fear him, upon those who hope for his kind-ness,
3. Our soul waits for the LORD, who is our help and our shield.

Blessed the nation whose God is the LORD,
to deliver them from death
May your kindness, O LORD, be up - on us

the people he has chosen for his own in - her - i - tance.
and preserve them in spite of fam - ine.
who have put our hope in you.

Vigil of the Assumption

August 14, 2001

Psalm 132:6-7, 9-10, 13-14

1. Behold, we heard of it in Eph - ra - thah; we found it in the fields of Jaar.
2. May your priests be clothed with jus - tice; let your faithful ones shout merrily for joy.
3. For the LORD has chosen Zi - on; he prefers her for his dwell - ing.

Let us enter into his dwell - ing, let us worship at his foot - stool.
For the sake of Da - vid your ser - vant, reject not the plea of your a - noint - ed.
"Zion is my resting place for - ev - er; in her will I dwell, for I pre - fer her."

ASSUMPTION OF THE BLESSED VIRGIN MARY

August 15, 2001

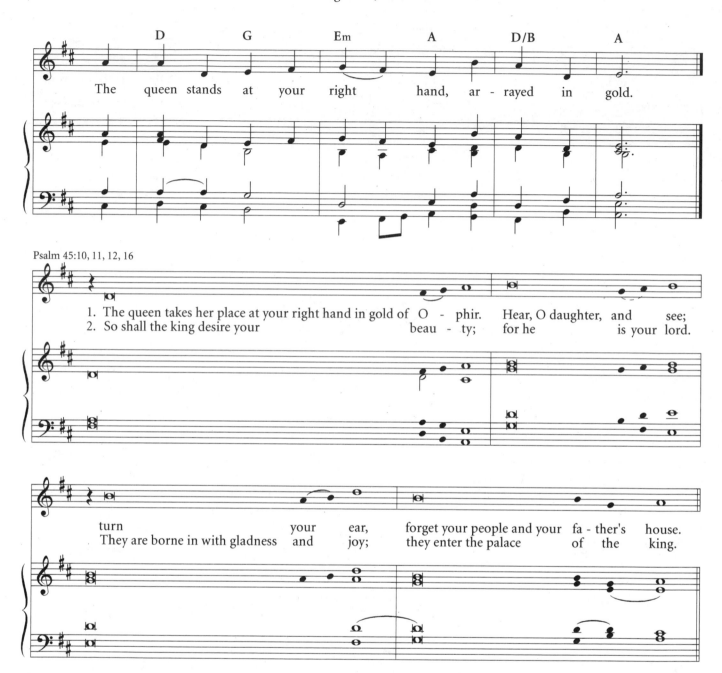

The queen stands at your right hand, ar - rayed in gold.

Psalm 45:10, 11, 12, 16

1. The queen takes her place at your right hand in gold of O - phir. Hear, O daughter, and see;
2. So shall the king desire your beau - ty; for he is your lord.

turn your ear, forget your people and your fa - ther's house.
They are borne in with gladness and joy; they enter the palace of the king.

TWENTIETH SUNDAY IN ORDINARY TIME

August 19, 2001

Psalm 40:2, 3, 4, 18

1. I waited, waited for the LORD,
2. The LORD heard my cry. He drew me out of the pit of destruction, out of the mud of the swamp;
3. And he put a new song into my mouth, a hymn to our God.
4. Though I am afflicted and poor, yet the LORD thinks of me.

and he stooped toward me.
he set my feet upon a crag; he made firm my steps.
Many shall look on in awe and trust in the LORD.
You are my help and my de - liverer; O my God, hold not back!

TWENTY-FIRST SUNDAY IN ORDINARY TIME

August 26, 2001

Go out to all the world and tell the good news.

Psalm 117:1, 2

1. Praise the LORD, all you nations; glorify him, all you peoples!
2. For steadfast is his kindness toward us, and the fidelity of the LORD endures for - ever.

TWENTY-SECOND SUNDAY IN ORDINARY TIME

September 2, 2001

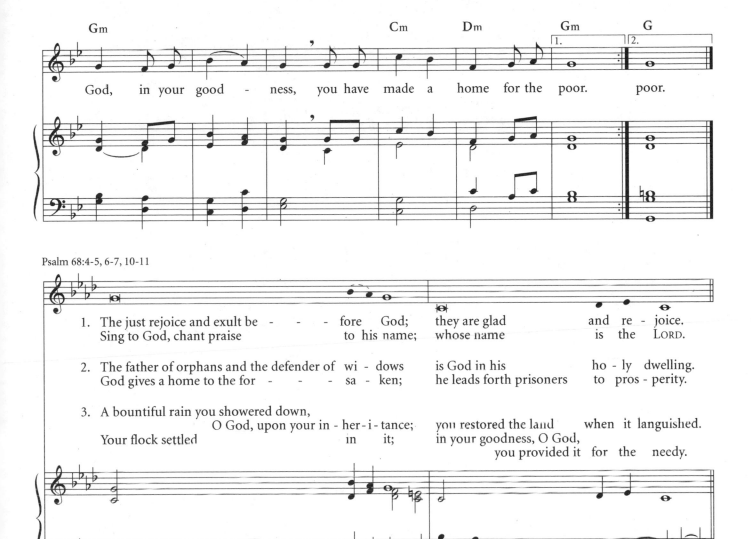

God, in your good - ness, you have made a home for the poor. poor.

Psalm 68:4-5, 6-7, 10-11

1. The just rejoice and exult be - - - fore God; they are glad and re - joice.
   Sing to God, chant praise to his name; whose name is the LORD.

2. The father of orphans and the defender of wi - dows is God in his ho - ly dwelling.
   God gives a home to the for - - - sa - ken; he leads forth prisoners to pros - perity.

3. A bountiful rain you showered down,
      O God, upon your in - her - i - tance; you restored the land when it languished.
   Your flock settled in it; in your goodness, O God,
      you provided it for the needy.

TWENTY-THIRD SUNDAY IN ORDINARY TIME
September 9, 2001

In ev-ery age, O Lord, you have been our ref-uge,

1. you have been our ref - uge.

2. you have been our ref - - - uge.

Psalm 90:3-4, 5-6, 12-13, 14-17

1. You turn man back to dust, saying, "Return, O children of men." For a thousand years in your sight are as yesterday, now that it is past, or as a watch of the night.

2. You make an end of them in their sleep; the next morning they are like the chang - ing grass, which at dawn springs up a - new, but by evening wilts and fades.

3. Teach us to number our days a - right, that we may gain wisdom of heart. Return, O LORD! How long? Have pity on your servants!

4. Fill us at daybreak with your kindness, that we may shout for joy and gladness all our days. And may the gracious care of the LORD our God be ours; prosper the work of our hands for us! Prosper the work of our hands!

Twenty-fourth Sunday in Ordinary Time

September 16, 2001

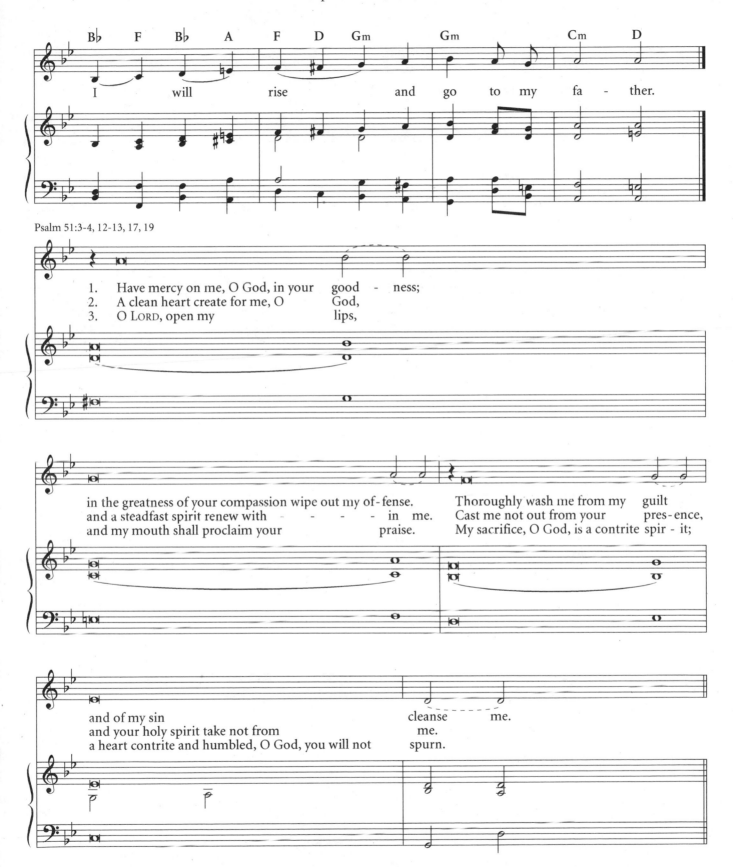

I will rise and go to my fa- ther.

Psalm 51:3-4, 12-13, 17, 19

1. Have mercy on me, O God, in your good-ness;
2. A clean heart create for me, O God,
3. O LORD, open my lips,

in the greatness of your compassion wipe out my of-fense.
and a steadfast spirit renew with – – – in me.
and my mouth shall proclaim your praise.

Thoroughly wash me from my guilt
Cast me not out from your pres-ence,
My sacrifice, O God, is a contrite spir- it;

and of my sin
and your holy spirit take not from
a heart contrite and humbled, O God, you will not

cleanse me.
me.
spurn.

TWENTY-FIFTH SUNDAY IN ORDINARY TIME
September 23, 2001

Praise the Lord who lifts up the poor.

Psalm 113:1-2, 4-6, 7-8

1. Praise, you servants of the LORD, praise the name of the LORD.
2. High above all nations is the LORD; above the heavens is the glory.
3. He raises up the lowly from the dust; from the dunghill he lifts up the poor

Blessed be the name of the LORD both now and for - ever.
Who is like the LORD,
        our God, who is en - throned on high and looks upon the heavens and the earth be - low?
to seat them with prin - ces, with the princes of his own people.

TWENTY-SIXTH SUNDAY IN ORDINARY TIME
September 30, 2001

Psalm 146:7, 8-9, 9-10

1. Blessed is he who keeps faith for - ev - er, secures justice for the op - pressed,
2. The LORD gives sight to the blind. The LORD raises up those who were bowed down;
3. The fatherless and the widow he sus - tains, but the way of the wicked he thwarts.

gives food to the hun - gry. The LORD sets cap - tives free.
the LORD loves the just. The LORD protects stran - gers.
The LORD shall reign for - ev - er; your God, O Zion, through all generations. Alle - lu - ia.

TWENTY-SEVENTH SUNDAY IN ORDINARY TIME

October 7, 2001

If to-day you hear his voice, hard-en not your hearts.

If to-day you hear his voice, hard-en not your hearts.

Psalm 95:1-2, 6-7, 7-9

1. Come, let us sing joyfully to the LORD; let us acclaim the Rock of our sal-va-tion.
2. Come, let us bow down in wor-ship; let us kneel before the LORD who made us,
3. Oh, that today you would hear his voice: "Harden not your hearts as at Meri-bah,

Let us come into his presence with thanks-giv-ing;
For he is our God, and we are the people he shep-herds,
as in the day of Massah in the desert, where your fathers tempt-ed me;

84

let us joyfully sing   psalms   to him.
the   flock   he guides.
they tested me though they had   seen   my works."

Twenty-eighth Sunday in Ordinary Time

October 14, 2001

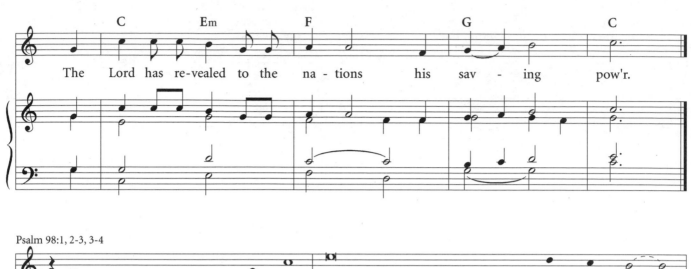

The Lord has re-vealed to the na - tions his sav - ing pow'r.

Psalm 98:1, 2-3, 3-4

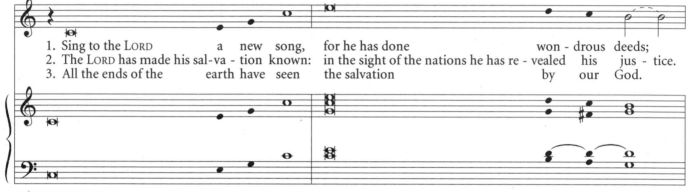

1. Sing to the LORD a new song, for he has done won - drous deeds;
2. The LORD has made his sal-va - tion known: in the sight of the nations he has re - vealed his jus - tice.
3. All the ends of the earth have seen the salvation by our God.

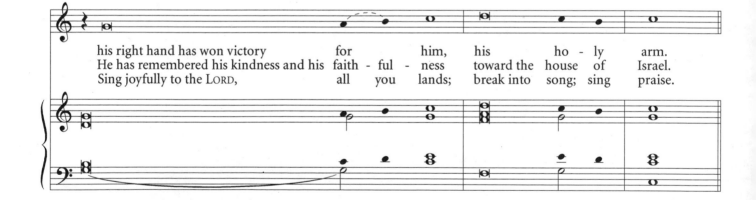

his right hand has won victory for him, his ho - ly arm.
He has remembered his kindness and his faith - ful - ness toward the house of Israel.
Sing joyfully to the LORD, all you lands; break into song; sing praise.

TWENTY-NINTH SUNDAY IN ORDINARY TIME

October 21, 2001

Our help is from the Lord who made heaven and earth.

Psalm 121:1-2, 3-4, 5-6, 7-8

1. I lift up my eyes toward the moun - tains; whence
2. May he not suffer your foot to slip; may he slumber not
3. The LORD is your guardian; the LORD is your shade; he is beside you at
4. The LORD will guard you from all e - vil; he will

shall help come to me? My help is from the LORD,
who guards you: In - deed he neither slumbers nor sleeps,
your right hand. The sun shall not harm you by day,
guard your life. The LORD will guard your coming and your going,

who made heaven and earth.
the guardian of Is - ra - el.
nor the moon at night.
both now and for - ev - er.

87

THIRTIETH SUNDAY IN ORDINARY TIME

October 28, 2001

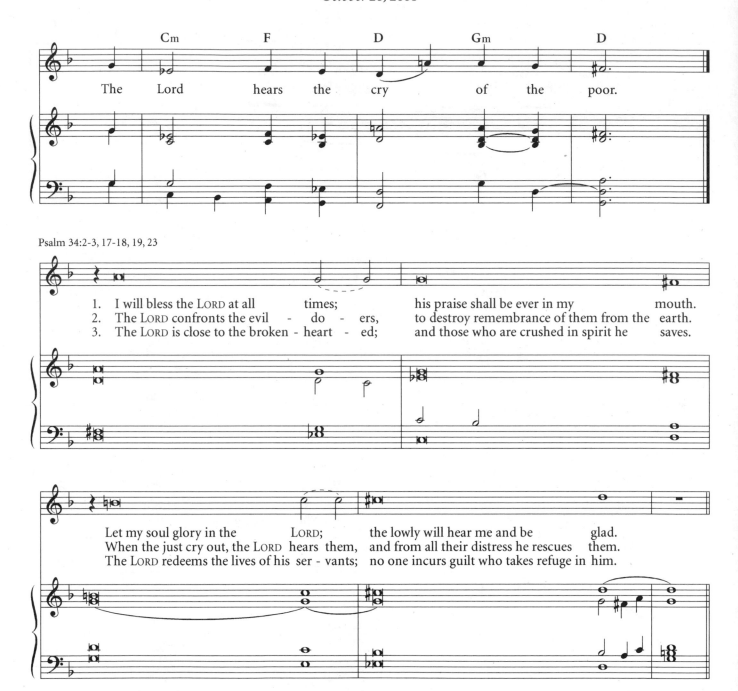

The Lord hears the cry of the poor.

Psalm 34:2-3, 17-18, 19, 23

1. I will bless the LORD at all times; his praise shall be ever in my mouth.
2. The LORD confronts the evil - do - ers, to destroy remembrance of them from the earth.
3. The LORD is close to the broken - heart - ed; and those who are crushed in spirit he saves.

Let my soul glory in the LORD; the lowly will hear me and be glad.
When the just cry out, the LORD hears them, and from all their distress he rescues them.
The LORD redeems the lives of his ser - vants; no one incurs guilt who takes refuge in him.

ALL SAINTS

November 1, 2001

Lord, this is the peo - ple that longs to see your face.

Psalm 24:1-2, 3-4, 5-6

1. The LORD's are the earth and its full - ness; the world and those who dwell in it.
2. Who can ascend the mountain of the LORD? or who may stand in his ho - ly place?
3. He shall receive a blessing from the LORD, a reward from God his sav - ior.

For he founded it up - - - on the seas and established it upon the riv - - - ers.
One whose hands are sinless, whose heart is clean, who desires not what is vain.
Such is the race that seeks for him, that seeks the face of the God of Ja - cob.

THE COMMEMORATION OF ALL THE FAITHFUL DEPARTED (ALL SOULS)

November 2, 2001

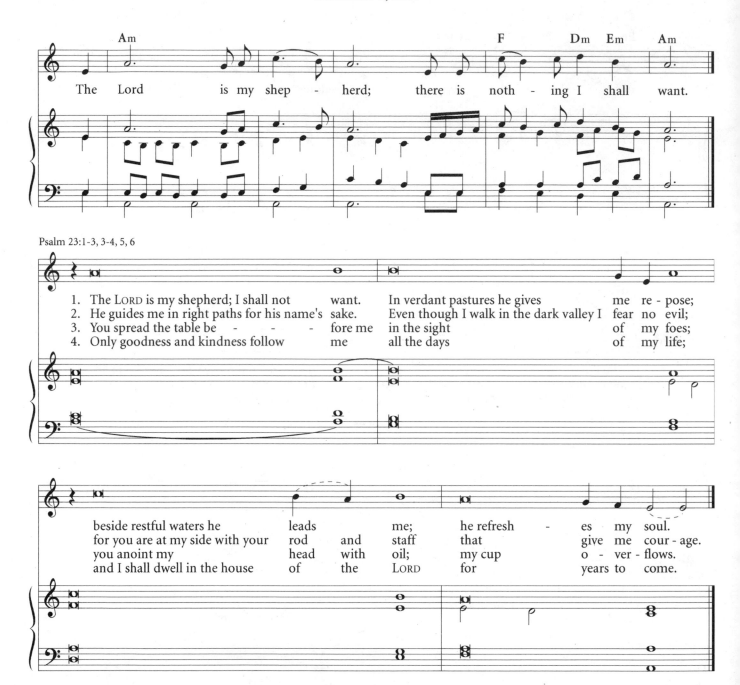

Psalm 23:1-3, 3-4, 5, 6

1. The LORD is my shepherd; I shall not want. In verdant pastures he gives me re - pose;
2. He guides me in right paths for his name's sake. Even though I walk in the dark valley I fear no evil;
3. You spread the table be - - - fore me in the sight of my foes;
4. Only goodness and kindness follow me all the days of my life;

beside restful waters he leads me; he refresh - es my soul.
for you are at my side with your rod and staff that give me cour - age.
you anoint my head with oil; my cup o - ver - flows.
and I shall dwell in the house of the LORD for years to come.

THIRTY-FIRST SUNDAY IN ORDINARY TIME
November 4, 2001

Psalm 145:8-9, 10-11, 12-13

1. I will extol you, O my God and King,
   and I will bless your name forever and ever.
2. The LORD is gracious and mer - ci - ful,
   slow to anger and of great kindness.
3. Let all your works give you thanks, O LORD,
   and let your faithful ones bless you.
4. The LORD is faithful in all his words
   and holy in all his works.

Every day will I bless you,
and I will praise your name forever and ever.
The LORD is good to all
and compassionate toward all his works.
Let them discourse of the glory of your kingdom
and speak of your might.
The LORD lifts up all who are falling
and raises up all who are bowed down.

THIRTY-SECOND SUNDAY IN ORDINARY TIME
November 11, 2001

Lord, when your glo - ry ap - pears, my joy will be full.

Psalm 17:1, 5-6, 8, 15

1. Hear, O LORD, a just suit; attend to my out - cry;
hearken to my prayer from lips without de - ceit.

2. My steps have been steadfast in your paths, my feet have not faltered.
I call upon you, for you will answer me, O God; incline your ear to me; hear my word.

3. Keep me as the apple of your eye, hide me in the shadow of your wings.
But I in justice shall behold your face; on waking, I shall be content in your presence.

THIRTY-THIRD SUNDAY IN ORDINARY TIME

November 18, 2001

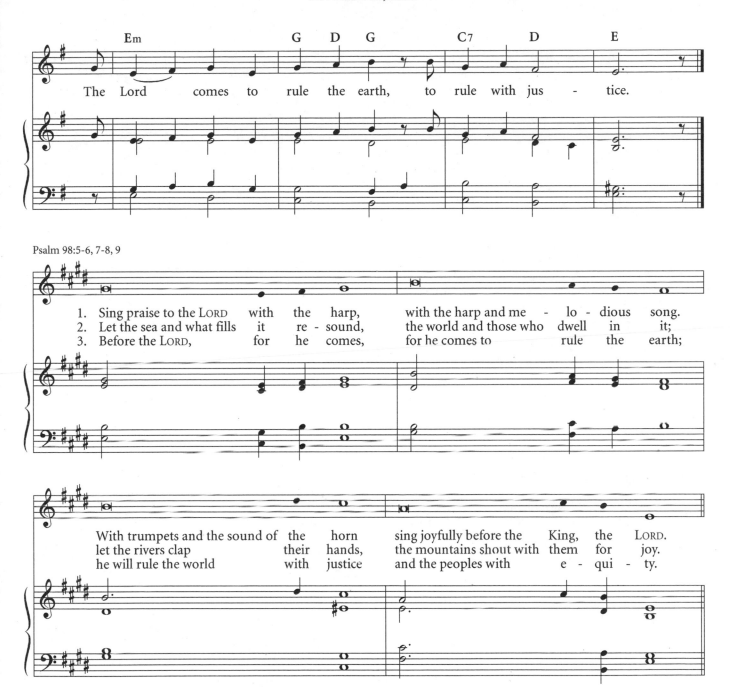

Psalm 98:5-6, 7-8, 9

1. Sing praise to the LORD with the harp, with the harp and me - lo - dious song.
2. Let the sea and what fills it re - sound, the world and those who dwell in it;
3. Before the LORD, for he comes, for he comes to rule the earth;

With trumpets and the sound of the horn sing joyfully before the King, the LORD.
let the rivers clap their hands, the mountains shout with them for joy.
he will rule the world with justice and the peoples with e - qui - ty.

THANKSGIVING DAY
November 22, 2001

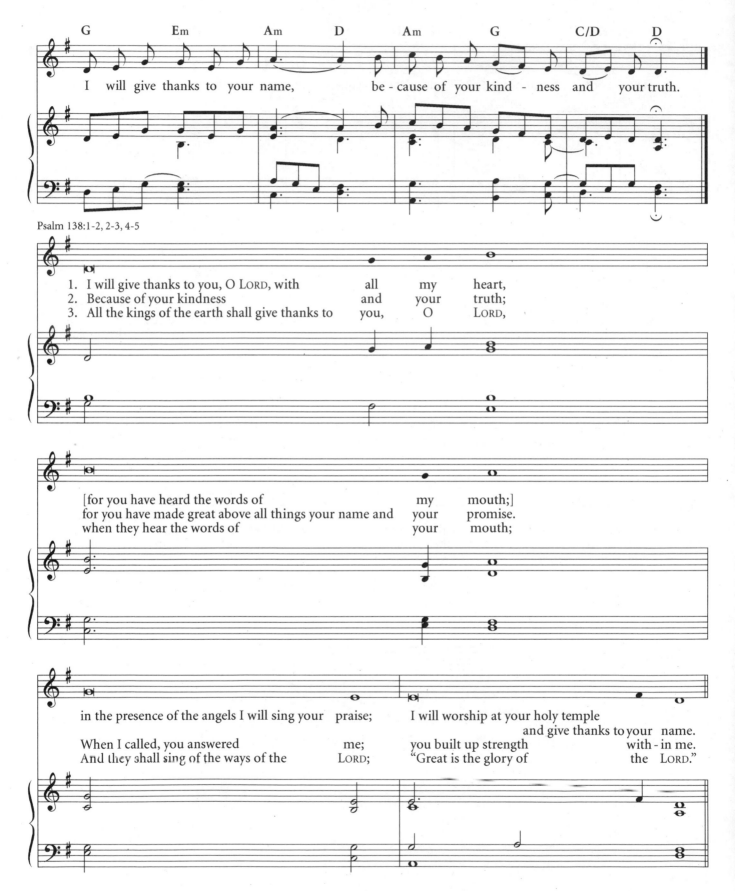

I will give thanks to your name, be - cause of your kind - ness and your truth.

Psalm 138:1-2, 2-3, 4-5

1. I will give thanks to you, O LORD, with all my heart,
2. Because of your kindness and your truth;
3. All the kings of the earth shall give thanks to you, O LORD,

[for you have heard the words of my mouth;]
for you have made great above all things your name and your promise.
when they hear the words of your mouth;

in the presence of the angels I will sing your praise; I will worship at your holy temple
and give thanks to your name.
When I called, you answered me; you built up strength with - in me.
And they shall sing of the ways of the LORD; "Great is the glory of the LORD."

CHRIST THE KING

November 25, 2001

Let us go re-joic-ing to the house of the Lord.

Psalm 122:1-2, 3-4, 4-5

1. I re-joiced be-cause they said to me, "We will
2. Je-ru-sa-lem built as a cit - - y with
3. Ac-cord-ing to the de-cree for Is-ra-el, to give

go up to the house of the LORD." And now we have set
com-pact u - ni - ty. To it the tribes go
thanks to the name of the LORD. In it are set up judg-ment

foot with - in your gates, O Je - ru - sa - lem.
up, with the tribes of the LORD.
seats, seats for the house of Da - - vid.

WORLD MISSION SUNDAY
October 21, 2001

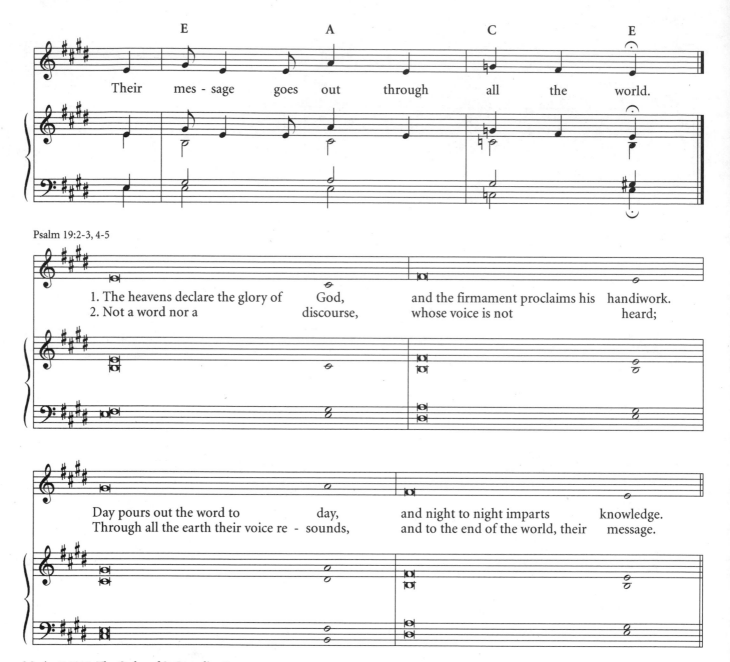

E · · · · · · A · · · · · · C · · · · · · E

Their mes - sage goes out through all the world.

Psalm 19:2-3, 4-5

1. The heavens declare the glory of God, and the firmament proclaims his handiwork.
2. Not a word nor a discourse, whose voice is not heard;

Day pours out the word to day, and night to night imparts knowledge.
Through all the earth their voice re - sounds, and to the end of the world, their message.

Music: © 2000, The Order of St. Benedict, Inc.

GREGORIAN CHANT PSALMODY

FIRST SUNDAY OF ADVENT

December 3, 2000

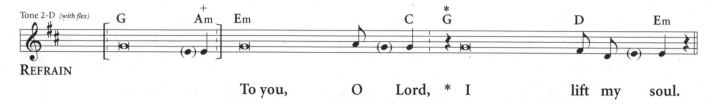

Tone 2-D *(with flex)*

REFRAIN

To you, O Lord, * I lift my soul.

VERSES   Psalm 25:4-5, 8-9, 10, 14

Your ways, O LORD make known <u>to</u> me; * teach <u>me</u> your paths,
guide me in your truth and <u>teach</u> me, +
   for you are God <u>my</u> savior; * and for you I wait <u>all</u> the day.

Good and upright is <u>the</u> LORD; * thus he shows sin<u>ners</u> the way.
He guides the humble <u>to</u> justice, * and teaches the hum<u>ble</u> his way.

All the paths of the LORD are kindness <u>and</u> constancy *
   toward those who keep his covenant and <u>his</u> decrees.
The friendship of the LORD is with those <u>who</u> fear him, *
   and his covenant, for <u>their</u> instruction.

IMMACULATE CONCEPTION

December 8, 2000

Tone 5-F

REFRAIN

Sing to the Lord a new song, * for he has done mar - ve-lous deeds.

VERSES   Psalm 98:1, 2-3, 3-4

Sing to the LORD <u>a</u> new song, * for he has done <u>wondrous</u> deeds;
his right hand has won victory <u>for</u> him, * his <u>holy</u> arm.

The LORD has made his sal<u>vation</u> known: * in the sight of the nations he has re<u>vealed</u> his justice.
He has remembered his kindness and <u>his</u> faithfulness * toward the <u>house</u> of Israel.

All the ends of the earth <u>have</u> seen * the salvation <u>by</u> our God.
Sing joyfully to the LORD, all <u>you</u> lands; * break into <u>song</u>; sing praise.

SECOND SUNDAY OF ADVENT

December 10, 2000

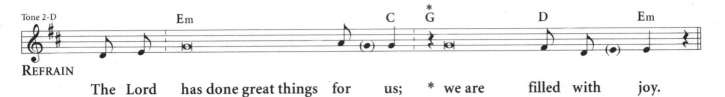

REFRAIN

The Lord has done great things for us; * we are filled with joy.

VERSES   Psalm 126:1-2, 2-3, 4-5, 6

When the LORD brought back the captives <u>of</u> Zion, * we were <u>like</u> men dreaming.
Then our mouth was filled <u>with</u> laughter, * and our tongue <u>with</u> rejoicing.

Then they said among <u>the</u> nations, * "The LORD has done great <u>things</u> for them."
The LORD has done great things <u>for</u> us; * we are <u>glad</u> indeed.

Restore our fortunes, <u>O</u> LORD, * like the torrents in the <u>southern</u> desert.
Those that sow <u>in</u> tears * shall <u>reap</u> rejoicing.

Although they go <u>forth</u> weeping, * carrying the seed <u>to</u> be sown,
they shall come back <u>rejoic</u>ing, * carry<u>ing</u> their sheaves.

THIRD SUNDAY OF ADVENT

December 17, 2000

REFRAIN

Cry out with joy and glad-ness; * for among you is the great and Holy One of Is-ra-el.

VERSES   Psalm 12:2-3, 4, 5-6

God indeed is <u>my</u> savior; * I am confident and <u>un</u>afraid.
my strength and my courage is <u>the</u> LORD, * and he has <u>been</u> my savior.
With joy you will <u>draw</u> water * at the fountain <u>of</u> salvation.

Give thanks to the LORD, acclaim his <u>name</u>; +
   among the nations make known <u>his</u> deeds, * proclaim how exalted <u>is</u> his name.

Sing praise to the LORD for his glorious <u>achieve</u>ment; * let this be known throughout <u>all</u> the earth.
Shout with exultation, O city of <u>Zion</u>, +
   for great in <u>your</u> midst * is the Holy <u>One</u> of Israel!

99

FOURTH SUNDAY OF ADVENT
December 24, 2000

REFRAIN

Lord, make us turn to you, let us see your face * and we shall be saved.

VERSES   Psalm 80:2-3, 15-16, 18-19

O shepherd of Israel, hearken, * from your throne upon the cherubim, shine forth.
Rouse your power, * and come to save us.

Once again, O Lord of hosts, * look down from heaven, and see;
take care of this vine, +
   and protect what your right hand has planted,* the son of man whom you yourself made strong.

May your help be with the man of your right hand,* with the son of man whom you yourself made strong.
Then we will no more withdraw from you; * give us new life, and we will call upon your name.

THE VIGIL OF CHRISTMAS
December 24, 2000

REFRAIN

For - ev - er I will sing * the goodness of the Lord.

VERSES   Psalm 89:4-5, 16-17, 27, 29

I have made a covenant with my chosen one, * I have sworn to David my servant:
forever will I confirm your posterity * and establish your throne for all generations.

Blessed the people who know the joyful shout; * in the light of your countenance, O Lord, they walk.
At your name they rejoice all the day, * and through your justice they are exalted.

He shall say of me, "You are my father, * my God, the rock, my savior."
Forever I will maintain my kindness toward him, * and my covenant with him stands firm.

CHRISTMAS

December 25, 2000

MASS AT MIDNIGHT

REFRAIN

To - day is born our Sav - ior, * Christ the Lord.

VERSES Psalm 96:1-2, 2-3, 11-12, 13

Sing to the LORD a <u>new</u> song; +
  sing to the LORD, all <u>you</u> lands. * Sing to the LORD: <u>bless</u> his name.

Announce his salvation, day after <u>day</u>. +
  Tell his glory among <u>the</u> nations; * among all peoples, his <u>won</u>drous deeds.

Let the heavens be glad and the earth <u>re</u>joice; * let the sea and what fills <u>it</u> resound;
let the plains be joyful and all that <u>is</u> in them! * Then shall all the trees of the for<u>est</u> exult.

They shall exult before the LORD, for <u>he</u> comes; * for he comes to <u>rule</u> the earth.
He shall rule the world <u>with</u> justice * and the peoples <u>with</u> his constancy.

CHRISTMAS

December 25, 2000

MASS AT DAWN

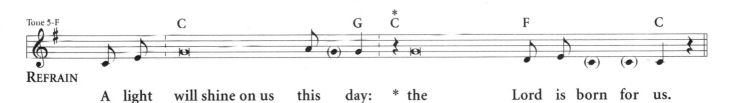

REFRAIN

A light will shine on us this day: * the Lord is born for us.

VERSES Psalm 97:1, 6, 11-12

The LORD is king; let the earth <u>re</u>joice; * let the many is<u>lands</u> be glad.
The heavens proclaim <u>his</u> justice, * and all peoples <u>see</u> his glory.

Light dawns for <u>the</u> just; * and gladness, for the up<u>right</u> of heart.
Be glad in the LORD, <u>you</u> just, * and give thanks to his <u>holy</u> name.

CHRISTMAS
December 25, 2000
MASS DURING THE DAY

Tone 7-G

REFRAIN

All the ends of the earth have seen * the saving pow'r of God.

VERSES Psalm 98:1, 2-3, 3-4, 5-6

Sing to the LORD a new song, * for he has done wondrous deeds;
his right hand has won victory for him, * his holy arm.

The LORD has made his salvation known: * in the sight of the nations he has revealed his justice.
He has remembered his kindness and his faithfulness * toward the house of Israel.

All the ends of the earth have seen * the salvation by our God.
Sing joyfully to the LORD, all you lands; * break into song; sing praise.

Sing praise to the LORD with the harp, * with the harp and melodious song.
With trumpets and the sound of the horn * sing joyfully before the King, the LORD.

HOLY FAMILY
December 31, 2000
SUNDAY IN THE OCTAVE OF CHRISTMAS

Tone 5-F *(with flex)*

REFRAIN

Blessed are those who fear the Lord * and walk in his ways.

VERSES Psalm 128:1-2, 3, 4-5

Blessed is everyone who fears the LORD, * who walks in his ways!
For you shall eat the fruit of your handiwork; * blessed shall you be, and favored.

Your wife shall be like a fruitful vine * in the recesses of your home;
your children like olive plants * around your table.

Behold, thus is the man blessed * who fears the LORD.
The LORD bless you from Zion: +
    may you see the prosperity of Jerusalem * all the days of your life.

SOLEMNITY OF MARY, MOTHER OF GOD
January 1, 2001
OCTAVE OF CHRISTMAS

Tone 7-G *(with flex)*

REFRAIN

May_____ God bless us * in his mer-cy.

VERSES   Psalm 67:2-3, 5, 6, 8

May God have pity on us <u>and</u> bless us; * may he let his face <u>shine</u> upon us.
So may your way be known up<u>on</u> earth; * among all nations, <u>your</u> salvation.

May the nations be glad and <u>exult</u> +
   because you rule the peoples <u>in</u> equity; * the nations on the <u>earth</u> you guide.

May the peoples praise you, <u>O</u> God; * may all the <u>peoples</u> praise you!
May <u>God</u> bless us, * and may all the ends of <u>the</u> earth fear him!

EPIPHANY
January 7, 2001

Tone 2-D

REFRAIN

Lord, ev - 'ry nation on earth * will a - dore you.

VERSES   Psalm 72:1-2, 7-8, 10-11, 12-13

O God, with your judgment endow <u>the</u> king, * and with your justice, <u>the</u> king's son;
he shall govern your people <u>with</u> justice * and your afflicted <u>ones</u> with judgment.

Justice shall flower in <u>his</u> days, * and profound peace, till the moon <u>be</u> no more.
May he rule from sea <u>to</u> sea, * and from the River to the ends <u>of</u> the earth.

The kings of Tarshish and the Isles shall <u>offer</u> gifts; * the kings of Arabia and Seba <u>shall</u> bring tribute.
All kings shall pay <u>him</u> homage, * all na<u>tions</u> shall serve him.

For he shall rescue the poor when he <u>cries</u> out, * and the afflicted when he has no <u>one</u> to help him.
He shall have pity for the lowly and <u>the</u> poor; * the lives of the poor <u>he</u> shall save.

Baptism of the Lord

January 8, 2001

Refrain

The Lord will bless his peo - ple * with peace.

Verses Psalm 29:1-2, 3-4, 3, 9-10

Give to the Lord, you sons <u>of</u> God, * give to the Lord glo<u>ry</u> and praise,
give to the Lord the glory due <u>his</u> name; * adore the Lord in ho<u>ly</u> attire.

The voice of the Lord is over <u>the</u> waters, * the Lord, ov<u>er</u> vast waters.
The voice of the Lord <u>is</u> mighty; * the voice of the Lord <u>is</u> majestic.

The God of glo<u>ry</u> thunders, * and in his temple <u>all</u> say, "Glory!"
The Lord is enthroned above <u>the</u> flood; * the Lord is enthroned as <u>king</u> forever.

Second Sunday in Ordinary Time

January 14, 2001

Refrain

Pro - claim his marvel - ous deeds * to all the na - tions.

Verses Psalm 96:1-2, 2-3, 7-8, 9-10

Sing to the Lord a <u>new</u> song; * sing to the Lord, <u>all</u> you lands.
Sing to <u>the</u> Lord * <u>bless</u> his name.

Announce his salvation, day after <u>day</u>. +
  Tell his glory among <u>the</u> nations; * among all peoples, his <u>won</u>drous deeds.

Give to the Lord, you families of <u>na</u>tions, +
  give to the Lord glory <u>and</u> praise; * give to the Lord the glory <u>due</u> his name!

Worship the Lord in holy <u>at</u>tire. * Tremble before him, <u>all</u> the earth;
say among the nations: The Lord <u>is</u> king. * He governs the peo<u>ples</u> with equity.

THIRD SUNDAY IN ORDINARY TIME
January 21, 2001

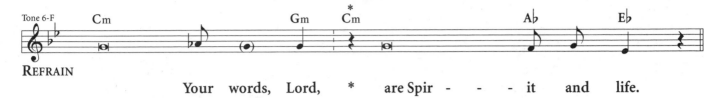

REFRAIN

Your words, Lord, * are Spir - - - it and life.

VERSES   Psalm 19:8, 9, 10, 15

The law of the LORD is perfect, * refreshing the soul;
the decree of the LORD is trustworthy, * giving wisdom to the simple.

The precepts of the LORD are right, * rejoicing the heart;
the command of the LORD is clear, * enlightening the eye.

The fear of the LORD is pure, * enduring forever;
the ordinances of the LORD are true, * all of them just.

Let the words of my mouth and the thought of my heart * find favor before you,
O LORD, my rock * and my redeemer.

FOURTH SUNDAY IN ORDINARY TIME
January 28, 2001

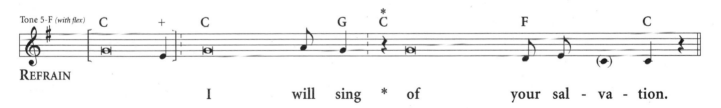

REFRAIN

I will sing * of your sal - va - tion.

VERSES   Psalm 71:1-2, 3-4, 5-6, 15, 17

In you, O LORD, I take refuge; * let me never be put to shame.
In your justice rescue me, and deliver me; * incline your ear to me, and save me.

Be my rock of refuge, +
  a stronghold to give me safety, * for you are my rock and my fortress.
  O my God, rescue me * from the hand of the wicked.

For you are my hope, O LORD; * my trust, O God, from my youth.
On you I depend from birth; * from my mother's womb you are my strength.

My mouth shall declare your justice, * day by day your salvation.
O God, you have taught me from my youth, * and till the present I proclaim your wondrous deeds.

PRESENTATION OF THE LORD
February 2, 2001
BLESSING AND LIGHTING OF CANDLES

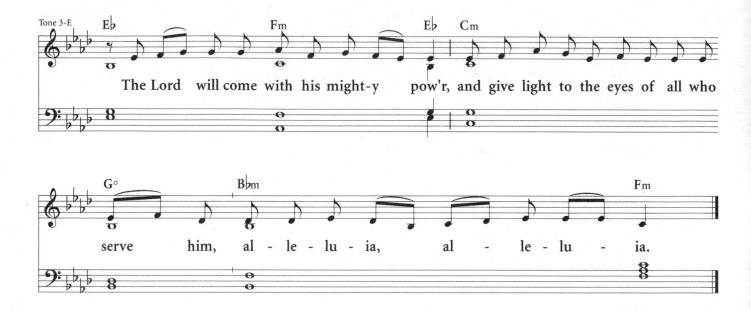

The Lord will come with his might-y pow'r, and give light to the eyes of all who serve him, al-le-lu-ia, al-le-lu-ia.

PRESENTATION OF THE LORD
February 2, 2001
PROCESSION

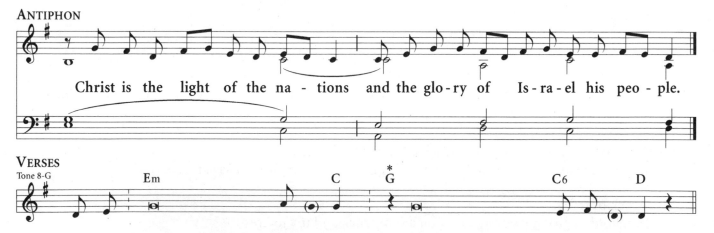

ANTIPHON

Christ is the light of the na - tions and the glo-ry of Is-ra-el his peo-ple.

VERSES

Now, Lord, you have kept <u>your</u> word: * let your servant <u>go</u> in peace.

With my own eyes I have seen the salvation * which you have prepared in the sight of <u>every</u> people.

A light to reveal you to <u>the</u> nations * and the glory of your <u>people</u> Israel.

106

Presentation of the Lord
February 2, 2001

Refrain

Who is the king of glo-ry? * It is the Lord!

Verses Psalm 24:7, 8, 9, 10

Lift up, O gates, your <u>lin</u>tels; +
 reach up, you an<u>cient</u> portals, * that the king of glory <u>may</u> come in!

Who is this king of <u>glo</u>ry? +
 The LORD, strong <u>and</u> mighty, * the LORD, migh<u>ty</u> in battle.

Lift up, O gates, your <u>lin</u>tels; +
 reach up, you an<u>cient</u> portals, * that the king of glory <u>may</u> come in!

Who is this king <u>of</u> glory? * The LORD of hosts; he is the <u>king</u> of glory.

Fifth Sunday in Ordinary Time
February 4, 2001

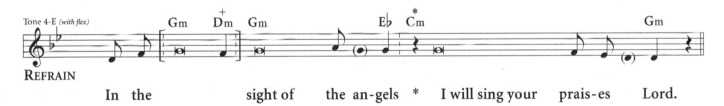

Refrain

In the sight of the an-gels * I will sing your prais-es Lord.

Verses Psalm 138:1-2, 2-3, 4-5, 7-8

I will give thanks to you, O LORD, with all my <u>heart</u>, +
 for you have heard the words of <u>my</u> mouth; * in the presence of the angels I will <u>sing</u> your praise;
I will worship at your ho<u>ly</u> temple * and give thanks <u>to</u> your name.

Because of your kindness and your <u>truth</u>; +
 for you have made great above <u>all</u> things * your name <u>and</u> your promise.
 When I called, you an<u>swered</u> me; * you built up <u>strength</u> within me.

All the kings of the earth shall give thanks to you, <u>O</u> LORD, * when they hear the words <u>of</u> your mouth;
and they shall sing of the ways of <u>the</u> LORD: * "Great is the glory <u>of</u> the LORD."

Your right <u>hand</u> saves me. * The LORD will complete what he has <u>done</u> for me;
your kindness, O LORD, endures <u>for</u>ever; * forsake not the work <u>of</u> your hands.

SIXTH SUNDAY IN ORDINARY TIME
February 11, 2001

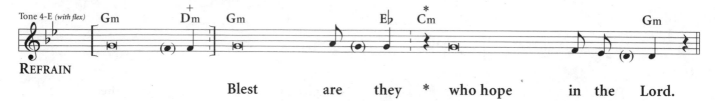

REFRAIN

Blest are they * who hope in the Lord.

VERSES   Psalm 1:1-2, 3, 4 and 6

Blessed the man who fol<u>lows</u> not * the counsel <u>of</u> the wicked,
nor walks in the way <u>of</u> sinners, * nor sits in the company <u>of</u> the insolent,
but delights in the law of <u>the</u> Lord * and meditates on his law <u>day</u> and night.

He is like <u>a</u> tree * planted near <u>run</u>ning water,
that yields its fruit in due <u>sea</u>son, +
    and whose leaves ne<u>ver</u> fade. * Whatever <u>he</u> does, prospers.

Not so the wicked, <u>not</u> so; * they are like chaff which the wind <u>drives</u> away.
For the Lord watches over the way of <u>the</u> just, * but the way of the <u>wick</u>ed vanishes.

SEVENTH SUNDAY IN ORDINARY TIME
February 18, 2001

The Lord is kind and mer - ci - ful.

VERSES   Psalm 103:1-2, 3-4, 8, 10, 12-13

Bless the Lord, O <u>my</u> soul: * and all my being, bless his <u>ho</u>ly name.
Bless the Lord, O <u>my</u> soul, * and forget not <u>all</u> his benefits.

He pardons all your in<u>iqui</u>ties, * heals <u>all</u> your ills.
He redeems your life from de<u>struc</u>tion, * crowns you with kindness <u>and</u> compassion.

Merciful and gracious is <u>the</u> Lord, * slow to anger and a<u>bound</u>ing in kindness.
Not according to our sins does he deal <u>with</u> us, * nor does he requite us according <u>to</u> our crimes.

As far as the east is from <u>the</u> west, * so far has he put our trans<u>gres</u>sions from us.
As a father has compassion on <u>his</u> children, * so the Lord has compassion on <u>those</u> who fear him.

EIGHTH SUNDAY IN ORDINARY TIME
February 25, 2001

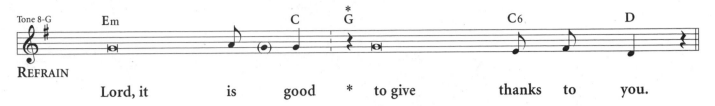

REFRAIN Lord, it is good * to give thanks to you.

VERSES Psalm 92:2-3, 13-14, 15-16

It is good to give thanks to the LORD, * to sing praise to your name, Most High,
to proclaim your kindness at dawn * and your faithfulness throughout the night.

The just one shall flourish like the palm tree, * like a cedar of Lebanon shall he grow.
They that are planted in the house of the LORD * shall flourish in the courts of our God.

They shall bear fruit even in old age; * vigorous and sturdy shall they be,
declaring how just is the Lord, * my rock, in whom there is no wrong.

ASH WEDNESDAY
February 28, 2001

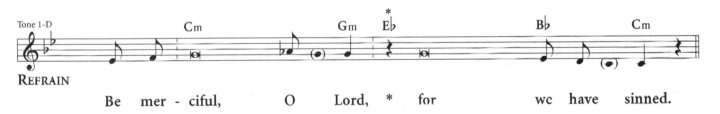

REFRAIN Be mer - ci - ful, O Lord, * for we have sinned.

VERSES Psalm 51:3-4, 5-6, 12-13, 14, 17

Have mercy on me, O God, in your goodness; * in the greatness of your compassion wipe out my offense.
Thoroughly wash me from my guilt * and of my sin cleanse me.

For I acknowledge my offense, * and my sin is before me always:
"Against you only have I sinned, * and done what is evil in your sight."

A clean heart create for me, O God, * and a steadfast spirit renew within me.
Cast me not out from your presence, * and your holy spirit take not from me.

Give me back the joy of your salvation, * and a willing spirit sustain in me.
O Lord, open my lips, * and my mouth shall proclaim your praise.

ASH WEDNESDAY

February 28, 2001

BLESSING AND GIVING OF ASHES

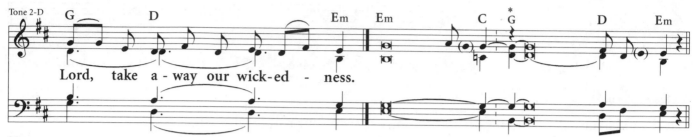

Lord, take a - way our wick-ed - ness.

VERSES Psalm 51:3-4, 5-6, 12-13, 14, 17

Have mercy on me, O God, in your goodness; * in the greatness of your compassion wipe out my offense.
Thoroughly wash me from my guilt * and of my sin cleanse me.

For I acknowledge my offense, * and my sin is before me always:
"Against you only have I sinned, * and done what is evil in your sight."

A clean heart create for me, O God, * and a steadfast spirit renew within me.
Cast me not out from your presence, * and your holy spirit take not from me.

Give me back the joy of your salvation, * and a willing spirit sustain in me.
O Lord, open my lips, * and my mouth shall proclaim your praise.

FIRST SUNDAY OF LENT

March 4, 2001

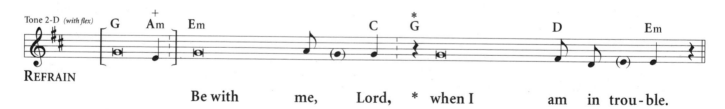

REFRAIN

Be with me, Lord, * when I am in trou - ble.

VERSES Psalm 91:1-2, 10-11, 12-13, 14-15

You who dwell in the shelter of the Most High, * who abide in the shadow of the Almighty,
say to the Lord, "My refuge and fortress, * my God in whom I trust."

No evil shall befall you, * nor shall affliction come near your tent,
for to his angels he has given command about you, * that they guard you in all your ways.

Upon their hands they shall bear you up, * lest you dash your foot against a stone.
You shall tread upon the asp and the viper; * you shall trample down the lion and the dragon.

Because he clings to me, I will deliver him; * I will set him on high because he acknowledges my name.
He shall call upon me, and I will answer him; +
    I will be with him in distress; * I will deliver him and glorify him.

SECOND SUNDAY OF LENT
March 11, 2001

REFRAIN

The Lord is my light * and my sal - va - tion.

VERSES   Psalm 27:1, 7-8, 8-9, 13-14

The LORD is my light and my salvation; * whom should I fear?
The LORD is my life's refuge; * of whom should I be afraid?

Hear, O LORD, the sound of my call; +
    have pity on me, and answer me. * Of you my heart speaks; you my glance seeks.

Your presence, O LORD, I seek. * Hide not your face from me;
do not in anger repel your servant. * You are my helper: cast me not off.

I believe that I shall see the bounty of the LORD * in the land of the living.
Wait for the LORD with courage; * be stouthearted, and wait for the LORD.

THIRD SUNDAY OF LENT
March 18, 2001

The Lord is kind and mer - ci - ful.

VERSES   Psalm 103:1-2, 3-4, 6-7, 8, 11

Bless the LORD, O my soul: * and all my being, bless his holy name.
Bless the LORD, O my soul, * and forget not all his benefits.

He pardons all your iniquities, * heals all your ills.
He redeems your life from destruction, * crowns you with kindness and compassion.

The LORD secures justice * and the rights of all the oppressed.
He has made known his ways to Moses, * and his deeds to the children of Israel.

Merciful and gracious is the LORD, * slow to anger and abounding in kindness.
For as the heavens are high above the earth, * so surpassing is his kindness toward those who fear him.

111

FOURTH SUNDAY OF LENT
March 25, 2001

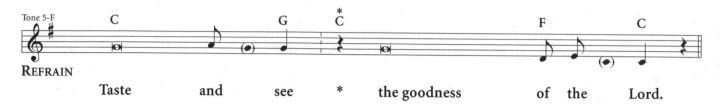

REFRAIN

Taste and see * the goodness of the Lord.

VERSES Psalm 34:2-3, 4-5, 6-7

I will bless the LORD <u>at</u> all times; * his praise shall be ever <u>in</u> my mouth.
Let my soul glory in <u>the</u> LORD; * the lowly will hear me <u>and</u> be glad.

Glorify the LORD <u>with</u> me, * let us together ex<u>tol</u> his name.
I sought the LORD, and <u>he</u> answered me * and delivered me from <u>all</u> my fears.

Look to him that you may be radiant <u>with</u> joy, * and your faces may not <u>blush</u> with shame.
When the poor one called out, the <u>LORD</u> heard, * and from all his dis<u>tress</u> he saved him.

FIFTH SUNDAY OF LENT
April 1, 2001

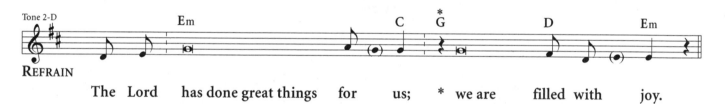

REFRAIN

The Lord has done great things for us; * we are filled with joy.

VERSES Psalm 126:1-2, 2-3, 4-5, 6

When the LORD brought back the captives <u>of</u> Zion, * we were <u>like</u> men dreaming.
Then our mouth was filled <u>with</u> laughter, * and our tongue <u>with</u> rejoicing.

Then they said among <u>the</u> nations, * "The LORD has done great <u>things</u> for them."
The LORD has done great things <u>for</u> us; * we are <u>glad</u> indeed.

Restore our fortunes, <u>O</u> LORD, * like the torrents in the <u>south</u>ern desert.
Those that sow <u>in</u> tears * shall <u>reap</u> rejoicing.

Although they go <u>forth</u> weeping, * carrying the seed <u>to</u> be sown,
they shall come back re<u>joic</u>ing, * carry<u>ing</u> their sheaves.

Palm Sunday of the Lord's Passion

April 8, 2001

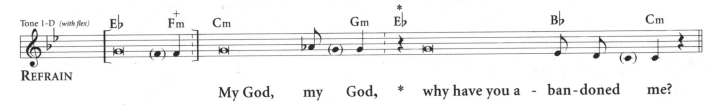

REFRAIN

My God, my God, * why have you a - ban - doned me?

VERSES   Psalm 22:8-9, 17-18, 19-20, 23-24

All who see me scoff <u>at</u> me; * they mock me with parted lips, they <u>wag</u> their heads:
"He relied on <u>the</u> LORD * let him de<u>liv</u>er him."

Indeed, many dogs <u>sur</u>round me, * a pack of evildoers closes in u<u>pon</u> me;
they have pierced my hands and <u>my</u> feet; * I can count <u>all</u> my bones.

They divide my garments <u>a</u>mong them, * and for my vesture <u>they</u> cast lots.
But you, O LORD, be not far from me; * O my help, hasten to aid me.

I will proclaim your name to <u>my</u> brethren; * in the midst of the assembly <u>I</u> will praise you:
"You who fear the LORD, <u>praise</u> him; +
   all you descendants of Jacob, give glory <u>to</u> him; * revere him, all you descen<u>dants</u> of Israel!"

Holy Thursday

April 12, 2001

EVENING MASS OF THE LORD'S SUPPER

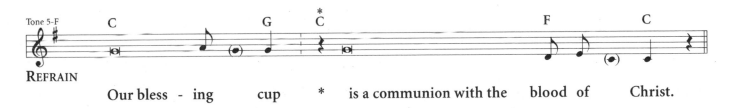

REFRAIN

Our bless - ing cup * is a communion with the blood of Christ.

VERSES   Psalm 116:12-13, 15-16, 17-18

How shall I make a return to <u>the</u> LORD * for all the good he has <u>done</u> for me?
The cup of salvation I <u>will</u> take up, * and I will call upon the name <u>of</u> the LORD.

Precious in the eyes of <u>the</u> LORD * is the death of his <u>faith</u>ful ones.
I am your servant, the son of <u>your</u> handmaid; * you have <u>loosed</u> my bonds.

To you will I offer sacrifice of <u>thanks</u>giving, * and I will call upon the name <u>of</u> the LORD.
My vows to the LORD I <u>will</u> pay * in the presence of <u>all</u> his people.

113

GOOD FRIDAY
April 13, 2001
CELEBRATION OF THE LORD'S PASSION

REFRAIN Fa-ther, into your hands * I com-mend my Spir-it.

VERSES Psalm 31:2, 6, 12-13, 15-16, 17, 25

In you, O LORD, I take refuge; * let me never be put to shame.
In your justice rescue me. +
 Into your hands I commend my spirit; * you will redeem me, O LORD, O faithful God.

For all my foes I am an object of reproach, +
 a laughingstock to my neighbors, and a dread to my friends; * they who see me abroad flee from me.
I am forgotten like the unremembered dead; * I am like a dish that is broken.

But my trust is in you, O LORD; * I say, "You are my God.
In your hands is my destiny; rescue me * from the clutches of my enemies and my persecutors."

Let your face shine upon your servant; * save me in your kindness.
Take courage and be stouthearted, * all you who hope in the LORD.

THE EASTER VIGIL
April 14, 2001

A   **After First Reading (Genesis 1:1–2:2)**

REFRAIN Lord, send out your Spir-it, * and renew the face of the earth.

VERSES Psalm 104:1, 24, 29-30, 31, 34

Bless the LORD, O my soul! * O LORD, my God, you are great indeed!
How manifold are your works, O LORD! * The earth is full of your creatures.

If you take away their breath, they perish * and return to their dust.
When you send forth your spirit, they are created, * and you renew the face of the earth.

May the glory of the LORD endure forever; * may the LORD be glad in his works!
Pleasing to him be my theme; * I will be glad in the LORD.

THE EASTER VIGIL
April 14, 2001

B **After First Reading (Genesis 1:1–2:2)**

REFRAIN

The earth is full * of the goodness of the Lord.

VERSES   Psalm 33:4-5, 6-7, 12-13, 20-22

Upright is the word of the LORD, * and all his works are trustworthy.
He loves justice and right; * of the kindness of the LORD the earth is full.

By the word of the LORD the heavens were made; * by the breath of his mouth all their host.
He gathers the waters of the sea as in a flask; * in cellars he confines the deep.

Blessed the nation whose God is the LORD, * the people he has chosen for his own inheritance.
From heaven the LORD looks down; * he sees all mankind.

Our soul waits for the LORD, * who is our help and our shield.
May your kindness, O LORD, be upon us * who have put our hope in you.

THE EASTER VIGIL
April 14, 2001

After Second Reading (Genesis 22:1-18)

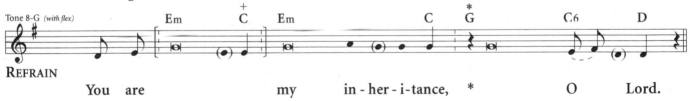

REFRAIN

You are my in - her - i - tance, * O Lord.

VERSES   Psalm 16:5, 8, 9-10, 11

O LORD, my allotted portion and my cup, * you it is who hold fast my lot.
I set the LORD ever before me; * with him at my right hand I shall not be disturbed.

Therefore my heart is glad and my soul rejoices, * my body, too, abides in confidence;
because you will not abandon my soul to the netherworld, *
  nor will you suffer your faithful one to undergo corruption.

You will show me the path to life, +
  fullness of joys in your presence, * the delights at your right hand forever.

THE EASTER VIGIL

April 14, 2001

After Third Reading (Exodus 14:15–15:1)

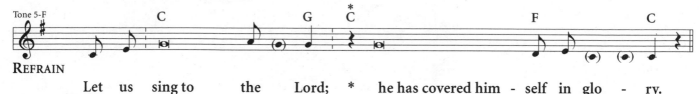

REFRAIN

Let us sing to the Lord; * he has covered him - self in glo - ry.

VERSES   Exodus 15:1-2, 3-4, 5-6, 17-18

I will sing to the LORD, for he is gloriously triumphant; * horse and chariot he has cast into the sea.
My strength and my courage is the LORD, * and he has been my savior.
He is my God, I praise him; * the God of my father, I extol him.

The LORD is a warrior, * LORD is his name!
Pharaoh's chariots and army he hurled into the sea; *
  the elite of his officers were submerged in the Red Sea.

The flood waters covered them, * they sank into the depths like a stone.
Your right hand, O LORD, magnificent in power, * your right hand, O LORD, has shattered the enemy.

You brought in the people you redeemed * and planted them on the mountain of your inheritance—
the place where you made your seat, O LORD, * the sanctuary, LORD, which your hands established.
The LORD shall reign * forever and ever.

THE EASTER VIGIL

April 14, 2001

After Fourth Reading (Isaiah 54:5-14)

REFRAIN

I will praise you, Lord, * for you have res - cued me.

VERSES   Psalm 30:2, 4, 5-6, 11-12, 13

I will extol you, O LORD, for you drew me clear * and did not let my enemies rejoice over me.
O LORD, you brought me up from the netherworld; *
  you preserved me from among those going down into the pit.

Sing praise to the LORD, you his faithful ones, * and give thanks to his holy name.
For his anger lasts but a moment; * a lifetime, his good will.
At nightfall, weeping enters in, * but with the dawn, rejoicing.

Hear, O Lord, and have pity on me; * O LORD, be my helper.
You changed my mourning into dancing; * O LORD, my God, forever will I give you thanks.

THE EASTER VIGIL
April 14, 2001

After Fifth Reading (Isaiah 55:1-11)

REFRAIN

You will draw water joy - ful - ly * from the springs of sal - va - tion.

VERSES   Isaiah 12:2-3, 4, 5-6

God indeed is <u>my</u> savior; * I am confident and <u>un</u>afraid.
My strength and my courage is <u>the</u> LORD, * and he has <u>been</u> my savior.
With joy you will <u>draw</u> water * at the fountain <u>of</u> salvation.

Give thanks to the LORD, acclaim his <u>name</u>; +
    among the nations make known <u>his</u> deeds, * proclaim how exalted <u>is</u> his name.

Sing praise to the LORD for his glorious <u>achieve</u>ment; * let this be known throughout <u>all</u> the earth.
Shout with exultation, O city of <u>Zi</u>on, +
    for great in <u>your</u> midst * is the Holy <u>One</u> of Israel!

THE EASTER VIGIL
April 14, 2001

After Sixth Reading (Baruch 3:9-15, 32–4:4)

REFRAIN

Lord, you have the words * of ever - - last - ing life.

VERSES   Psalm 19:8, 9, 10, 11

The law of the LORD <u>is</u> perfect, * refresh<u>ing</u> the soul;
the decree of the LORD <u>is</u> trustworthy, * giving wisdom <u>to</u> the simple.

The precepts of the LORD <u>are</u> right, * rejoic<u>ing</u> the heart;
the command of the LORD <u>is</u> clear, * enlighten<u>ing</u> the eye.

The fear of the LORD <u>is</u> pure, * endur<u>ing</u> forever;
the ordinances of the LORD <u>are</u> true, * all <u>of</u> them just.

They are more precious <u>than</u> gold, * than a heap of <u>pur</u>est gold;
sweeter also <u>than</u> syrup * or honey <u>from</u> the comb.

THE EASTER VIGIL

April 14, 2001

A   After Seventh Reading (Ezekiel 36:16-17, 18-28)

REFRAIN

Like a deer that longs for run - ning streams, * my soul longs for you, my God.

VERSES   Psalm 42:3, 5; 43:3, 4

Athirst is my soul for God, the living God. * When shall I go and behold the face of God?

I went with the throng * and led them in procession to the house of God,
amid loud cries of joy and thanksgiving, * with the multitude keeping festival.

Send forth your light and your fidelity; * they shall lead me on
and bring me to your holy mountain, * to your dwelling-place.

Then will I go in to the altar of God, * the God of my gladness and joy;
then will I give you thanks upon the harp, * O God, my God!

THE EASTER VIGIL

April 14, 2001

B   After Seventh Reading (Ezekiel 36:16-17, 18-28)

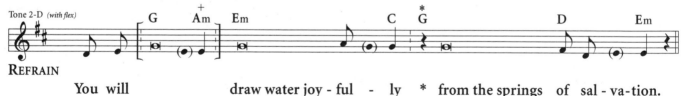

REFRAIN

You will draw water joy - ful - ly * from the springs of sal - va - tion.

VERSES   Isaiah 12:2-3, 4, 5-6

God indeed is <u>my</u> savior; * I am confident and <u>una</u>fraid.
My strength and my courage is <u>the</u> LORD, * and he has <u>been</u> my savior.
With joy you will <u>draw</u> water * at the fountain <u>of</u> salvation.

Give thanks to the LORD, acclaim his <u>name</u>; +
among the nations make known <u>his</u> deeds, * proclaim how exalted <u>is</u> his name.

Sing praise to the LORD for his glorious <u>a</u>chievement; * let this be known throughout <u>all</u> the earth.
Shout with exultation, O city of <u>Zion</u>, +
for great in <u>your</u> midst * is the Holy <u>One</u> of Israel!

THE EASTER VIGIL
April 14, 2001

C   After Seventh Reading (Ezekiel 36:16-17, 18-28)

REFRAIN   Cre - ate   a clean heart * in   me, O   God.

VERSES   Psalm 51:12-13, 14-15, 18-19

A clean heart create for me, <u>O</u> God, * and a steadfast spirit re<u>new</u> within me.
Cast me not out from <u>your</u> presence, * and your Holy Spirit take <u>not</u> from me.

Give me back the joy of your <u>sal</u>vation, * and a willing spirit sus<u>tain</u> in me.
I will teach transgressors <u>your</u> ways, * and sinners shall re<u>turn</u> to you.

For you are not pleased <u>with</u> sacrifices; * should I offer a holocaust, you would <u>not</u> accept it.
My sacrifice, O God, is a con<u>trite</u> spirit; * a heart contrite and humbled, O God, you <u>will</u> not spurn.

THE EASTER VIGIL
April 14, 2001

After Epistle (Romans 6:3-11)

Al - le - lu - ia, al - le - lu - ia, al - le - lu - ia.

Psalm 118:1-2, 16-17, 22-23

1. Give thanks to the LORD, for he is good, for his mercy en - - dures for - ev - er.
   Let the house of Is - - ra - el say, "His mercy en - - dures for - ev - er."

2. The right hand of the LORD has struck with power; the right hand of the LORD is ex - alt - ed.
   I shall not die, but live, and declare the works of the LORD.

3. The stone which the builders re - ject - ed has become the cor - ner - stone.
   By the LORD has this been done; it is wonder - - ful in our eyes.

EASTER SUNDAY
April 15, 2001

This is the day the Lord has made; let us re - - joice and be glad.

OR:

Al - le - lu - ia, al - le - lu - ia, al - le - lu - ia.

Psalm 118:1-2, 16-17, 22-23

1. Give thanks to the LORD, for   he   is   good,   for his mercy en - - dures for - ev - er.
   Let the house of Is - - - ra - el   say,   "His mercy en - - - dures for - ev - er."

2. The right hand of the LORD has   struck with power;   the right hand of the LORD   is   ex - alt - ed.
   I shall not   dic, but   live,   and declare the   works of   the LORD.

3. The stone which the builders   re - ject - ed   has become   the cor - ner - stone.
   By the LORD has   this   been done;   it is wonder - - - ful in   our eyes.

121

SECOND SUNDAY OF EASTER

April 22, 2001

REFRAIN

Give thanks to the Lord for he is good, * his love is ev - er - last - ing.

or: Al - le - lu - - - - - ia, * al - - - le - lu - ia.

VERSES Psalm 118:2-4, 13-15, 22-24

Let the house of Isra_el_ say, * "His mercy end_ures_ forever."
Let the house of Aar_on_ say, * "His mercy end_ures_ forever."
Let those who fear the LORD say, * "His mercy end_ures_ forever."

I was hard pressed and _was_ falling, * but the LORD helped me.
My strength and my courage is _the_ LORD, * and he has _been_ my savior.
The joyful shout _of_ victory * in the tents _of_ the just.

The stone which the builders _rejected_ * has be_come_ the cornerstone.
By the LORD has this _been_ done; * it is wonderful _in_ our eyes.
This is the day the LORD _has_ made; * let us be glad and re_joice_ in it.

THIRD SUNDAY OF EASTER

April 29, 2001

REFRAIN

I will praise you, Lord, * for you have res - cued me.

or: Al - le - lu - - - ia, * al - - - le - lu - - ia.

VERSES Psalm 30:2, 4, 5-6, 11-12, 13

I will extol you, O LORD, for you drew _me_ clear * and did not let my enemies rejoice _over_ me.
O LORD, you brought me up from _the_ netherworld; *
  you preserved me from among those going down in_to_ the pit.

Sing praise to the LORD, you _his_ faithful ones, * and give thanks to his _holy_ name.
For his anger lasts but _a_ moment; * a lifetime, _his_ good will.
At nightfall, weeping ent_ers_ in, * but with the _dawn_, rejoicing.

Hear, O Lord, and have pity _on_ me; * O LORD, _be_ my helper.
You changed my mourning in_to_ dancing; * O LORD, my God, forever will I _give_ you thanks.

FOURTH SUNDAY OF EASTER
May 6, 2001

REFRAIN

We are his peo - ple, * the sheep of his flock.
or: Al - le - - - - lu - - - - ia, * al - - - le - lu - ia.

VERSES   Psalm 100:1-2, 3, 5

Sing joyfully to the LORD, all you <u>lands</u>; +
  serve the LORD <u>with</u> gladness; * come before him with <u>joy</u>ful song.

Know that the LORD is <u>God</u>; +
  he made us, his <u>we</u> are; * his people, the <u>flock</u> he tends.

The LORD is <u>good</u>: +
  his kindness endures <u>for</u>ever, * and his faithfulness, to all <u>gen</u>erations.

FIFTH SUNDAY OF EASTER
May 13, 2001

REFRAIN

I will praise your name for - ev - er, * my king and my God.
or: Al - le - lu - - - - - ia, * al - - - le - lu - ia.

VERSES   Psalm 145:8-9, 10-11, 12-13

The LORD is gracious <u>and</u> merciful, * slow to anger and <u>of</u> great kindness.
The LORD is good <u>to</u> all * and compassionate toward <u>all</u> his works.

Let all your works give you thanks, <u>O</u> LORD, * and let your faith<u>ful</u> ones bless you.
Let them discourse of the glory of <u>your</u> kingdom * and speak <u>of</u> your might.

Let them make known your might to the children <u>of</u> Adam, * and the glorious splendor <u>of</u> your kingdom.
Your kingdom is a kingdom for <u>all</u> ages, * and your dominion endures through all <u>gen</u>erations.

Sixth Sunday of Easter
May 20, 2001

Tone 5-F *(with flex)*

REFRAIN

O God, * let all the na-tions praise you.

or: Al - le - - - lu - - - - ia, * al - - - le - lu - ia.

VERSES Psalm 67:2-3, 5, 6, 8

May God have pity on us <u>and</u> bless us; * may he let his face <u>shine</u> upon us.
So may your way be known up<u>on</u> earth; * among all nations, <u>your</u> salvation.

May the nations be glad and ex<u>ult</u> +
    because you rule the peoples <u>in</u> equity; * the nations on the <u>earth</u> you guide.

May the peoples praise you, <u>O</u> God; * may all the <u>peoples</u> praise you!
May <u>God</u> bless us, * and may all the ends of <u>the</u> earth fear him!

The Ascension of the Lord
May 24, 2001

Tone 8-G

REFRAIN

God mounts his throne to shouts of joy: * a blare of trumpets for the Lord.

or: Al - le - lu - - - - ia, * al - - - - le - lu - ia.

VERSES Psalm 47:2-3, 6-7, 8-9

All you peoples, clap <u>your</u> hands, * shout to God with <u>cries</u> of gladness,
for the LORD, the Most High, <u>the</u> awesome, * is the great king over <u>all</u> the earth.

God mounts his throne amid shouts <u>of</u> joy; * the LORD, amid <u>trumpet</u> blasts.
Sing praise to God, <u>sing</u> praise; * sing praise to our <u>king</u>, sing praise.

For king of all the earth <u>is</u> God; * sing <u>hymns</u> of praise.
God reigns over <u>the</u> nations, * God sits upon his <u>holy</u> throne.

SEVENTH SUNDAY OF EASTER
May 27, 2001

REFRAIN

The Lord is king, * the Most High over all the earth.
or: Al - le - lu - - - - ia, * al - - - - - le - lu - ia.

VERSES Psalm 97:1-2, 6-7, 9

The LORD is king; let the earth re<u>joi</u>ce; * let the many i<u>slands</u> be glad.
Justice <u>and</u> judgment * are the foundation <u>of</u> his throne.

The heavens proclaim <u>his</u> justice; * and all peoples <u>see</u> his glory.
<u>All</u> gods * are pro<u>strate</u> before him.

You, O LORD, are the Most High over all <u>the</u> earth, * exalted far a<u>bove</u> all gods.

THE VIGIL OF PENTECOST
June 2, 2001

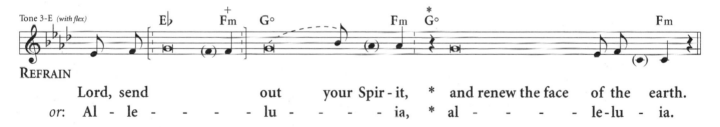

REFRAIN

Lord, send out your Spir - it, * and renew the face of the earth.
or: Al - le - - - - lu - - - ia, * al - - - - le-lu - ia.

VERSES Psalm 104:1-2, 24, 35, 27-28, 29, 30

Bless the LORD, O <u>my</u> soul! * O LORD, my God, you are <u>great</u> indeed!
You are clothed with majesty <u>and</u> glory, * robed in light as <u>with</u> a cloak.

How manifold are your works, O <u>LORD</u>! +
   In wisdom you have wrought <u>them</u> all— * the earth is full <u>of</u> your creatures;
bless the LORD, O <u>my</u> soul! * <u>Alle</u>luia.

Creatures all look <u>to</u> you * to give them food <u>in</u> due time.
When you give it to them, <u>they</u> gather it; * when you open your hand, they are <u>filled</u> with good things.

If you take away their breath, <u>they</u> perish * and return <u>to</u> their dust.
When you send forth your spirit, they <u>are</u> created, * and you renew the face <u>of</u> the earth.

PENTECOST
June 3, 2001
MASS DURING THE DAY

Tone 3-E *(with flex)*

REFRAIN

Lord, send out your Spir - it, * and renew the face of the earth.

or: Al - le - lu - - - ia, * al - - - - le - lu - ia.

VERSES Psalm 104:1, 24, 29-30, 31, 34

Bless the LORD, O <u>my</u> soul! * O LORD, my God, you are <u>great</u> indeed!
How manifold are your works, <u>O</u> LORD! * The earth is full <u>of</u> your creatures.

If you take away their breath, <u>they</u> perish * and return <u>to</u> their dust.
When you send forth your spirit, they <u>are</u> created, * and you renew the face <u>of</u> the earth.

May the glory of the LORD endure <u>forever</u>; * may the LORD be glad <u>in</u> his works!
Pleasing to him be <u>my</u> theme; * I will be glad <u>in</u> the LORD.

TRINITY SUNDAY
June 10, 2001

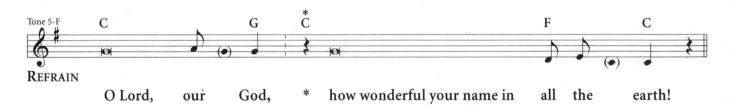

Tone 5-F

REFRAIN

O Lord, our God, * how wonderful your name in all the earth!

VERSES Psalm 8:4-5, 6-7, 8-9

When I behold your heavens, the work of <u>your</u> fingers, * the moon and the stars which you <u>set</u> in place—
what is man that you should be mindful <u>of</u> him, * or the son of man that you should <u>care</u> for him?

You have made him little less than <u>the</u> angels, * and crowned him with <u>glory</u> and honor.
You have given him rule over the works of <u>your</u> hands, * putting all things un<u>der</u> his feet:

All sheep <u>and</u> oxen, * yes, and the beasts <u>of</u> the field,
the birds <u>of</u> the air, the fishes of <u>the</u> sea, * and whatever swims the paths <u>of</u> the seas.

THE MOST HOLY BODY AND BLOOD OF CHRIST
June 17, 2001

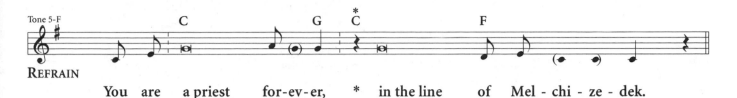

Tone 5-F

REFRAIN

You are a priest for-ev-er, * in the line of Mel - chi - ze - dek.

VERSES Psalm 110:1, 2, 3, 4

The Lord said to my Lord: "Sit at my right hand * till I make your enemies your footstool."

The scepter of your power the Lord will stretch forth from Zion: * "Rule in the midst of your enemies."

"Yours is princely power in the day of your birth, in holy splendor; *
    before the daystar, like the dew, I have begotten you."

The Lord has sworn, and he will not repent; *
    "You are a priest forever, according to the order of Melchizedek."

THE NATIVITY OF JOHN THE BAPTIST
June 23, 2001
VIGIL MASS

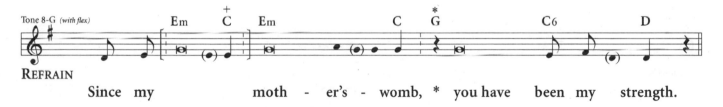

Tone 8-G *(with flex)*

REFRAIN

Since my moth - er's - womb, * you have been my strength.

VERSES Psalm 71:1-2, 3-4, 5-6, 15, 17

In you, O Lord, I take refuge; * let me never be put to shame.
In your justice rescue me, and deliver me; * incline your ear to me, and save me.

Be my rock of refuge, +
    a stronghold to give me safety, * for you are my rock and my fortress.
O my God, rescue me * from the hand of the wicked.

For you are my hope, O Lord; * my trust, O Lord, from my youth.
On you I depend from birth; * from my mother's womb you are my strength.

My mouth shall declare your justice, * day by day your salvation.
O God, you have taught me from my youth, * and till the present I proclaim your wondrous deeds.

THE NATIVITY OF JOHN THE BAPTIST
June 24, 2001
MASS DURING THE DAY

REFRAIN

I praise you, * for I am wonder - ful - ly made.

VERSES   Psalm 139:1-3, 13-14, 14-15

O LORD you have probed me and you <u>know</u> me; +
  you know when I sit and when <u>I</u> stand; * you understand my thoughts <u>from</u> afar.
My journeys and my rest <u>you</u> scrutinize, * with all my ways you <u>are</u> familiar.

Truly you have formed my in<u>most</u> being; * you knit me in my <u>mother's</u> womb.
I give you thanks that I am fearfully, wonderful<u>ly</u> made; * wonderful <u>are</u> your works.

My soul also you knew <u>full</u> well; * nor was my frame un<u>known</u> to you
when I was made <u>in</u> secret, * when I was fashioned in the depths <u>of</u> the earth.

THIRTEENTH SUNDAY IN ORDINARY TIME
July 1, 2001

REFRAIN

You are my in-her - i - tance, * O Lord.

VERSES   Psalm 16:1-2, 5, 7-8, 9-10, 11

Keep me, O God, for in you I <u>take</u> refuge; * I say to the LORD, "My <u>LORD</u> are you.
O LORD, my allotted portion and <u>my</u> cup, * you it is who hold <u>fast</u> my lot."

I bless the LORD <u>who</u> counsels me; * even in the night my <u>heart</u> exhorts me.
I set the LORD ever <u>before</u> me; * with him at my right hand I shall not <u>be</u> disturbed.

Therefore my heart is glad and my soul <u>rejoices</u>, * my body, too, a<u>bides</u> in confidence;
because you will not abandon my soul to <u>the</u> netherworld, *
  nor will you suffer your faithful one to <u>undergo</u> corruption.

You will show me the path to <u>life</u>, +
  fullness of joys in <u>your</u> presence, * the delights at your right <u>hand</u> forever.

Fourteenth Sunday in Ordinary Time

July 8, 2001

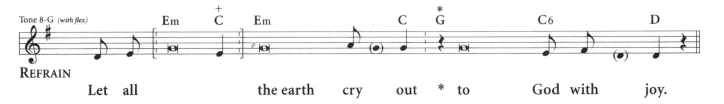

REFRAIN Let all the earth cry out * to God with joy.

VERSES Psalm 66:1-3, 4-5, 6-7, 16, 20

Shout joyfully to God, all the earth, +
  sing praise to the glory of his name; * proclaim his glorious praise.

"Let all on earth worship and sing praise to you, * sing praise to your name!"
Come and see the works of God, * his tremendous deeds among the children of Adam.

He has changed the sea into dry land; * through the river they passed on foot.
Therefore let us rejoice in him. * He rules by his might forever.

Hear now, all you who fear God, * while I declare what he has done for me.
Blessed be God who refused me not * my prayer or his kindness!

Fifteenth Sunday in Ordinary Time

July 15, 2001

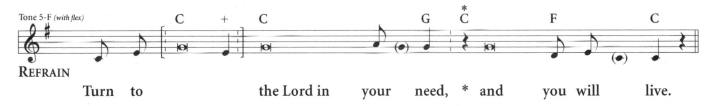

REFRAIN Turn to the Lord in your need, * and you will live.

VERSES Psalm 69:14, 17, 30-31, 33-34, 36, 37

I pray to you, O Lord, * for the time of your favor, O God!
In your great kindness answer me * with your constant help.
Answer me, O Lord, for bounteous is your kindness: * in your great mercy turn toward me.

I am afflicted and in pain; * let your saving help, O God, protect me.
I will praise the name of God in song, * and I will glorify him with thanksgiving.

"See, you lowly ones, and be glad; * you who seek God, may your hearts revive!
For the Lord hears the poor, * and his own who are in bonds he spurns not."

For God will save Zion * and rebuild the cities of Judah.
The descendants of his servants shall inherit it, * and those who love his name shall inhabit it.

Sixteenth Sunday in Ordinary Time
July 22, 2001

REFRAIN

He who does jus-tice * will live in the presence of the Lord.

VERSES   Psalm 15:2-3, 3-4, 5

One who walks blamelessly and does <u>jus</u>tice; +
   who thinks the truth in <u>his</u> heart * and slanders not <u>with</u> his tongue.

Who harms not his <u>fel</u>low man, * nor takes up a reproach a<u>gainst</u> his neighbor;
by whom the reprobate is <u>des</u>pised, * while he honors those who <u>fear</u> the Lord.

Who lends not his money <u>at</u> usury * and accepts no bribe a<u>gainst</u> the innocent.
One who does <u>these</u> things * shall never <u>be</u> disturbed.

Seventeenth Sunday in Ordinary Time
July 29, 2001

REFRAIN

Lord, on the day I called for help, * you an-swered me.

VERSES   Psalm 138:1-2, 2-3, 6-7, 7-8

I will give thanks to you, O Lord, with all my <u>heart</u>, +
   for you have heard the words of <u>my</u> mouth; * in the presence of the angels I will <u>sing</u> your praise;
I will worship at your ho<u>ly</u> temple * and give thanks <u>to</u> your name.

Because of your kindness and your <u>truth</u>; +
   for you have made great above <u>all</u> things * your name <u>and</u> your promise.
When I called you ans<u>wered</u> me; * you built up <u>strength</u> within me.

The Lord is exalted, yet the lowly <u>he</u> sees, * and the proud he knows <u>from</u> afar.
Though I walk amid distress, you <u>preserve</u> me; * against the anger of my enemies you <u>raise</u> your hand.

Your right <u>hand</u> saves me. * The Lord will complete what he has <u>done</u> for me;
your kindness, O Lord, endures <u>forever</u>; * forsake not the work <u>of</u> your hands.

EIGHTEENTH SUNDAY IN ORDINARY TIME

August 5, 2001

Tone 8-G *(with flex)*

REFRAIN

If to - - - day you hear his voice, * harden not your hearts.

VERSES Psalm 90:3-4, 5-6, 12-13

You turn man back <u>to</u> dust, * saying, "Return, O chil<u>dren</u> of men."
For a thousand years in your <u>sight</u> +
   are as yesterday, now that it <u>is</u> past * or as a watch <u>of</u> the night.

You make an end of them in <u>their</u> sleep; * the next morning they are like the <u>chang</u>ing grass,
which at dawn springs up a<u>new</u>, * but by evening <u>wilts</u> and fades.

Teach us to number our days a<u>right</u>, * that we may gain wis<u>dom</u> of heart.
Return, O LORD! <u>How</u> long? * Have pity <u>on</u> your servants!

Fill us at daybreak with <u>your</u> kindness, * that we may shout for joy and gladness <u>all</u> our days.
And may the gracious care of the LORD our God be <u>ours</u>; +
   prosper the work of our hands <u>for</u> us! * Prosper the work <u>of</u> our hands!

NINETEENTH SUNDAY IN ORDINARY TIME

August 12, 2001

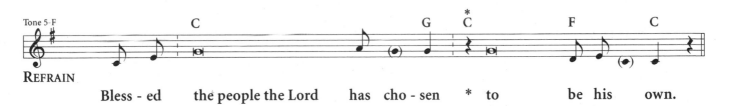

Tone 5-F

REFRAIN

Bless - ed the people the Lord has cho - sen * to be his own.

VERSES Psalm 33:1, 12, 18-19, 20-22

Exult, you just, in <u>the</u> LORD; * praise from the up<u>right</u> is fitting.
Blessed the nation whose God is <u>the</u> LORD, * the people he has chosen for his <u>own</u> inheritance.

See, the eyes of the LORD are upon those <u>who</u> fear him, * upon those who hope <u>for</u> his kindness,
to deliver them <u>from</u> death * and preserve them in <u>spite</u> of famine.

Our soul waits for <u>the</u> LORD, * who is our help <u>and</u> our shield.
May your kindness, O LORD, <u>be</u> upon us * who have put our <u>hope</u> in you.

VIGIL OF THE ASSUMPTION

August 14, 2001

REFRAIN

Lord, go up to the place of your rest, * you and the ark of your ho-li-ness.

VERSES Psalm 132:6-7, 9-10, 13-14

Behold, we heard of it <u>in</u> Ephrathah; * we found it in the <u>fields</u> of Jaar.
Let us enter into <u>his</u> dwelling, * let us worship <u>at</u> his footstool.

May your priests be clothed <u>with</u> justice; * let your faithful ones shout merri<u>ly</u> for joy.
For the sake of David <u>your</u> servant, * reject not the pleas of <u>your</u> anointed.

For the LORD has chos<u>en</u> Zion; * he prefers her <u>for</u> his dwelling.
"Zion is my resting place <u>for</u>ever; * in her will I dwell, for <u>I</u> prefer her."

ASSUMPTION OF THE BLESSED VIRGIN MARY

August 15, 2001

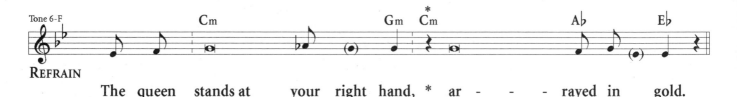

REFRAIN

The queen stands at your right hand, * ar - - - rayed in gold.

VERSES Psalm 45:10, 11, 12, 16

The queen takes her place at <u>your</u> right hand * in <u>gold</u> of Ophir.

Hear, O daughter, and see; turn <u>your</u> ear, * forget your people and your <u>fa</u>ther's house.

So shall the king desire <u>your</u> beauty; * for he <u>is</u> your lord.

They are borne in with gladness <u>and</u> joy; * they enter the palace <u>of</u> the king.

TWENTIETH SUNDAY IN ORDINARY TIME
August 19, 2001

Tone 4-E *(with flex)*

REFRAIN

Lord,_____ * come to my aid!

VERSES Psalm 40:2, 3, 4, 18

I have waited, waited for <u>the</u> LORD, * and he <u>stooped</u> toward me.

The LORD heard my <u>cry</u>. +
  He drew me out of the pit of <u>de</u>struction, * out of the mud <u>of</u> the swamp;
he set my feet upon <u>a</u> crag; * he made <u>firm</u> my steps.

And he put a new song into <u>my</u> mouth, * a hymn <u>to</u> our God.
Many shall look on <u>in</u> awe * and trust <u>in</u> the LORD.

Though I am afflicted <u>and</u> poor, * yet the LORD <u>thinks</u> of me.
You are my help and my de<u>liv</u>erer; * O my God, <u>hold</u> not back!

TWENTY-FIRST SUNDAY IN ORDINARY TIME
August 26, 2001

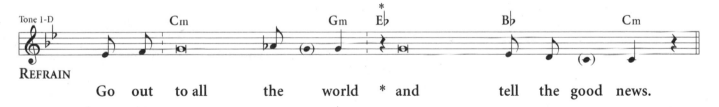

Tone 1-D

REFRAIN

Go out to all the world * and tell the good news.

VERSES Psalm 117:1, 2

Praise the LORD, all <u>you</u> nations; * glorify him, <u>all</u> you peoples!

For steadfast is his kindness <u>toward</u> us, * and the fidelity of the LORD en<u>dures</u> forever.

133

Twenty-second Sunday in Ordinary Time

September 2, 2001

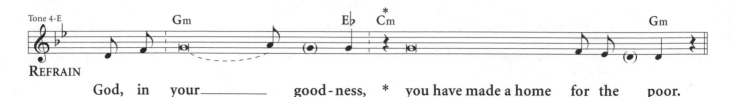

REFRAIN

God, in your_____ good-ness, * you have made a home for the poor.

VERSES Psalm 6:4-5, 6-7, 10-11

The just rejoice and exult be<u>fore</u> God; * they are glad <u>and</u> rejoice.
Sing to God, chant praise to <u>his</u> name; * whose name <u>is</u> the Lord.

The father of orphans and the defender <u>of</u> widows * is God in his <u>holy</u> dwelling.
God gives a home to the <u>for</u>saken; * he leads forth prisoners to pros<u>per</u>ity.

A bountiful rain you showered down, O God, upon your inheritance; *
   you restored the land <u>when</u> it languished.
your flock settled <u>in</u> it; * in your goodness, O God, you provided it <u>for</u> the needy.

Twenty-third Sunday in Ordinary Time

September 9, 2001

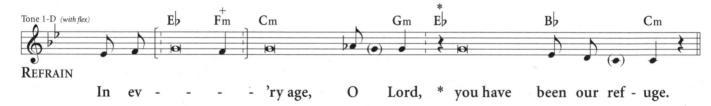

REFRAIN

In ev - - - - 'ry age, O Lord, * you have been our ref - uge.

VERSES Psalm 90:3-4, 5-6, 12-13, 14-17

You turn man back <u>to</u> dust, * saying, "Return, O chil<u>dren</u> of men."
For a thousand years in your <u>sight</u> +
   are as yesterday, now that it <u>is</u> past, * or as a watch <u>of</u> the night.

You make an end of them in <u>their</u> sleep; * the next morning they are like the <u>changing</u> grass,
which at dawn springs up a<u>new</u>, * but by evening <u>wilts</u> and fades.

Teach us to number our days a<u>right</u>, * that we may gain wis<u>dom</u> of heart.
Return, O LORD! <u>How</u> long? * Have pity <u>on</u> your servants!

Fill us at daybreak with <u>your</u> kindness, * that we may shout for joy and gladness <u>all</u> our days.
And may the gracious care of the LORD our God <u>be</u> ours; +
   prosper the work of our hands <u>for</u> us! * Prosper the work <u>of</u> our hands!

134

TWENTY-FOURTH SUNDAY IN ORDINARY TIME
September 16, 2001

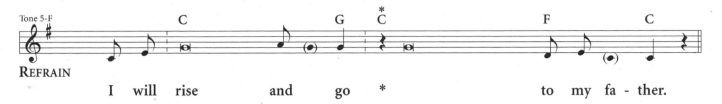

REFRAIN

I will rise and go * to my fa - ther.

VERSES Psalm 51:3-4, 12-13, 17, 19

Have mercy on me, O God, in your goodness; * in the greatness of your compassion wipe out my offense.
Thoroughly wash me from my guilt * and of my sin cleanse me.

A clean heart create for me, O God, * and a steadfast spirit renew within me.
Cast me not out from your presence, * and your holy spirit take not from me.

O LORD, open my lips, * and my mouth shall proclaim your praise.
My sacrifice, O God, is a contrite spirit; * a heart contrite and humbled, O God, you will not spurn.

TWENTY-FIFTH SUNDAY IN ORDINARY TIME
September 23, 2001

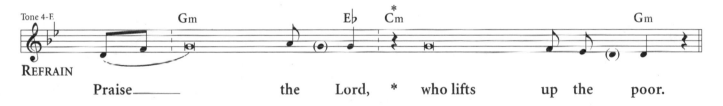

REFRAIN

Praise———— the Lord, * who lifts up the poor.

VERSES Psalm 113:1-2, 4-6, 7-8

Praise, you servants of the LORD; * praise the name of the LORD.
Blessed be the name of the LORD * both now and forever.

High above all nations is the LORD; * above the heavens is his glory.
Who is like the LORD, our God, who is enthroned on high *
    and looks upon the heavens and the earth below?

He raises up the lowly from the dust; * from the dunghill he lifts up the poor
to seat them with princes, * with the princes of his own people.

TWENTY-SIXTH SUNDAY IN ORDINARY TIME

September 30, 2001

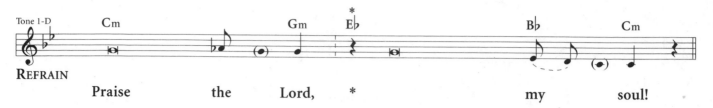

REFRAIN

Praise the Lord, * my soul!

VERSES Psalm 146:7, 8-9, 9-10

The LORD keeps faith <u>for</u>ever, * secures justice for <u>the</u> oppressed,
gives food to <u>the</u> hungry. * The LORD sets <u>cap</u>tives free.

The LORD gives sight to <u>the</u> blind; * the LORD raises up those who <u>were</u> bowed down.
The LORD loves <u>the</u> just; * the LORD <u>pro</u>tects strangers.

The fatherless and the widow he <u>sus</u>tains, * but the way of the wick<u>ed</u> he thwarts.
The LORD shall reign <u>for</u>ever; * your God, O Zion, through <u>all</u> generations.

TWENTY-SEVENTH SUNDAY IN ORDINARY TIME

October 7, 2001

REFRAIN

If to - - - day you hear his voice, * harden not your hearts.

VERSES Psalm 95:1-2, 6-7, 8-9

Come, let us sing joyfully to <u>the</u> LORD; * let us acclaim the rock of <u>our</u> salvation.
Let us come into his presence with <u>thanks</u>giving; * let us joyfully sing <u>psalms</u> to him.

Come, let us bow down <u>in</u> worship; * let us kneel before the <u>LORD</u> who made us.
For he is <u>our</u> God, * and we are the people he shepherds, the <u>flock</u> he guides.

Oh, that today you would hear his <u>voice</u>: +
   "Harden not your hearts as <u>at</u> Meribah, * as in the day of Massah <u>in</u> the desert,
where your fathers tempt<u>ed</u> me; * they tested me though they had <u>seen</u> my works."

Twenty-eighth Sunday in Ordinary Time

October 14, 2001

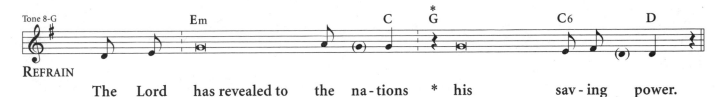

REFRAIN

The Lord has revealed to the na-tions * his sav-ing power.

VERSES Psalm 98:1, 2-3, 3-4

Sing to the LORD a new song, * for he has done wondrous deeds;
his right hand has won victory for him, * his holy arm.

The LORD has made his salvation known: * in the sight of the nations he has revealed his justice.
He has remembered his kindness and his faithfulness * toward the house of Israel.

All the ends of the earth have seen * the salvation by our God.
Sing joyfully to the LORD, all you lands; * break into song; sing praise.

Twenty-ninth Sunday in Ordinary Time

October 21, 2001

REFRAIN

Our help is from the Lord, * who made heav - en and earth.

VERSES Psalm 121:1-2, 3-4, 5-6, 7-8

I lift up my eyes toward the mountains; * whence shall help come to me?
My help is from the LORD, * who made heaven and earth.

May he not suffer your foot to slip; * may he slumber not who guards you:
indeed he neither slumbers nor sleeps, * the guardian of Israel.

The LORD is your guardian; the LORD is your shade; * he is beside you at your right hand.
The sun shall not harm you by day, * nor the moon by night.

The LORD will guard you from all evil; * he will guard your life.
The LORD will guard your coming and your going, * both now and forever.

THIRTIETH SUNDAY IN ORDINARY TIME
October 28, 2001

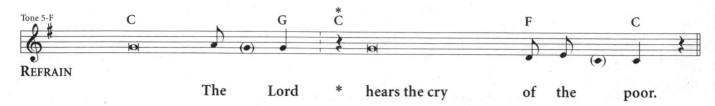

REFRAIN

The Lord * hears the cry of the poor.

VERSES   Psalm 34:2-3, 17-18, 19, 23

I will bless the Lord at all times; * his praise shall be ever in my mouth.
Let my soul glory in the Lord; * the lowly will hear me and be glad.

The Lord confronts the evildoers, * to destroy remembrance of them from the earth.
When the just cry out, the Lord hears them, * and from all their distress he rescues them.

The Lord is close to the brokenhearted; * and those who are crushed in spirit he saves.
The Lord redeems the lives of his servants; * no one incurs guilt who takes refuge in him.

ALL SAINTS
November 1, 2001

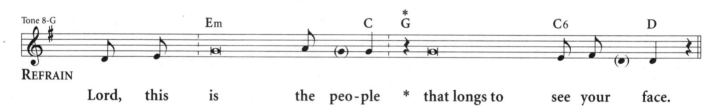

REFRAIN

Lord, this is the peo-ple * that longs to see your face.

VERSES   Psalm 24:1-2, 3-4, 5-6

The Lord's are the earth and its fullness; * the world and those who dwell in it.
For he founded it upon the seas * and established it upon the rivers.

Who can ascend the mountain of the Lord? * or who may stand in his holy place?
One whose hands are sinless, whose heart is clean, * who desires not what is vain.

He shall receive a blessing from the Lord, * a reward from God his savior.
Such is the race that seeks for him, * that seeks the face of the God of Jacob.

The Commemoration of All the Faithful Departed (All Souls)

November 2, 2001

Refrain

The Lord is my shep - herd; * there is nothing I shall want.

Verses Psalm 23:1-3, 3-4, 5, 6

The LORD is my shepherd; * I shall not want.
In verdant pastures he gives me repose; +
    beside restful waters he leads me; * he refreshes my soul.

He guides me in right paths * for his name's sake.
Even though I walk in the dark valley * I fear no evil; for you are at my side
with your rod and your staff * that give me courage.

You spread the table before me * in the sight of my foes;
you anoint my head with oil; * my cup overflows.

Only goodness and kindness follow me * all the days of my life;
and I shall dwell in the house of the LORD * for years to come.

Thirty-first Sunday in Ordinary Time

November 4, 2001

Refrain

I will praise your name for - ev - er, * my king and my God.

Verses Psalm 145:1-2, 8-9, 10-11, 13, 14

I will extol you, O my God and King, * and I will bless your name forever and ever.
Every day will I bless you, * and I will praise your name forever and ever.

The LORD is gracious and merciful, * slow to anger and of great kindness.
The LORD is good to all * and compassionate toward all his works.

Let all your works give you thanks, O LORD, * and let your faithful ones bless you.
Let them discourse of the glory of your kingdom * and speak of your might.

The LORD is faithful in all his words * and holy in all his works.
The LORD lifts up all who are falling * and raises up all who are bowed down.

THIRTY-SECOND SUNDAY IN ORDINARY TIME
November 11, 2001

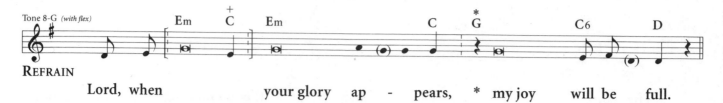

REFRAIN

Lord, when your glory ap - pears, * my joy will be full.

VERSES   Psalm 17:1, 5-6, 8, 15

Hear, O LORD, a just <u>suit</u>; +
    attend to <u>my</u> outcry; * hearken to my prayer from lips with<u>out</u> deceit.

My steps have been steadfast in <u>your</u> paths, * my feet <u>have</u> not faltered.
I call upon you, for you will answer me, <u>O</u> God; * incline your ear to me; <u>hear</u> my word.

Keep me as the apple of <u>your</u> eye, * hide me in the shadow <u>of</u> your wings.
But I in justice shall behold <u>your</u> face; * on waking I shall be content <u>in</u> your presence.

THIRTY-THIRD SUNDAY IN ORDINARY TIME
November 18, 2001

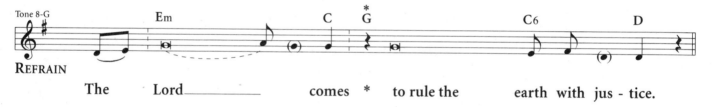

REFRAIN

The Lord_____ comes * to rule the earth with jus - tice.

VERSES   Psalm 98:5-6, 7-8, 9

Sing praise to the LORD with <u>the</u> harp, * with the harp and mel<u>o</u>dious song.
With trumpets and the sound of <u>the</u> horn * sing joyfully before the <u>King</u>, the LORD.

Let the sea and what fills it <u>resound</u>, * the world and those who <u>dwell</u> in it;
let the rivers clap <u>their</u> hands, * the mountains shout with <u>them</u> for joy.

Before the LORD, for <u>he</u> comes, * for he comes to <u>rule</u> the earth;
he will rule the world <u>with</u> justice * and the peo<u>ples</u> with equity.

THANKSGIVING DAY
November 22, 2001

Tone 5-F *(with flex)*

REFRAIN

The earth   has yielded   its   fruits; * God, our   God has blessed us.

VERSES   Psalm 67:2-3, 5, 7-8

May God have pity on us <u>and</u> bless us; * may he let his face <u>shine</u> upon us.
So may your way be known up<u>on</u> earth; * among all nations, <u>your</u> salvation.

May the nations be glad and ex<u>ult</u> +
   because you rule the peoples <u>in</u> equity; * the nations on the <u>earth</u> you guide.

The earth has yielded <u>its</u> fruits: * God, our <u>God</u>, has blessed us.
May <u>God</u> bless us, * and may all the ends of <u>the</u> earth fear him!

CHRIST THE KING
November 25, 2001

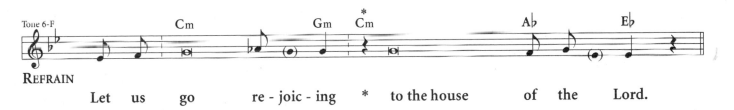

Tone 6-F

REFRAIN

Let   us   go   re - joic - ing   *   to the house   of   the   Lord.

VERSES   Psalm 122:1-2, 3-4, 4-5

I rejoiced because they said <u>to</u> me, * "We will go up to the house <u>of</u> the LORD."
And now we have <u>set</u> foot * within your gates, <u>O</u> Jerusalem.

Jerusalem, built as <u>a</u> city * with <u>com</u>pact unity.
To it the tribes <u>go</u> up, * the tribes <u>of</u> the LORD.

According to the decree <u>for</u> Israel, * to give thanks to the name <u>of</u> the LORD.
In it are set up jud<u>g</u>ment seats, * seats for the <u>house</u> of David.

WORLD MISSION SUNDAY
October 21, 2001

REFRAIN

Their mes - sage goes out * through all the world.

VERSES Psalm 19:2-3, 4-5

The heavens declare the glory of God, * and the firmament proclaims his handiwork.
Day pours out the word today, * and night to night imparts knowledge.

Not a word nor a discourse, * whose voice is not heard;
Through all the earth their voice resounds, * and to the ends of the world, their message.

GREGORIAN CHANT PSALMODY

Simplified and Adapted to the Accentuation of the English Language
with Modal Accompaniments

Fr. Bartholomew Sayles, O.S.B., and Sr. Cecile Gertken, O.S.B.

*   This sign is used after the middle cadence.

+   This sign after a word is used only in verses of extended length. It points out a drop (flex) in the voice to a lower pitch on the word accent. The flex when used appears only in the first half of a psalm or canticle verse. The majority of psalms do not use the flex note(s). In such cases the "measure" with the reciting tone followed by the flex note(s) is omitted.

__   A line under a syllable points out the first note of the middle or final cadence.

( )   The extra note(s) in parentheses are used for words or combinations of words where the word accent at the flex or cadence is either second last or third last.

N.B.   The first "measure" or the two "pick-up" notes at the beginning of each tone are used <u>only</u> with the refrain or antiphon and also with each line of a canticle. These two notes are <u>not</u> used with the lines of the psalm. Each line of the psalm begins on the reciting tone.

SERVICE MUSIC AND HYMNS

COMMON TEXTS FOR SUNG RESPONSORIALS

"The psalm as a rule is drawn from the *Lectionary* because the individual psalm texts are directly connected with the individual readings: the choice of psalm depends therefore on the readings.

"Nevertheless, in order that people may be able to join in the responsorial psalm more readily, some texts of responses and psalms have been chosen, according to the different seasons of the year and classes of saints, for optional use, whenever the psalm is sung, in place of the text corresponding to the reading (cf. General Instruction of the Roman Missal, n. 36)."

—Lectionary for Mass, The Liturgical Press, 1998, p. 1059

SEASON OF ADVENT

Refrain: To You, O Lord, I Lift My Soul; Verses: Psalm 25:4-5, 8-9, 10, 14
1. Same as First Sunday of Advent, Hunstiger, page 3.
2. Same as First Sunday of Advent, chant, page 98.

SEASON OF CHRISTMAS

Refrain: All the Ends of the Earth Have Seen; Verses: Psalm 98:1, 2-3, 3-4, 5-6
3. Same as Christmas: Mass during the Day, Hunstiger, page 12.
4. Same as Christmas: Mass during the Day, chant, page 102.

SEASON OF EPIPHANY

Refrain: Lord, Every Nation on Earth Will Adore You; Verses: Psalm 72:1-2, 7-8, 10-11, 12-13
5. Same as Epiphany, Hunstiger, page 16.
6. Same as Epiphany, chant, page 103.

SEASON OF LENT

Refrain: Be Merciful, O Lord, for We Have Sinned; Verses: Psalm 51:3-4, 5-6, 12-13, 14, 17
7. Same as Ash Wednesday, Hunstiger, page 27.
8. Same as Ash Wednesday, chant, page 109.

Refrain: Be with Me, Lord, When I Am in Trouble; Verses: Psalm 91:1-2, 10-11, 12-13, 14-15
9. Same as First Sunday of Lent, Hunstiger, page 28.
10. Same as First Sunday of Lent, chant, page 110.

SEASON OF EASTER

Refrain: This Is the Day the Lord Has Made; Verses: Psalm 118:1-2, 16-17, 22-23
11. Same as Easter Sunday, Hunstiger, page 53.
12. Same as Easter Sunday, chant, page 121.

Refrain: Let All the Earth Cry Out to God with Joy; Verses: Psalm 66:1-3, 4-5, 6-7, 16, 20
13. Same as Fourteenth Sunday in Ordinary Time, Hunstiger, page 68.
14. Same as Fourteenth Sunday in Ordinary Time, chant, page 129.

Refrain: Sing a New Song to the Lord; Verses: Psalm 98:1, 2-3, 3-4
15. Same as Immaculate Conception, Hunstiger, page 4.
16. Same as Immaculate Conception, chant, page 98.

Refrain: The Lord Is Kind and Merciful; Verses: Psalm 103:1-2, 3-4, 8, 10, 12-13
17. Same as Seventh Sunday in Ordinary Time, Hunstiger, page 25.
18. Same as Seventh Sunday in Ordinary Time, chant, page 108.

Refrain: The Lord Is My Light and My Salvation; Verses: Psalm 27:1, 7-8, 9, 13-14
19. Same as Second Sunday of Lent, Hunstiger, page 11.
20. Same as Second Sunday of Lent, chant, page 111.

Refrain: Lord, You Have the Words of Everlasting Life; Verses: Baruch 3:9-15, 32–4:4
21. Same as Easter Vigil, Response to Reading VI, Hunstiger, page 46.
22. Same as Easter Vigil, Response to Reading VI, chant, page 117.

Refrain: We Are His People, the Sheep of His Flock; Verses: Psalm 100:1-2, 3, 5
23. Same as Fourth Sunday of Easter, Hunstiger, page 56.
24. Same as Fourth Sunday of Easter, chant, page 123.

Refrain: I Will Praise Your Name Forever; Verses: Psalm 145:8-9, 10-11, 12-13
25. Same as Thirty-first Sunday in Ordinary Time, Hunstiger, page 91.
26. Same as Thirty-first Sunday in Ordinary Time, chant, page 139.

MASS OF CREATION

Marty Haugen

27. BLESSING AND SPRINKLING OF HOLY WATER

VERSES

Text: *Mass of Creation,* Marty Haugen
Music: *Mass of Creation,* Marty Haugen, © 1984, GIA Publications, Inc.

28. Kyrie

Lord, have mer-cy. Christ, have mer-cy.

Capo 3: (Em)   (D)
Gm   F

Lord, have mer-cy.

(C)   (Em)   (Bm7) (Em)   (Bm7) (Em)
Eb   Gm   Dm7   Gm   Dm7   Gm

mf   *mp*   *p*

Last time rit.

Optional Verses*

Cantor or priest:

1. God   of   all   cre - a - tion,   earth   and   sea   and   sky,
2. God   of   ev - 'ry   na - tion,   God   of   grace   and   peace,
3. God   of   our   sal - va - tion,   God   of   grace   and   peace,

Last time rit.

God   of   all   e - ter - ni - ty: hear   us,   hear   us.
God   of   wis - dom   and   of   love: hear   us,   hear   us.
God   of   wis - dom   and   of   love: hear   us,   hear   us.

*May be sung over ostinato Kyrie, or in alternation with the Kyrie using the same accompaniment.

Text: *Mass of Creation*, Marty Haugen
Music: *Mass of Creation*, Marty Haugen, © 1984, GIA Publications, Inc.

29. Gloria

Music: *Mass of Creation*, Marty Haugen, © 1984, GIA Publications, Inc.

30. Gospel Acclamation

Alternate Verses: Speak, O Lord, your servant listens, yours the word of life eternal:
To the humble and the lowly you reveal the Kingdom's myst'ry:
Praise the Word who lived among us, made us children of the Kingdom:
You are light, Lord, for our darkness, break upon our waiting spirits:
Gentle shepherd, you who know us, call us all into your presence:
Be our way, Lord, be our truth, Lord, be our hope of life eternal:
We who love you, seek your truth, Lord, come and make your home within us:
We shall watch, Lord, we shall pray, Lord, for we know not when you cometh:

Text: *Mass of Creation*, Marty Haugen
Music: *Mass of Creation*, Marty Haugen, © 1984, GIA Publications, Inc.

31. Lenten Acclamation

REFRAIN

Descant: 𝄋 *f –ff*

Praise to you, Lord Je - sus Christ, king of end - less glo - ry!

Melody in soprano: 𝄋

Praise to you, Lord Je - sus Christ, king of end - less glo - ry!

Capo 3: (Gm) (D) (Em) (Bm) (C) (Bm) (Em) (D) (G) (D) (Em) (Am) (D) (G) (D) (Em)
Em F Gm Dm Eb Dm Gm F Bb F Gm Cm F Bb F Gm

f *f –ff*

VERSES *mp*

Cantor or choir: D.S.

1st Sun.	We do not live on bread a - lone, but we live on ev - 'ry word from our God.
2nd Sun.	From the shin-ing cloud a voice is heard— "This is my be - lov - ed Son, hear his words."
3rd Sun.	"Come, take the wa - ter that I give, if you drink you will nev - er thirst a - gain."
4th Sun.	"I am the Light of all the world, all who fol - low me will have the light of life."
5th Sun.	"I am the Res - ur - rec - tion, I am life to all who trust in my name."
6th Sun.	Christ was o - be-dient un - to death, e - ven death on the wood of the cross.
General	Turn to the Lord with all your heart, for the time of sal - va - tion is here.

(C) (G) (D) (Am/C) (Em) (B) (Fm) (Am) (B7)
Eb Bb F Cm/Eb Gm D Gm Cm D7

D.S.

mp

Music: *Mass of Creation*, Marty Haugen, © 1984, GIA Publications, Inc.

32. GENERAL INTERCESSIONS

For (intention) let us pray to the Lord.

Lord, hear our prayer. prayer.

Capo 3: (Em) (D/E) (G/E) (D/E) (C) (Bm7) (A) (E)
Gm F/G Bb/G F/G Eb Dm7 C G

Music: *Mass of Creation*, Marty Haugen, © 1984, GIA Publications, Inc.

33. EUCHARISTIC PRAYER

The Lord be with you. And al-so with you. Lift up your hearts. We lift them up to the Lord.

Capo 3: (Gadd9) (Bm7) (C) (Am7) (D)
Bbadd9 Dm7 Eb Cm7 F

Let us give thanks to the Lord, our God. It is right to give him thanks and praise.

(Gadd9) (Bm7) (C) (Am7) (D)
Bbadd9 Dm7 Eb Cm7 F

Music: *Mass of Creation*, Marty Haugen, © 1984, GIA Publications, Inc.

34. Sanctus

Music: *Mass of Creation*, Marty Haugen, © 1984, GIA Publications, Inc.

35. MEMORIAL ACCLAMATION: CHRIST HAS DIED

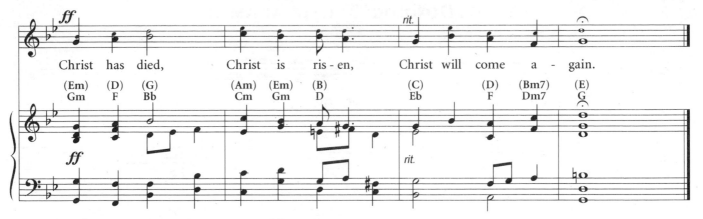

Music: *Mass of Creation*, Marty Haugen, © 1984, GIA Publications, Inc.

36. MEMORIAL ACCLAMATION: WHEN WE EAT THIS BREAD

Let us pro-claim the mys-ter-y of faith: When we eat this bread, when we drink this cup, we pro-claim your death, Lord Je-sus, un-til you come in glo-ry.

Music: *Mass of Creation*, Marty Haugen, © 1993, GIA Publications, Inc.

37. DOXOLOGY AND GREAT AMEN

Priest: Through him, with him, in him, in the unity of the Holy Spir-it, all glory and honor is yours al-

Capo 3: (Em)   (D/E)   (C/E)
Gm   F/G   Eb/G

might - y Fa - ther, for ev - er and ev - er.

(D/E) (Em)   (Am7) (Bm7)   (Em) (C) (Bm7)
F/G Gm   Cm7 Dm7   Gm Eb Dm7

Descant:

All:
Melody: A - men, a - men, a - - - men.

(Em) (D) (G)   (Am) (Em) (B)   (C)   (D)   (A)
Gm F Bb   Cm Gm D   Eb   F   C

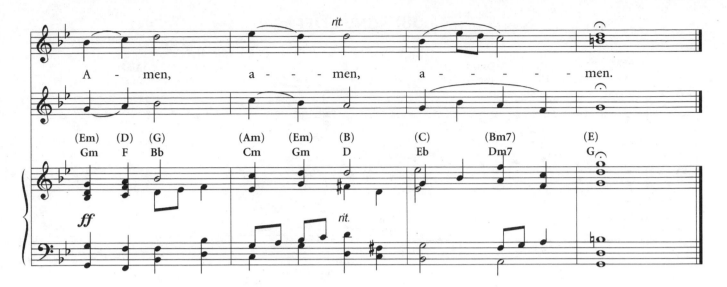

Music: *Mass of Creation,* Marty Haugen, © 1984, GIA Publications, Inc.

38. AGNUS DEI

1. Je-sus, Lamb of God,
2. Je-sus, Bread of Life, you take a-way the sins of the world: have mer-cy on
3. Je-sus, Prince of Peace,

us.   Je-sus, Lamb of God, you take a-way the

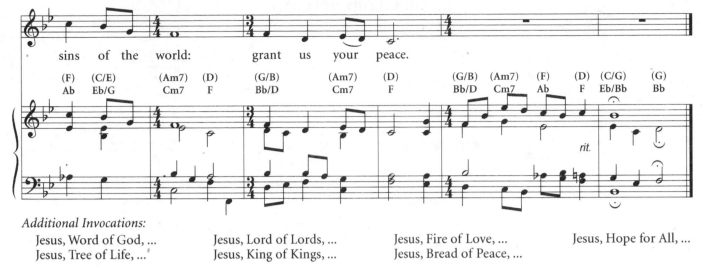

sins of the world: grant us your peace.

Additional Invocations:

Jesus, Word of God, ...   Jesus, Lord of Lords, ...   Jesus, Fire of Love, ...   Jesus, Hope for All, ...
Jesus, Tree of Life, ...   Jesus, King of Kings, ...   Jesus, Bread of Peace, ...

Music: *Mass of Creation,* Marty Haugen, © 1984, GIA Publications, Inc.

ST. BENEDICT MASS

Robert LeBlanc

39. LORD, HAVE MERCY

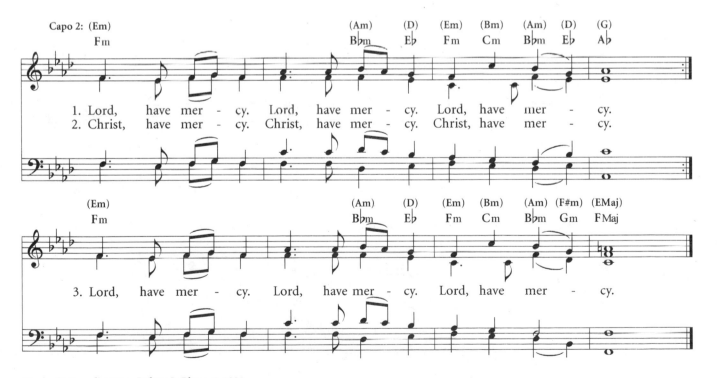

1. Lord, have mer - cy. Lord, have mer - cy. Lord, have mer - cy.
2. Christ, have mer - cy. Christ, have mer - cy. Christ, have mer - cy.

3. Lord, have mer - cy. Lord, have mer - cy. Lord, have mer - cy.

Music: *St. Benedict Mass,* Robert LeBlanc, © 1991

40. GLORY TO GOD

Glo - ry to God in the high - est, and peace to his peo - ple on earth.

Capo 2: (G) (D7) (G) (D) (Em) (D) (G) (C/E) (Bm7) (Am) (G) (D)
Ab Eb7 Ab Eb Fm Eb Ab Db/F Cm7 Bbm Ab Eb

Lord God, heav - en - ly King, al - might - y God and Fa - ther, we

(G) (C) (G) (Em) (BMaj) (Em) (D) (Em) (C) (G) (D) (G)
Ab Db Ab Fm CMaj Fm Eb Fm Db Ab Eb Ab

wor - ship you, we give you thanks, we praise you for your glo - ry.

(C) (G) (C) (F#dim) (G) (C) (F#dim) (G) (B)
Db Ab Db Gdim Ab Db Gdim Ab C

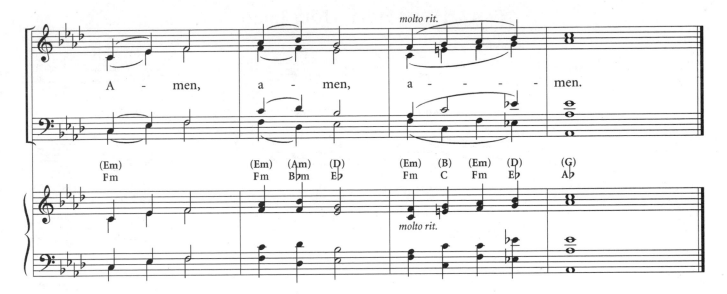

A - men, a - men, a - - - men.

Music: *St. Benedict Mass*, Robert LeBlanc, © 1991

41. ALLELUIA

Al - le - lu - ia, al - le - lu - ia, al - le - lu - - ia.

Music: *St. Benedict Mass*, Robert LeBlanc, © 1991

42. HOLY, HOLY, HOLY LORD

Ho - ly, ho - ly, ho - ly Lord, God of pow-er and might. Heav - en and earth are

full of your glo - ry. Ho - san - na in the high - est. Bless-ed is he who

comes in the name of the Lord. Ho - san - na in the high - est.

Music: *St. Benedict Mass*, Robert LeBlanc, © 1991

43. MEMORIAL ACCLAMATION: CHRIST HAS DIED

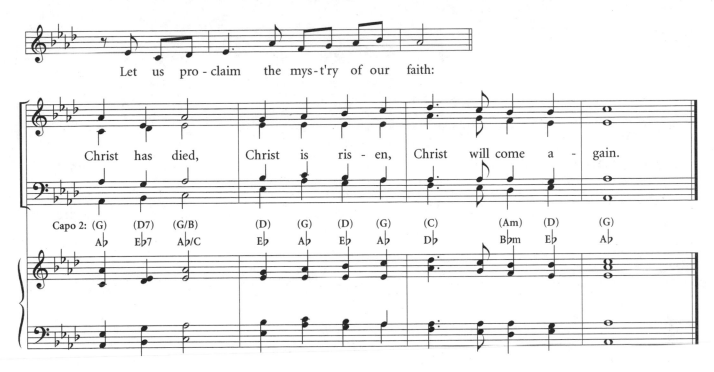

Let us pro-claim the mys-t'ry of our faith:

Christ has died, Christ is ris - en, Christ will come a - gain.

Music: *St. Benedict Mass,* Robert LeBlanc, © 1991

44. AMEN

A - men, a - men, a - - - men.

Music: *St. Benedict Mass,* Robert LeBlanc, © 1991

45. LAMB OF GOD

1.2. Lamb of God, you take a-way the sins of the world: have mer-cy on us.

3. Lamb of God, you take a-way the sins of the world: grant us peace.

Music: *St. Benedict Mass*, Robert LeBlanc, © 1991

MASS OF THE GOOD SHEPHERD

Stephen Somerville

46. LORD, HAVE MERCY

Lord, have mer-cy. Christ, have mer-cy. Lord, have mer-cy.

47. GLORY TO GOD IN THE HIGHEST

Glo-ry to God in the high-est, and peace to his peo-ple on earth. Lord God,

heav-en-ly King, al-might-y God and Fa-ther, we wor-ship you, we give you thanks, we

praise you for your glo-ry. Lord Je-sus Christ, on-ly Son of the Fa-ther,

Lord God, Lamb of God, you take a-way the sin of the world: have

48. HOLY, HOLY, HOLY

Ho - ly, ho - ly, ho - ly Lord, God of pow'r and might, heav - en and earth are full of your glo - ry. Ho - san - na in the high - est. Bless - ed is he who comes in the name of the Lord. Ho - san - na in the high - est.

49. Lamb of God

Lamb of God, you take a-way the sins of the world: have mer - cy on us.

Lamb of God, you take a-way the sins of the world: have mer - cy on us.

Lamb of God, you take a-way the sins of the world: grant us peace.

TRINITY MASS

Becket Senchur, O.S.B.

50. HOLY, HOLY, HOLY

Ho - ly, ho - ly, ho - ly Lord, God of pow-er and might. Heav - en and earth are full, full of your glo - ry. Ho - san - na, ho - san - na, ho - san - na in the high - est. Bless - ed is he who comes in the name of the Lord. Ho - san - na, ho - san - na, ho - san - na in the high - est.

51. Memorial Acclamation: Christ Has Died

Christ has died, Christ is ris-en, Christ will come a-gain.

52. Memorial Acclamation: When We Eat This Bread

When we eat this bread and drink this cup, we pro-claim your death, Lord Je-sus, un-til you come in glo - - - ry.

53. MEMORIAL ACCLAMATION: LORD, BY YOUR CROSS

Lord, by your cross and res - ur - rec - tion, you have set us free. You are the Sav - ior of the world.

54. AMEN

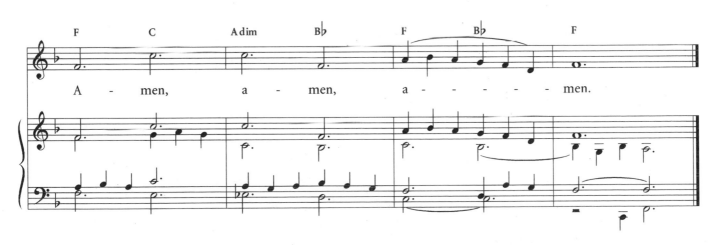

A - men, a - men, a - - - - - men.

55. LAMB OF GOD

1. 2. Lamb of God, you take a - way the sins of the world: have mer - cy on us.

3. Lamb of God, you take a - way the sins of the world: grant us peace, grant us peace.

MISSA LAUDIS

Becket Senchur, O.S.B.

56. LORD HAVE MERCY

57. GLORY TO GOD

REFRAIN

Glo-ry to God in the high - est, and peace to his peo-ple on earth.

VERSE 1 *Cantor:*

Lord God, heav-en-ly King, al-might-y God and Fa - ther: we wor-ship you, we

Choir:

give you thanks, we praise you for your glo - ry.

To refrain

VERSE 2 *Cantor:*

Lord Je-sus Christ, on-ly Son of the

Fa - ther, Lord God, Lamb of God, you take a-way the sin of the world:

58. HOLY, HOLY, HOLY

Ho - ly, ho - ly, ho - ly Lord, God of pow-er and might.

Heav-en and earth are full of your glo - ry. Ho - san - na, ho-san -

na in the high - est. Bless-ed is he who comes in the name

of the Lord. Ho - san - na, ho-san - na in the high - est.

59. MEMORIAL ACCLAMATION: YOUR DEATH, O LORD

Your death, O Lord, is a birth to e-ter-nal life: you have set us free, al-le-lu-ia!

60. AMEN

A - - - - men, a - - - men.

61. Lamb of God

Lamb of God, you take a - way the sins of the world: have mer - cy on us.

Lamb of God, you take a - way the sins of the world: have mer - cy on us.

Lamb of God, you take a - way the sins of the world: grant us peace.

MASS OF THE TRINITY

Annette Lackaff, O.S.B.

62. ALLELUIA

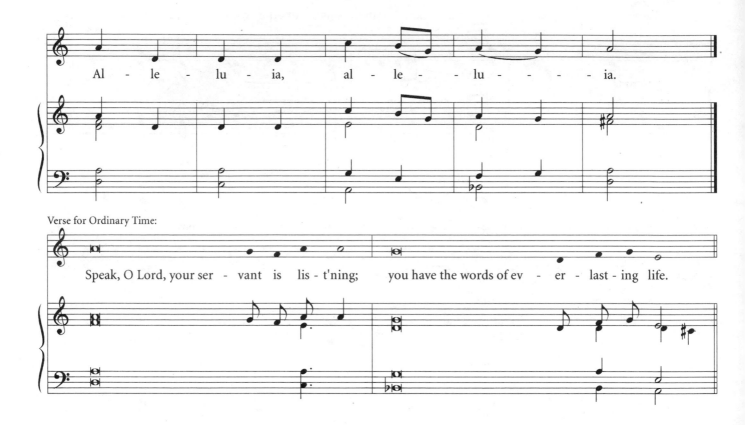

Al - le - lu - ia, al - le - lu - - ia.

Verse for Ordinary Time:

Speak, O Lord, your ser - vant is lis - t'ning; you have the words of ev - er - last - ing life.

63. HOLY, HOLY, HOLY

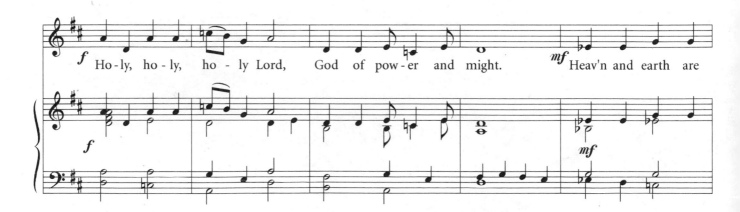

Ho - ly, ho - ly, ho - ly Lord, God of pow - er and might. Heav'n and earth are

full of your glo - ry. *f* Ho - san - na in the high - est. *mf* Blest is he who

comes in the name of the Lord. *f* Ho - san - na in the high - - est.

64. MEMORIAL ACCLAMATION

Christ has died, Christ is ris - en, Christ will come a - gain.

189

65. Amen

A - - - men, a - men, a - men.

66. Lamb of God

Lamb of God, you take a - way the sins of the world: have mer - cy on us.

Lamb of God, you take a - way the sins of the world: have mer - cy on us.

Lamb of God, you take a - way the sins of the world: grant us peace.

67. GLORY TO GOD

Mass of Hope by Becket Senchur, O.S.B.

REFRAIN

Glo - ry to God in the high - est, and peace to his peo - ple on earth. peo - ple on earth.

VERSE 1

Lord God, heav - en - ly King, al - might - y God and Fa - ther, we wor - ship you, we give you thanks, we praise you for your glo - ry.

VERSE 2

Lord Je-sus Christ, on - ly Son of the Fa - ther, Lord God, Lamb of God, you

take a - way the sin of the world: have mer - cy on us; you are

To refrain

seat - ed at the right hand of the Fa - ther: re - ceive our prayer.

VERSE 3

For you a - lone are the Ho - ly One, you a - lone are the Lord,

you a-lone are the Most High, Je - - - sus Christ, with the
Ho - ly Spir - it, in the glo - ry of God the Fa - ther.
A - - - - - - - - men.

To refrain

68. Glory to God

Tobias Colgan, O.S.B.

REFRAIN

Glo-ry to God in the high - est, and peace to his peo-ple on earth.

VERSE 1

Lord God, heav-en-ly King, al-might-y God and Fa - ther.

VERSE 2

We wor-ship you, we give you thanks, we praise you for your glo - ry.

VERSE 3

Lord Je-sus Christ, on - ly Son of the Fa - ther, Lord God,

Lamb of God, you take a - way the sin of the world: have mer -

To refrain VERSE 4

cy on us. You are seat - ed at the right hand of the

To refrain VERSE 5

Fa - ther: re - ceive our pray'r. For you a - lone are the

Ho - ly One, You a - lone are the Lord. You a - lone are the Most

High, Je - - - sus Christ. With the Ho - ly Spir - it,

in the glo-ry of God the Fa - ther. — A - - - - men.

To refrain

69. ALLELUIA

Jay F. Hunstiger

Al - le - lu - ia, al - le - lu - ia, al - le - lu - ia, al - le - lu - ia. Al - le -

lu - ia, al - le - lu - ia, al - le - lu - ia, al - le - lu - ia.

70. ALLELUIA

Traditional Chant

Al - le - lú - ia, al - le - lú - ia, al - le - lú - ia.

71. ALLELUIA

Mass of Saint Oliver Plunkett by Edward J. McKenna

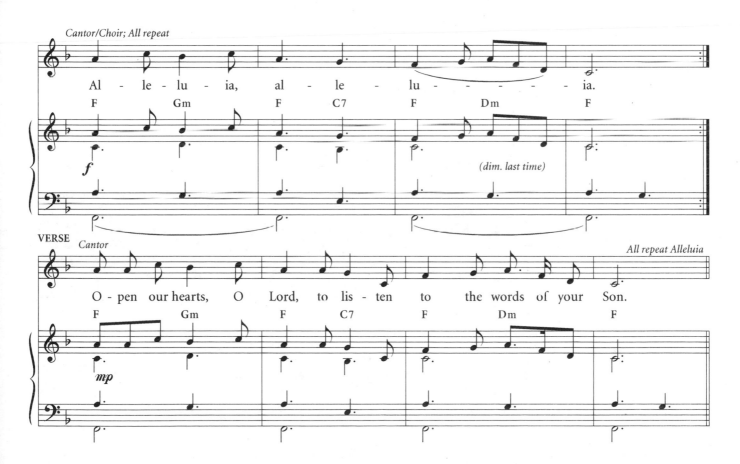

Cantor/Choir; All repeat

Al - le - lu - ia, al - le - lu - ia.

VERSE

Cantor

O - pen our hearts, O Lord, to lis - ten to the words of your Son.

All repeat Alleluia

72. ALLELUIA

WITH VERSE FOR EASTER

Chant, Tone 5-F

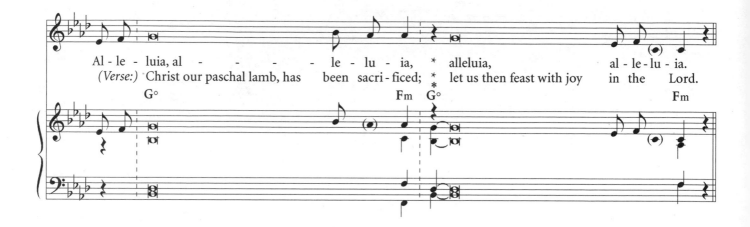

Al - le - luia, al - - - - le - lu - ia, * alleluia, al - le - lu - ia.

(Verse:) Christ our paschal lamb, has been sacri-ficed; * let us then feast with joy in the Lord.

G° Fm G° Fm

73. ALLELUIA

WITH VERSE FOR EASTER

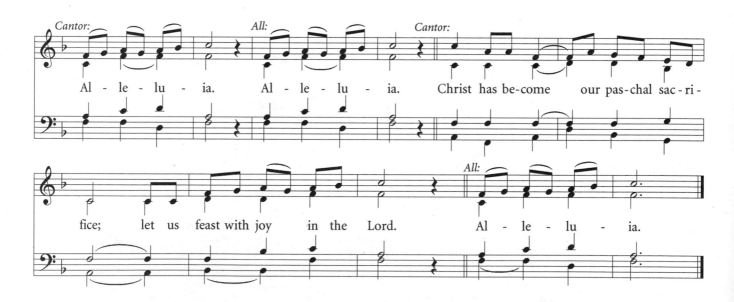

Cantor: Al - le - lu - ia. *All:* Al - le - lu - ia. *Cantor:* Christ has be-come our pas-chal sac-ri -

fice; let us feast with joy in the Lord. *All:* Al - le - lu - ia.

74. Praise to You, Lord Jesus Christ
(Lenten Acclamation)

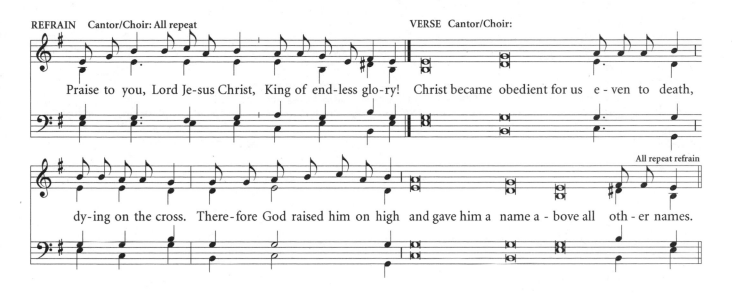

REFRAIN Cantor/Choir: All repeat

Praise to you, Lord Je-sus Christ, King of end-less glo-ry!

VERSE Cantor/Choir:

Christ became obedient for us e-ven to death,

dy-ing on the cross. There-fore God raised him on high and gave him a name a-bove all oth-er names.

All repeat refrain

75. Amen

Chant, Mode VI

A - - - - men, a - men, a - - - - men.

76. Amen

Mass of Hope by Eugene Englert

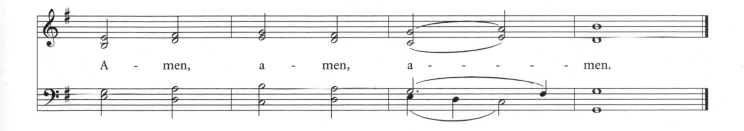

A - men, a - men, a - - - - men.

77. Lord's Prayer

adapt. Robert J. Snow

Celebrant:

[A] Let us pray with confidence to the Fa - ther in the words our Sav - ior gave us.
[B] Je - sus taught us to call God our Fa - ther and so we have the cour - - age to say:
[C] Let us ask our Father to for - give our sins and to bring us to forgive those who sin a - gainst us.
[D] Let us pray for the coming of the king - dom as Je - sus taught us.

All:

Our Fa - ther who art in heav - en hal - lowed be thy name; thy king - dom come; thy

will be done on earth as it is in heav - en. Give us this day our dai - ly bread,

and for - give us our tres - pass - es as we for - give those who tres - pass a - gainst us; and

lead us not in - to temp - ta - tion, but de - liv - er us from e - vil.

78. COMFORT, COMFORT YE MY PEOPLE

1. Com - fort, com - fort ye, my peo - ple, Speak ye peace, thus says our God:
2. For the her - ald's voice is cry - ing In the des - ert far and near,
3. Make ye straight what long was crook - ed, Make the rough - er plac - es plain:

Com - fort those who sit in dark - ness Bowed be - neath their sor - row's load;
Bid - ding all to seek re - pen - tance Since the king - dom now is near.
Let your hearts be true and hum - ble As be - fits his ho - ly reign;

Speak ye to Je - ru - sa - lem Of the peace that waits for them: Tell her that her
O that warn - ing cry o - bey! Now pre - pare for God a way; Let the val - leys
For the glo - ry of the Lord Now o'er earth is shed a - broad, And all flesh shall

sins I cov - er, And her war - fare now is o - ver.
rise to meet him, And the hills bow down to greet him.
see the to - ken That his word is nev - er bro - ken.

Text: Johann Olearius, tr. Catherine Winkworth
Music: BOURGEOIS, 87 87 77 88, Louis Bourgeois

203

79. O Come, Divine Messiah

1. O come, Di- vine Mes- si- ah; The world in si- lence waits the day
2. O Christ, whom na- tions sigh for, Whom priest and proph- et long fore- told,
3. You come in peace and meek- ness And low- ly will your cra- dle be;

When hope shall sing its tri- umph And sad- ness flee a- way.
Come, break the cap- tives' fet- ters, Re- deem the long lost fold.
All clothed in hu- man weak- ness Shall we your God- head see.

REFRAIN

Dear Sav- ior, haste! Come, come to earth. Dis- pel the night and show your face, And bid us

hail the dawn of grace. O come, Di- vine Mes- si- ah; The world in si- lence

waits the day When hope shall sing its tri - umph And sad - ness flee a - way.

Text: Abbé Pellegrin, 1663–1745; tr. Sister Mary of St. Phillip
Music: VENEZ, DIVIN MESSIE, Irregular with Refrain, 16th cent. Noel, c. 1544; arr. Arthur Hutchings, b. 1906, ©

80. CREATOR OF THE STARS OF NIGHT

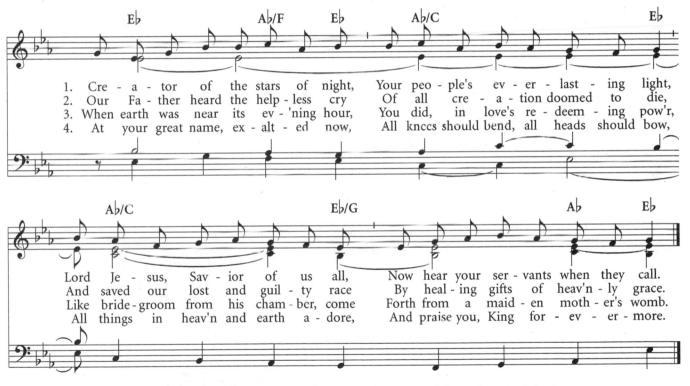

1. Cre - a - tor of the stars of night, Your peo - ple's ev - er - last - ing light,
2. Our Fa - ther heard the help - less cry Of all cre - a - tion doomed to die,
3. When earth was near its ev - 'ning hour, You did, in love's re - deem - ing pow'r,
4. At your great name, ex - alt - ed now, All knees should bend, all heads should bow,

Lord Je - sus, Sav - ior of us all, Now hear your ser - vants when they call.
And saved our lost and guil - ty race By heal - ing gifts of heav'n - ly grace.
Like bride - groom from his cham - ber, come Forth from a maid - en moth - er's womb.
All things in heav'n and earth a - dore, And praise you, King for - ev - er - more.

5. To you, O holy One, we pray,
   Our judge in that tremendous day,
   Ward off, while yet we dwell below,
   The weapons of our crafty foe.

6. To God the Father, God the Son,
   And God the Spirit, three in one,
   Praise, honor, might, and glory be
   From age to age eternally.

Text: Latin, 9th cent.; John Mason Neale, 1818–1866, alt.
Music: CONDITOR ALME SIDERUM, 88 88, *Plainchant, Mode IV*

81. Bedew Us

Be - dew us, heav-ens from a - bove! O clouds, rain down the Just One!

1. With-hold your wrath from us, O Lord, and re-mem-ber no more our e - vil-do - ing.

Lo, the cit - y of the Ho - ly One is made a des-ert, Si - on a des - ert is be-come.

Je - ru - sa-lem waste and des - o - late: the house of your ho - ly pres-ence,

and of your glo - ry, where of old our fa - thers sang your prais - es.

2. We all have sinned, and are be-come like un - to one un - clean. We have fal - len low,

as a dy - ing leaf falls earth - ward; and our in - i - qui-ties, as a wind have

swept us swift - ly far. You have hid - den your face from us, your peo - ple;

you have bro - ken us by the weight of our own sin - ning,

3. Be-hold, O Lord, the af-flic-tion of your peo - ple. Send quick - ly him who is to come.

Send forth the Lamb who rules all earth - ly king - doms,

From Pe - tra in the des - ert, to the Mount of the daugh - ter of Si - on;

that he may take a - way the griev-ous yoke of our sub - jec - tion.

4. Be now com-fort-ed, be now com-fort - ed, O you my peo - ple; for most speed - i - ly

comes sal - va - tion. Why are you con-sumed with sor - row - ing, so that your grief has quite

trans - formed you? I come to save, be no more fear - ful. For know you not

that I am your God and Mas - ter, Is - rael's Ho - ly One, your sole Re - deem - er.

Music: RORATE CAELI, Chant, Mode I

82. COME, THOU LONG-EXPECTED SAVIOR

1. Come, thou long-expected Savior, Born to set thy people free;
2. Born thy people to deliver, Born a child and yet a King,

From our fears and sins release us; Let us find our rest in thee.
Born to reign in us forever, Now thy gracious kingdom bring.

Israel's strength and consolation, Hope of all the earth thou art;
By thine own eternal Spirit Rule in all our hearts alone;

Fond desire of ev'ry nation, Joy of ev'ry longing heart.
By thine all-sufficient merit Raise us to thy glorious throne.

Text: Charles Wesley, 1707–1788
Music: HYFRYDOL, 87 87 87 87, Rowland H. Prichard, 1811–1887

83. HARK, THE GLAD SOUND

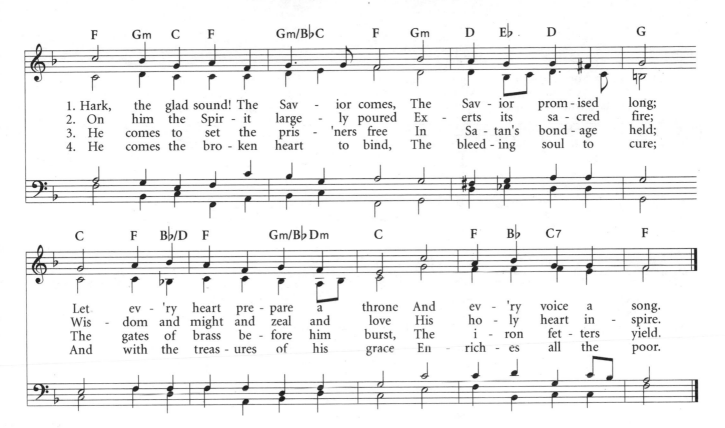

1. Hark, the glad sound! The Sav-ior comes, The Sav-ior prom-ised long;
2. On him the Spir-it large-ly poured Ex-erts its sa-cred fire;
3. He comes to set the pris-'ners free In Sa-tan's bond-age held;
4. He comes the bro-ken heart to bind, The bleed-ing soul to cure;

Let ev-'ry heart pre-pare a throne And ev-'ry voice a song.
Wis-dom and might and zeal and love His ho-ly heart in-spire.
The gates of brass be-fore him burst, The i-ron fet-ters yield.
And with the treas-ures of his grace En-rich-es all the poor.

5. His silver trumpets publish loud
The jub'lee of the Lord,
Our debts are all remitted now,
Our heritage restored.

6. Our glad hosannas, Prince of peace,
Your welcome shall proclaim,
And heav'n's exalted arches ring
With your beloved name.

Text: Philip Doddridge, 1705–1751
Music: BRISTOL, 86 86, *Thomas Ravenscroft's Psalmes,* 1621

84. HE WILL COME

1. Keep on look-ing, go on seek-ing, don't stop hop-ing, He will come.
2. Bless - ed an - gels, saints and sin - ners, all re - joice to see this day;
3. Hearts will won - der, eyes must o - pen, ears shall catch His ev - 'ry word;

Keep a - wake now, watch and pray now, trust and see that He will come.
Poor or wealth - y, high or low - ly, all must help to clear His way.
Words of thun - der, words of wis - dom, words like these were nev - er heard.

Shake off slum - ber, dawn is break - ing, come with full ex - pec - tan - cy!
Down a - mong us He has chos - en here to taste our cup of life;
Through the a - ges we've been wait - ing, count - less prayers a - bove did fly;

Years of grop-ing, years of hop-ing, all ful-filled when He will come.
Who would guess that he'd be com-ing, here to share both joy and strife?
Now He's com-ing down a-mong us, here to live and here to die.

Text: Willard F. Jabusch, b. 1930, ©
Music: Welsh Folk Song; acc. S. R. Rudcki, b. 1928, ©

85. HARK, A HERALD VOICE IS CALLING

1. Hark! A her-ald voice is call-ing: "Christ is near," it seems to say,
2. Star-tled at the sol-emn warn-ing Let the earth-bound soul a-rise;
3. Lo, the Lamb so long ex-pect-ed Comes with par-don down from heav'n;
4. So when love comes forth in judg-ment, Debts and doubts and wrongs to clear,

"Cast a-way the dreams of dark-ness, Wak-en chil-dren of the day!"
Christ, her sun, all sloth dis-pel-ling, Shines up-on the morn-ing skies.
Let us meet him with re-pen-tance, Pray that we may be for-giv'n.
Faith-ful may he find his ser-vants Watch-ing till the dawn ap-pear.

Text: Anon.; tr. Edward Caswall, 1814–1878, and others
Music: MERTON, 87 87, William Henry Monk, 1823–1889

86. O Come, O Come, Emmanuel

1. (Dec. 21) O come, O come, Em-man - u - el, And ran-som cap - tive Is - ra - el,
2. (Dec. 17) O come, thou wis - dom from on high, And or - der all things far and nigh;
3. (Dec. 18) O come, thou ho - ly Lord of might, Who to thy tribes on Si - nai's height
4. (Dec. 19) O come, thou rod of Jes - se's stem, From ev - 'ry foe de - liv - er them.
5. (Dec. 20) O come, thou key of Da - vid, come, And o - pen wide our heav'n - ly home,
6. (Dec. 22, 23) O come, de - sire of na - tions, bind In one the hearts of hu - man-kind;
7. (Dec. 24) O come, thou day-spring, come and cheer our spir - its by thine ad - vent here;

That mourns in lone - ly ex - ile here Un - til the Son of God ap - pear.
To us the path of knowl - edge show, And teach us in her ways to go.
In an - cient times did give the law, In cloud and ma - jes - ty and awe.
From death and sin thy peo - ple save, And give them vic - t'ry o'er the grave.
Make safe the way that leads on high, And close the path to mis - er - y.
Bid ev - 'ry sad di - vi - sion cease And be thy - self our Prince of peace.
Dis - perse the gloom - y clouds of night And death's dark shad-ow put to flight.

Re-joice! Re-joice! Em-man-u-el shall come to thee, O Is-ra-el.

alternate accompaniment

Text: *O Antiphons,* 12th cent.; tr. John Mason Neale, 1818–1866
Music: VENI, VENI, EMMANUEL, 88 88 with Refrain, Thos. Helmore, 1811–1890, 15th cent. *Plainchant,* adapt; acc. Edward J. McKenna, b. 1939, ©

87. ON JORDAN'S BANK

1. On Jor-dan's bank the Bap-tist's cry An-noun-ces that the Lord is nigh;
2. Then cleansed be ev-'ry heart from sin; make straight the way of God with-in.
3. For you are our sal-va-tion, Lord, Our ref-uge and our great re-ward;
4. To God the Son all glo-ry be! His ad-vent set all na-tions free.

A-wake and heark-en for he brings Glad tid-ings of the King of kings.
Let ev-'ry one a home pre-pare For Christ to come and en-ter there.
Once more up-on your peo-ple shine, And fill the world with love di-vine.
Him with the Fa-ther we a-dore, And Ho-ly Spir-it ev-er-more.

Text: Charles Coffin, 1676–1749; tr. John Chandler, 1806–1876
Music: Vehe, 1537, alt.

88. PEOPLE, LOOK EAST

1. Peo - ple, look East, The time is near Of the crown - ing of the
2. Stars, keep the watch. When night is dim. One more light the bowl shall
3. An - gels, an - nounce with shouts of mirth Him who brings new life to

year. Make your house fair as you are a - ble, Trim the hearth, and set the
brim. Shin - ing be - yond the frost - y weath - er, Bright as the sun and moon to -
earth. Set ev - 'ry peak and val - ley hum - ming With the word, "The Lord is

ta - ble. Peo - ple look East, and sing to - day: Love, the Guest, is on the way.
geth - er, Peo - ple look East, and sing to - day: Love, the Star, is on the way.
com - ing." Peo - ple look East, and sing to - day: Love, the Lord, is on the way.

Text: Eleanor Farjeon, 1881–1965, ©
Music: BESACON CAROL, 87 98 87, French Carol, arr. John Stainer, 1840–1901, ©

89. Savior of the Nations Come

1. Sav - ior of the na - tions come; Vir - gin's Son, make here your home.
2. From the Fa - ther forth he came, And re - turns un - to the same,
3. You, the Fa - ther's on - ly Son, Have o'er sin the vic - t'ry won.
4. Dew from hea - ven, gen - tly come; Bring our bar - ren land to bloom.
5. Long de - sired of a - ges past, Show your - self to us at last;
6. Bright - ly does your man - ger shine; Glo - rious is its light di - vine.

Mar - vel now, O heav'n and earth, That the Lord chose such a birth.
Cap - tive lead - ing death and hell, High the song of tri - umph swell.
Bound - less shall your king - dom be; When shall we its glor - ies see?
Melt our moun - tains, bless - ed rain; Let proud hills be lev - el plain.
And from sin's cap - ti - vi - ty, Call us back and set us free.
Let not sin o'er cloud this light; Ev - er be our faith thus bright.

Text: St. Ambrose, 340–397; para. Martin Luther, 1483–1546; tr. William M. Reynolds, 1812–1876, vv. 1–3 & 6; Sr. Delores Dufner, O.S.B., b. 1939, vv. 4 & 5, ©
Music: NUN KOMM, DER HEIDEN HEILAND, 77 77, *Erfurt Enchiridia*, 1524; harm. Melchior Vulpius, 1560?–1616

90. Infant Wrapped in God's Own Light

1. In - fant wrapped in God's own light, Sav - ior sent to con - quer night,
2. Light of all the na - tions, shine! Show to us who wait a sign.
3. Ser - vant Sav - ior, chos - en one, You are God's be - lov - ed Son.
4. Ra - diance of the Fa - ther's face, Shine his love in ev - ery place.

King be - fore whom kings bowed low, Let a star be - fore us go.
God on earth, our host and guest, Be in flesh made man - i - fest.
Let your Spir - it on us rest; Be in us made man - i - fest.
Splen - dor of God's glo - ry bright, Lead us to e - ter - nal light!

Text: Sr. Delores Dufner, O.S.B., b. 1939, ©
Music: NUN KOMM, DER HEIDEN HEILAND, 77 77, *Erfurt Enchiridia*, 1524; harm. Melchior Vulpius, 1560?–1616

91. HAIL TO THE LORD'S ANOINTED

1. Hail to the Lord's A - noint - ed, Great Da - vid's great - er Son!
2. He shall come down like show - ers up - on the fruit - ful earth,
3. Kings shall bow down be - fore him And gold and in - cense bring;
4. O'er ev - 'ry foe vic - to - ri - ous, He on his throne shall rest,

Hail, in the time ap - point - ed, His reign on earth be - gun!
And joy and hope, like flow - ers, Spring in his path to birth.
All na - tions shall a - dore him, His praise all peo - ples sing;
From age to age more glo - rious, All bless - ing and all - blest,

He comes to break op - pres - sion, To set the cap - tive free,
Be - fore him on the moun - tains Shall peace, the her - ald, go
To him shall prayer un - ceas - ing And dai - ly vows as - cend,
The tide of time shall nev - er His cov - e - nant re - move;

To take a - way trans - gres - sion, And rule in eq - ui - ty.
And right-eous - ness, in foun - tains, From hill to val - ley flow.
His king-dom still in - creas - ing, A king - dom with - out end.
His name shall stand for - ev - er, That name to us is love.

Text: James Montgomery, 1771–1854; *Psalm 72*
Music: ELLACOMBE, 76 76 D, *Gesangbuch der Herzogl*, 1784, adapt. 1863; harm. William Henry Monk, 1823–1889

217

92. THE ADVENT WREATH

1. Ev - 'ry ta - per, ev - 'ry can - dle flame, Or an - y blaz-ing light Re - minds us of Christ, the Light of the world, Who gives our blind-ed vi - sion sight. May ev - 'ry Ad-vent flame Lead us to God: We ask in Je - sus' name. name.

VERSES

1. (First Sunday) The Church in ex-pec-ta-tion waits For Je-sus to come up-on our earth. In
2. (Second Sunday) The sec-ond can-dle on our wreath, The Beth-le-hem Can-dle, now is lit. The
3. (Third Sunday) We light the An-gel Can-dle now, For "Glo-ry to God" will soon be heard. The
4. (Fourth Sunday) We light four can-dles on this day; The cir-cle of light is now com-plete. Soon
5. (Christmas) The can-dle num-ber five is saved For Christ-mas, when glad-ly it is lit. We

four long weeks we will fore-see The in-fant Je-sus' low-ly birth. We
ho-ly pair must leave their home; Their wills to God's do they sub-mit. Now
song an-nouc-es God's Good News, Ful-fill-ing An-gel Ga-briel's word. The
in the sta-ble we shall see Di-vin-i-ty with our flesh meet. The
praise the one we wait-ed for, Our Lord and King, the In-fi-nite. With

light the can-dle, first of all; The Proph-e-cy Can-dle is its name. The
Jo-seph and his wife de-part For Beth-le-hem, where his tax is due. On
Scrip-tures teach us we can hope With pa-tience and cour-age as we wait. We
Shep-herd's Can-dle is the fourth, The last of the Ad-vent wicks we light. We
ex-pec-ta-tion we have watched. Our pa-tience and wait-ing now are past. We

proph - ets have fore - told his birth, And Good News Je - sus would pro - claim.
don - key and on foot they went; What lay a - head they lit - tle knew.
pray for vir - tues such as these, And God will be our ad - vo - cate.
look to Je - sus, who will come To change to day our dark - est night.
wel - come Je - sus to our earth To stay and live with us at last.

Text: Omer Westendorf, b. 1916, ©
Music: Robert Kreutz, b. 1922, ©

93. THE ADVENT OF OUR GOD

1. The ad - vent of our God   With ea - ger prayers we greet.
2. The ev - er - last - ing Son   Came down to make us free;
3. Daugh - ter of Si - on, rise   To meet your low - ly King;
4. As judge on clouds of light,   He soon will come a - gain,

And sing - ing, haste up - on his road His com - ing reign to meet.
And he a ser - vant's form put on To gain our lib - er - ty.
Nor let your faith - less heart de - spise The peace he comes to bring.
His scat - tered peo - ple to u - nite, With them in heav'n to reign.

5. Then evil flee away
Before the rising dawn!
Let this old Adam day by day
God's image still put on.

6. Praise to th'incarnate Son
Who comes to set us free,
With Father, Spirit, ever one.
To all eternity.

Text: Charles Coffin, 1676–1749; tr. John Chandler, 1806–1876, alt.
Music: FRANCONIA, 66 86, Johann B. Konig, 1691–1758; adapt. and harm. William Henry Havergal, 1793–1870

94. The King Shall Come

1. The King shall come when morn-ing dawns And light tri-um-phant breaks,
2. Not as of old a lit-tle child, To bear and fight and die,
3. Oh, bright-er than the ris-ing morn When Christ, vic-to-rious, rose
4. Oh, bright-er than that glo-rious morn Shall dawn up-on our race
5. The King shall come when morn-ing dawns And light and beau-ty brings.

When beau-ty gilds the east-ern hills And life to joy a-wakes.
But crowned with glo-ry like the sun That lights the morn-ing sky.
And left the lone-some place of death, De-spite the rage of foes.
The day when Christ in splen-dor comes, And we shall see his face.
Hail, Christ the Lord! Your peo-ple pray: Come quick-ly, King of kings.

Text: John Brownlie, alt.
Music: MORNING SONG, 86 86, *Kentucky Harmony*

95. WAKE, AWAKE, FOR NIGHT IS FLYING

1. Wake, a-wake, for night is fly - ing; The watch-men on the heights are cry - ing, A-wake, Je - ru - sa - lem, a - rise! Mid-night's sol - emn hour is toll - ing; His char - iot wheels are near - er roll - ing; He comes! O Church, lift up thine eyes! Rise up, with will - ing feet; Go

2. Zi - on hears the watch-men sing - ing; Her heart with deep de - light is spring - ing, She wakes, she ris - es from her gloom, For her Lord comes down all glo - rious, In grace ar - rayed, by truth vic - to - rious; Her star is risen, her light is come! Ah, come thou bless - ed One, God's

3. Now let all the heavens a - dore thee, And men and an - gels sing be - fore thee With harp and cym - bal's clear - est tone; Of one pearl each shin - ing por - tal, Where we shall join the choirs im - mor - tal In prais - es round thy glo - rious throne; No vi - sion ev - er brought, No

222

forth, the Bride-groom meet: Al - le - lu - ia! Lo, great and small, We
own be - lov - ed Son, Al - le - lu - ia! We haste a - long, An
ear hath ev - er caught Such great glo - ry! There - fore will we, e -

an - swer all; We fol - low where thy voice shall call.
ea - ger throng, And glad - some join the ad - vent song.
ter - nal - ly, Sing hymns of joy and praise to thee.

Text: Philipp Nicolai, 1556–1608
Music: WACHET AUF, Irregular, Melody, Hans Sach, 1494–1576; adapt. Philipp Nicolai; acc. J. S. Bach, 1685–1750

96. Lift Up Your Heads, You Mighty Gates

1. Lift up your heads, you might-y gates; Be - hold the King of glo - ry waits! The
2. O blest the land, the cit - y blest, Where Christ the rul - er is con - fessed! O
3. Fling wide the por - tals of your heart; Make it a tem - ple set a - part; Loud
4. So come, my Sov - 'reign; en - ter in! Let new and no - bler life be - gin; Your

King of kings is draw - ing near; The Sav - ior of the world is here.
hap - py hearts and hap - py homes To whom this King of tri - umph comes!
al - le - lu - ias now em - ploy, Sing out with prayer and love and joy.
Ho - ly Spir - it guide us on Un - til the glo - rious crown be won.

Text: Based on *Psalm 24*, Georg Weissel, 1590–1635, tr. Catherine Winkworth, 1827–1878
Music: TRURO, LM, *Psalmodia Evangelica*, 1789

97. A Christmas Anthem

1. Sing we the sto-ry of the shep-herds; Wise men three tell us of a
2. Stars shine a-round the man-ger ta-ble; Glo-ry of hea-ven rings the
3. Cold be the win-ter of our birth-place; High be the vi-sion of this
4. Christ leads us to our com-mon Par-ent, Mak-ing us one in what we

star; Gos-pel of peace is more than mere words. God through this
world: Hearts join as one to there as-sem-ble. Christ is re-
night; Wis-dom from God to flesh in pure grace, Word leaps down
do. Borne from the womb to life tran-scend-ent, Love comes to

child shows who we are: Chil-dren of Beth-le-hem!
born a thou-sand-fold. Come, ye to Beth-le-hem!
from her bed of light. Born we in Beth-le-hem!
live with us a-new. Make we for Beth-le-hem!

Text: Edward J. McKenna, b. 1939, ©
Music: MARYHAVEN, 98 98 6, Edward J. McKenna, b. 1939, ©

98. A Child Is Born / The Magi Kings

1. A child is born in Beth - le - hem, al - le - lu - ia;
2. Our broth - er in the flesh is he, al - le - lu - ia;
3. By grace this child is born a - gain, al - le - lu - ia;
4. The Ma - gi kings come from a - far, al - le - lu - ia;
5. Gold, in - cense, myrrh, they of - fer him, al - le - lu - ia;

Re - joice, re - joice Je - ru - sa - lem, al - le - lu - ia, al - le - lu - ia.
Our King for all e - ter - ni - ty, al - le - lu - ia, al - le - lu - ia.
In ev - 'ry heart he frees from sin, al - le - lu - ia, al - le - lu - ia.
Led on by faith in heav - en's star, al - le - lu - ia, al - le - lu - ia.
And bend - ing low they wor - ship him, al - le - lu - ia, al - le - lu - ia.

1.-5. Let grate - ful hearts now sing A song of joy and ho - ly praise To Christ the new - born King!

Text: *Puer natus,* 14th cent., tr. Irvin Udulutsch, O.F.M., Cap., b. 1920, ©
Music: PUER NATUS, 88 with Alleluias and Refrain, *Plainchant, Mode I;* acc. Irvin Udulutsch, O.F.M., Cap., b. 1920, ©

99. ONCE IN ROYAL DAVID'S CITY

5. And our eyes at last shall see him,
   Through his own redeeming love;
   For that child who seemed so helpless
   Is our Lord in heav'n above;
   And he leads his children on
   To the place where he is gone.

6. Not in that poor lowly stable,
   With the oxen standing round,
   We shall see him; but in heaven,
   Where his saints his throne surround:
   Christ, revealed to faithful eye,
   Set at God's right hand on high.

Text: Cecil Frances Alexander, 1818–1895, alt. vv. 1–2, 4–6; James Waring McCrady, b. 1938, v. 3, ©
Music: IRBY, 87 87 77, Henry John Gauntlett, 1805–1876; harm. Arthur Henry Mann, 1850–1929, ©

100. SILENT NIGHT

Text: Joseph Mohr, 1792–1848; tr. John Freeman Young, 1820–1885
Music: STILLE NACHT, Irregular, Franz Gruber, 1787–1863

101. HARK! THE HERALD ANGELS SING

1. Hark! the her - ald an - gels sing, Glo - ry to the new - born King!
2. Christ, by high - est heav'n a - dored, Christ, the ev - er - last - ing Lord,
3. Mild he lays his glo - ry by, Born that we no more may die,
4. What good news the an - gels bring, What glad ti - dings of our King!

Peace on earth and mer - cy mild, God and sin - ners rec - on - ciled!
Late in time be - hold him come, Off - spring of the Vir - gin's womb.
Born to raise us from the earth, Born to give us sec - ond birth.
Christ the Lord is born to - day, Christ who takes our sins a - way!

Joy - ful, all ye na - tions, rise, Join the tri - umph of the skies;
Veiled in flesh the God - head see; Hail th'In - car - nate De - i - ty,
Ris'n with heal - ing in his wings, Light and life to all he brings.
He who rules both heav'n and earth Hath in Beth - le - hem his birth;

With th'an - gel - ic host pro - claim, "Christ is born in Beth - le - hem!"
Pleased as man with us to dwell, Je - sus our Em - man - u - el!
Hail, the Sun of Right - eous - ness! Hail, the heav'n - born Prince of Peace!
With th'an - gel - ic host pro - claim, "Christ is born in Beth - le - hem!"

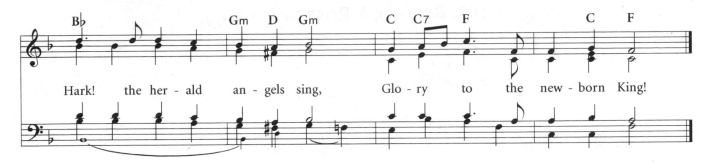

Hark! the her - ald an - gels sing, Glo - ry to the new - born King!

Text: Charles Wesley, 1707–1788, alt. vv. 1–3; William Hammond, 1719–1783, v. 4
Music: MENDELSSOHN, 77 77 D and Refrain, Felix Mendelssohn, 1808–1847; adapt. William H. Cummings, 1831–1915

102. AWAY IN A MANGER

1. A - way in a man - ger, no crib for a bed, The lit - tle Lord
2. The cat - tle are low - ing, the ba - by a - wakes, But lit - tle Lord
3. Be near me, Lord Je - sus, I ask thee to stay Close by me for -

Je - us laid down his sweet head. The stars in the sky looked
Je - sus, no cry - ing he makes. I love thee, Lord Je - sus, look
ev - er, and love me, I pray. Bless all the dear chil - dren in

down where he lay, The lit - tle Lord Je - sus, a - sleep on the hay.
down from the sky, And stay by my cra - dle till morn - ing is nigh.
thy ten - der care. And fit us for heav - en to live with thee there.

Text: John Thomas McFarland, 1851–1913, v. 3; anon., vv. 1–2
Music: AWAY IN A MANGER, 11 11 11 11, James R. Murray, 1841–1905

103. Behold, A Rose of Judah

1. Be - hold a rose of Ju - dah from ten - der branch has sprung! A
2. This rose of roy - al beau - ty of which I - sa - iah sings, Is
3. We pray thee, Vir - gin Moth - er, the Queen of heav'n and earth: Ob -

rose from root of Jes - se, as proph - ets long had sung. It bore a flow - er
Mar - y, maid - en Moth - er, and Christ the flow'r she brings. By God's u - nique de -
tain for us from Je - sus the bless - ings of his birth. By his hu - mil - i -

bright, that blos - somed in the win - ter when half - spent was the night.
sign, re - main - ing still a vir - gin, she bore her Child di - vine.
ty, may we live as God's chil - dren, in peace and u - ni - ty.

Text: German, 15th cent.
Music: ES IST EIN ROS, 76 76 676

104. GO TELL IT ON THE MOUNTAIN

Go tell it on the moun - tain, O - ver the hills and ev - 'ry - where;

Go tell it on the moun - tain That Je - sus Christ is born!

1. While shep - herds kept their watch - ing O'er si - lent flocks by night,
2. The shep - herds feared and trem - bled When lo! A - bove the earth
3. Down in a low - ly man - ger The hum - ble Christ was born,

Be - hold through - out the heav - ens There shone a ho - ly light.
Rang out the an - gel cho - rus That hailed our Sav - ior's birth.
And God sent us sal - va - tion That bless - ed Christ - mas morn.

Text: Afro-American Spiritual, 19th cent.; adapt. tr John W. Work, b. 1901, ©
Music: GO TELL IT ON THE MOUNTAIN, 76 76 with Refrain, Afro-American Spiritual; acc. John W. Work, b. 1901, ©

105. Angels We Have Heard on High

Text: Traditional French Carol, tr. anon.
Music: GLORIA, 77 77 with Refrain, Traditional French Carol

106. O Come, All Ye Faithful
107. Adeste Fideles

1. O come, all ye faith-ful, joy-ful and tri-um-phant, O come ye, O come ye to
2. God of God, Light of Light, Lo! He comes forth from the
1. Ad-é-ste fi-dé-les, lae-ti, tri-um-phán-tes, Ve-ní-te, ve-ní-te in
2. De-um de De-o, Lu-men de Lú-mi ne Ge-stant pu-é- lae

Beth - le - hem; Come and be-hold him, born the King of an - gels:
Vir - gin's womb. Our ver - y God, be - got-ten not cre - a - ted,
Béth - le - hem. Na-tum vi - dé - te, Re-gem an-ge-ló - rum.
ví - sce - ra. De - um ve - rum, Gé - ni-tum, non fac - tum.

O come, let us a-dore him, O come, let us a-dore him, O come, let us a - dore him, Christ, the Lord!
Ve - ní-te a-do-ré-mus, ve-ní - te a-do-ré-mus, ve-ní - te a-do-ré-mus Dó - mi-num.

3. Sing, choirs of angels, sing in exultation,
   Sing, all ye citizens of heav'n above!
   Glory to God, all glory in the highest;

4. Yea, Lord, we greet thee,
   Born this happy morning,
   Jesus, to thee be glory giv'n.

3. Cantet nunc Io! Chorus angelórum,
   Cantet nunc aula caeléstium.
   Glória, glória, in excélsis Deo.

4. Ergo qui natus Die hodiérna
   Jesus tibi sit glória.
   Patris aetérni verbum caro factum.

Text: John F. Wade, c. 1711–1786; tr. Frederick Oakeley, 1802–1880, alt.
Music: ADESTE FIDELES, Irregular with Refrain, John F. Wade, c. 1711–1786; arr. David Wilcocks, b. 1919, ©

108. GOD REST YOU MERRY, GENTLEMEN

1. God rest you merry, gentlemen, let nothing you dismay;
2. From God our heav'nly Father a blessed angel came
3. "Fear not, then," said the angel, "Let nothing you affright;
4. Now to the Lord sing praises, all you within this place,

Remember Christ our Savior was born on Christmas Day,
And unto certain shepherds brought tidings of the same:
This day is born a Savior of a pure virgin bright,
And with true love and charity each other now embrace;

To save us all from Satan's pow'r when we were gone astray.
How that in Bethlehem was born the Son of God by name.
To free all those who trust in him from Satan's pow'r and might."
This holy tide of Christmas doth bring redeeming grace.

O tidings of comfort and joy, comfort and joy; O tidings of comfort and joy!

Text: 18th cent. English Carol
Music: GOD REST YOU MERRY, 76 76 86 with Refrain, 18th cent. English Carol; harm. John Stainer, 1840–1901

234

109. RESONET IN LAUDIBUS

1. Ré - son - et in laú - di - bus Cum ju - cún - dis pláu - si - bus,
2. Si - on lau - da Dó - mi - num Sal - va - tó - rem ó - mni - um;
3. Na - tus est Em - má - nu - el, Quem prae - dí - xit Gá - bri - el,
4. San - cta ti - bi Trí - ni - tas Os ó - mni - um grá - ti - as

Si - on cum fi - dé - li - bus.
Vir - go pa - rit Fí - li - um.
Te - stis est E - zé - chi - el.
Ré - son - et al - tís - si - mas.

Ap - pá - ru - it quem gé - nu - it Ma - rí - a.

Gau - dé - te, gau - dé - te, Chri-stus na - tus hó - di - e! Gau - dé - te, gau - dé - te, ex Ma - rí - a Vír - gi - ne.

Text: Anon., 14th cent.
Music: *Plainchant, Mode V;* acc. Jean-Hebert Desrocquettes, O.S.B., ©

235

110. FROM HEAVEN ABOVE TO EARTH

1. From heav'n a-bove to earth I come To bring good news to ev-ery-one!
2. To you this night is born a child Of Ma-ry, cho-sen vir-gin mild;
3. This is the Christ, God's Son most high, Who hears your sad and bit-ter cry;
4. The bless-ing which the Fa-ther planned The Son holds in his in-fant hand,

Glad tid-ings of great joy I bring To all the world and glad-ly sing.
This new-born Child of low-ly birth Shall be the joy of all the earth.
He will him-self your Sav-ior be And from all sin will set you free.
That in his king-dom bright and fair, You may with us his glo-ry share.

Text: Martin Luther, 1483–1546; tr. *Lutheran Book of Worship*, 1978, ©
Music: VOM HIMMEL HOCH, 88 88, Martin Luther, 1483–1546, attr.; harm. Hans Leo Hassler, 1564–1612

236

111. IT CAME UPON THE MIDNIGHT CLEAR

1. It came up-on the mid-night clear, That glo-rious song of old,
2. Still through the clo-ven skies they come, With peace-ful wings un-furled,
3. Yet with the woes of sin and strife, The world has suf-fered long;
4. For, lo, the days are has-t'ning on, By proph-ets seen of old,

From an-gels bend-ing near the earth To touch their harps of gold:
And still their heav'n-ly mu-sic floats O'er all the wea-ry world:
Be-neath the heav'n-ly hymn have rolled Two thou-sand years of wrong;
When with the ev-er-cir-cling years Shall come the time fore-told,

"Peace on the earth, good will to all From heav-'en's all gra-cious King."
A-bove its sad and low-ly plains They bend on hov-'ring wing,
And war-ring hu-man-kind hears not The ti-dings which they bring;
When peace shall o-ver all the earth Its an-cient splen-dors fling,

The world in sol-emn still-ness lay, To hear the an-gels sing.
And ev-er o'er its ba-bel sounds The bless-ed an-gels sing.
O hush the noise and cease your strife And hear the an-gels sing.
And all the world give back the song Which now the an-gels sing.

Text: Edmund Hamilton Sears, 1810–1876, alt.
Music: CAROL, 86 86 86 86, Richard S. Willis, 1819–1900

112. JOY TO THE WORLD

1. Joy to the world! the Lord is come; Let earth re-ceive her King; Let
2. Joy to the world! the Sav-ior reigns; Let earth her songs em-ploy; While
3. He rules the world with truth and grace And makes the na-tions prove The
4. His name shall be the Prince of Peace, The ev-er-last-ing Lord, The
5. "Glo-ry to God," the sound-ing skies With joy their an-thems ring: "Peace

ev - 'ry heart pre-pare him room And heav'n and na-ture sing, And
fields and floods, rocks, hills and plains Re-peat the sound-ing joy, Re-
glo - ries of his right-eous-ness, And won-ders of his love, And
Won - der-ful, the Coun-sel-lor, The God by all a-dored, The
to the earth, good will to all," From heav'n's e-ter-nal King. From

heav'n and na-ture sing, And heav'n, and heav'n and na-ture sing.
peat the sound-ing joy, Re - peat, re-peat the sound-ing joy.
won - ders of his love, And won - ders, won-ders of his love.
God by all a-dored, The God, the God by all a-dored.
heav'n's e-ter-nal King. From heav'n's, from heav'n's e-ter-nal King.

Text: Isaac Watts, 1674–1748, alt.
Music: ANTIOCH, 86 86 with Repeat, George F. Handel, 1685–1759; adapt. and arr. Lowell Mason, 1792–1872

113. WINTER'S SNOW

1. See a - mid the win - ter's snow, Born for us on earth be - low;
2. Lo, with - in a man - ger lies He who built the star - ry skies;
3. Say, you ho - ly shep - herds, say, Tell your joy - ful news to - day,
4. As we watched at dead of night, Lo, we saw a won - drous light:

See the ten - der Lamb ap - pears, Pro - mised from e - ter - nal years:
He who, throned in height sub - lime, Sits a - mid the cher - u - bim:
Why have you now left your sheep On the lone - ly moun - tain steep?
An - gels sing - ing "Peace on earth" Told us of the Sav - ior's birth:

REFRAIN

Hail, thou ev - er bless - ed morn; Hail, re - demp - tion's hap - py dawn;

Sing through all Je - ru - sa - lem, Christ is born in Beth - le - hem.

5. Sacred infant, all divine,
   What a tender love was thine.
   Thus to come from highest bliss
   Down to such a world as this: *Refrain*

6. Teach, O teach us, holy Child,
   By thy face so meek and mild,
   Teach us to resemble thee,
   In thy sweet humility: *Refrain*

Text: Edward Caswall, 1814–1878
Music: HUMILITY, 77 77 with Refrain, John Goss, 1800–1880

114. OF THE FATHER'S LOVE BEGOTTEN

1. Of the Fa - ther's love be - got - ten, Ere the worlds be - gan to be,
2. Bless - ed was the day for ev - er When the Vir - gin full of grace,
3. This is he whom seers in old time Chant - ed of with one ac - cord,
4. O ye heights of heav'n, a - dore him; An - gel hosts, his prais - es sing;
5. Glo - ry be to God the Fa - ther, Glo - ry be to God the Son,

He is Al - pha and O - me - ga, He the source the end - ing he,
By the Ho - ly Ghost con - ceiv - ing, Bore the Sav - ior of our race,
Whom the voic - es of the proph - ets Prom - ised in their faith - ful word;
All do - min - ions, bow be - fore him, And ex - tol our God and King;
Glo - ry to the Ho - ly Spir - it, Per - sons three, yet God - head One.

Of the things that are, that have been, And that fu - ture years shall see,
And the child, the world's Re - deem - er, First re - vealed his sa - cred face,
Now he shines, the long ex - pect - ed; Let cre - a - tion praise the Lord,
Let no tongue on earth be si - lent, Ev - 'ry voice in con - cert ring,
Glo - ry be from all cre - a - tion While e - ter - nal a - ges run,

Ev - er - more and ev - er - more.
Ev - er - more and ev - er - more.
Ev - er - more and ev - er - more.
Ev - er - more and ev - er - more.
Ev - er - more and ev - er - more. A - men.

Text: Aurelius Clemens Prudentius, 348–413, tr. John Mason Neale, 1818–1866, et al.
Music: CORDE NATUS (DIVINUM), 87 87 87 with Refrain, Didrik Pedersen of Abo, harm. Rev. Percy Jones, ©

115. I Wonder As I Wander

1. I won - der as I wan - der out un - der the sky, How Je - sus, the
2. When Ma - ry birthed Je - sus, 'twas in a cows' stall, With wise - men and
3. If Je - sus had want - ed for an - y wee thing; A star in the
4. I won - der as I wan - der out un - der the sky, How Je - sus, the

Sav - ior, did come for to die, For poor, or - n'ry peo - ple like you and like
far - mers and shep - herds and all, But high from God's heav - en a star's light did
sky, or a bird on the wing; Or all of God's an - gels in heav - en to
Sav - ior, did come for to die. For poor, or - n'ry peo - ple like you and like

I. I won - der as I wan - der, Out un - der the sky.
fall, And the prom - ise of a - ges It then did re - call.
sing, He sure - ly could have had it, 'Cause He was the King!
I, I won - der as I wan - der, Out un - der the sky.

Text: Appalachian Carol; collected by John Jacob Niles
Music: Appalachian Folk Song; adapt. John Jacob Niles; arr. Fred Bock, ©

241

116. THE FIRST NOWELL

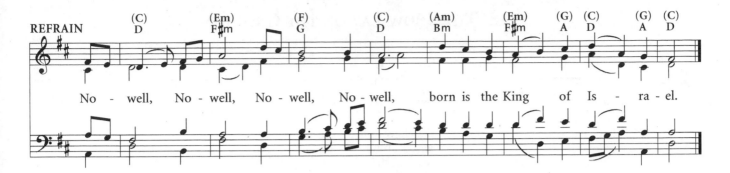

6. Then let us all with one accord
   sing praises to our heav'nly Lord;
   that hath made heav'n and earth of nought,
   and with his blood our life hath bought. *Refrain*

Text: English Carol, 18th cent.
Music: THE FIRST NOWELL, Irregular with Refrain, English Carol, 17th cent.; harm. John Stainer, 1840–1901

117. While Shepherds Watched Their Flocks

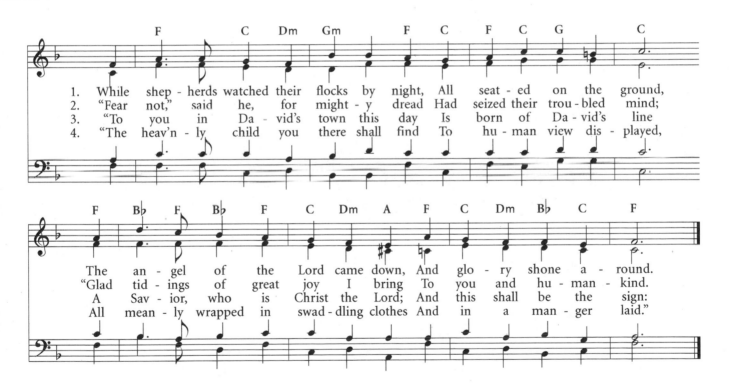

5. Thus spoke the seraph; and forthwith
   Appeared a shining throng
   Of angels praising God, who thus
   Addressed their joyful song:

6. "All glory be to God on high,
   And on the earth be peace:
   Good will henceforth from heav'n to all
   Begin and never cease."

Text: *New Version of the Psalms*, 1696; tr. Nahum Tate, 1652–1715, and Nicholas Brady, 1659–c. 1726
Music: WINCHESTER OLD, 86 86, George Kirbye, c. 1560–1634, attr.

118. The Snow Lay on the Ground

1. The snow lay on the ground, the stars shone bright, When that
2. 'Twas Ma - ry, daugh - ter pure of ho - ly Ann, that
   She laid Him in a stall at Beth - le - hem; The
3. Saint Jo - seph too was by to tend the Child, To
   The An - gels hov - er'd round and sang this song, Ve -
4. And then that man - ger poor be - came a throne, For
   Oh, come, then, let us join the heav'n - ly host, To

Christ our Lord was born on Christ - mas night. *(to refrain)*
brought in - to this world on the God made man. *(to refrain)*
ass and ox - en shared the roof with them. *(to refrain)*
guard Him and pro - tect His Moth - er mild.
ni - te ad - o - re - mus Do - mi - num. *(to refrain)*
He whom Ma - ry bore was God the Son.
praise the Fa - ther, Son and Ho - ly Ghost. *(to refrain)*

REFRAIN
Ve - ni - te ad - o - re - mus Do - mi - num, Ve - ni - te ad - o - re - mus Do - mi - num.

Old English Carol
VENITE, ADOREMUS, Irregular with Refrain

244

119. O Come, Little Children

1. O come, lit-tle chil-dren; O come one and all, Who lies in the man-ger in Beth-le-hem's stall; For there, lit-tle chil-dren on this hol-iest night, Our God sends from heav-en his Son, your de-light.

2. He lies there, be-fore you, a-sleep in the hay, With Ma-ry and Jo-seph to guard him and pray. The won-der-ing shep-herds look in at the door, And see-ing the in-fant they kneel and a-dore.

3. A-dore like the shep-herds! Your glad voi-ces raise With those of the an-gels who sing in his praise. Your cho-rus will ech-o from earth to the sky, With "Glo-ry to God in his heav-en most high."

Text: Johann Christoph von Schmid, 1768–1854; tr. Edward C. Currie, d. 1967, ©
Music: IHR KINDERLEIN, KOMMET, 11 11 11 11, Johann A. P. Schulz, 1747–1800; harm. J. Alfred Schehl, 1882–1959, alt., ©

120. Oh, Sleep Now, Holy Babe

1. Oh, sleep now, holy baby, with your head against my breast; meanwhile the
pangs of my sorrow are soothed and put to rest.
2. You need not fear King Herod, he will bring no harm to you; so rest in the
arms of your mother who sings you a la ru.

1. Duer-me-te, Niño lindo, en los brazos del amor duerme y descansa la pena de mi dolor.
2. No te-mas al rey Herodes que nada te ha de hacer; en los brazos de tu madre y ahi nadie te ha de ofender.

A la ru, a la me, a la ru, a la me, a la
ru, a la me, a la ru, a la ru, a la me.

Music: A LA RU, © 1954, used with permission

121. O Little Town of Bethlehem

1. O lit-tle town of Beth-le-hem, How still we see thee lie!
2. For Christ is born of Ma - ry, And gath-ered all a - bove,
3. How si - lent - ly, how si - lent - ly The won-drous gift is giv'n!
4. O ho - ly Child of Beth - le - hem, De - scend to us, we pray;

A - bove thy deep and dream - less sleep The si - lent stars go by;
While mor - tals sleep, the an - gels keep Their watch of won - d'ring love.
So God im - parts to hu - man hearts The bless - ings of his heav'n.
Cast out our sin and en - ter in; Be born in us to - day.

Yet in thy dark streets shin - eth The ev - er - last - ing Light;
O morn - ing stars, to - geth - er Pro - claim the ho - ly birth;
No ear may hear his com - ing, But in this world of sin,
We hear the Christ - mas an - gels The great glad ti - dings tell;

The hopes and fears of all the years Are met in thee to - night.
And prais - es sing to God the King, And peace to all on earth.
Where meek souls will re - ceive him, still The dear Christ en - ters in.
O come to us, a - bide with us, Our Lord Em - man - u - el!

Text: Phillip Brooks, 1835–1908
Music: ST. LOUIS, 86 86 86 86, Lewis H. Redner, 1831–1908

122. WHAT CHILD IS THIS?

1. What child is this, who laid to rest, On Mary's lap is sleep - ing? Whom
2. Why lies he in such mean es - tate Where ox and ass are feed - ing? Good
3. So bring him in - cense, gold, and myrrh, Come, peas - ant, king, to own him. The

an - gels greet with an - thems sweet, While shep - herds watch are keep - ing?
Chris - tian, fear; for sin - ners here The si - lent Word is plead - ing.
King of kings sal - va - tion brings. Let lov - ing hearts en - throne him.

This, this is Christ the King, Whom shep - herds guard and an - gels sing;

Haste, haste to bring him laud, The babe, the son of Ma - ry.

Text: William Chatterton Dix, 1837–1898
Music: GREENSLEEVES, 87 87 with Refrain, English Melody, 1580

123. WHEN BLOSSOMS FLOWERED 'MID THE SNOWS

1. When blos - soms flow - 'red 'mid the snows Up-
gain the heart with rap - ture glows To

on a win - ter night, Was born the Child, the Christ - mas Rose, The
greet the ho - ly night, That gave the world its Christ - mas Rose, Its

King of Love and Light. The an - gels sang, the shep - herds sang, The
King of Love and Light. Let ev - 'ry voice ac - claim His name, The

grate - ful earth re - joiced; And at His bless - ed
grate - ful cho - rus swell. From par - a - dise to

birth the stars Their ex - ul - ta - tion voiced.
earth He came That we with Him might dwell. O

Non troppo lento

come let us a - dore Him, O come let us a -

dore Him, O come let us a - dore Him

Christ the Lord. 2. A-

Text: Pietro Alessandro Yon, 1866–1943; tr. Frederick H. Martens, 1874–1932, ©
Music: GESU BAMBINO, 86 86 86 86 with Refrain, Pietro Alessandro Yon, 1866–1943, ©

251

124. As with Gladness Men of Old

1. As with glad-ness men of old Did the guid-ing star be-hold,
2. As with joy-ful steps they sped To that low-ly man-ger bed,
3. As they of-fered gifts most rare At that man-ger rude and bare,
4. Christ Re-deem-er, with us stay, Help us live your ho-ly way;

As with joy they hailed its light, Lead-ing on-ward, beam-ing bright,
There to bend the knee be-fore Him whom heav'n and earth a-dore,
So may we with ho-ly joy, Pure and free from sin's al-loy,
And when earth-ly things are past, Bring our ran-somed souls at last

So, most gra-cious God, may we Ev-er-more be led to thee.
So may we with will-ing feet Ev-er seek thy mer-cy seat.
All our cost-liest treas-ures bring, Christ, to thee our heav'n-ly King.
Where they need no star to guide, Where no clouds your glo-ry hide.

Text: William Chatterton Dix, 1837–1898
Music: DIX, 77 77 77, Conrad Kocher, 1786–1872; arr. William Henry Monk, 1823–1889

125. WE THREE KINGS OF ORIENT ARE

1. We three kings of O - ri - ent are, Bear - ing gifts we tra - verse a - far,
2. Born a King on Beth - le - hem's plain, Gold I bring to crown him a - gain,
3. Frank - in - cense to of - fer have I, In - cense owns a De - i - ty nigh,
4. Myrrh is mine; its bit - ter per - fume Breathes a life of gath - er - ing gloom;
5. Glo - rious now be - hold him a - rise, King, and God, and Sac - ri - fice;

Field and foun - tain, Moor and moun - tain, Fol - low - ing yon - der star.
King for ev - er, Ceas - ing nev - er O - ver us all to reign.
Prayer and prais - ing, All are rais - ing, Wor - ship him, God on high.
Sor - rowing, sigh - ing, Bleed - ing, dy - ing, Sealed in the stone - cold tomb.
Heav'n sings "Al - le - lu - ia"; "Al - le - lu - ia", earth re - plies.

O star of won - der, star of night, Star with roy - al beau - ty bright;

West - ward lead - ing, Still pro - ceed - ing, Guide us to thy per - fect light!

Text: John Henry Hopkins, Jr., 1820–1891
Music: KINGS OF ORIENT (Hopkins), 88 86 with Refrain, John Henry Hopkins, Jr., 1820 1891

253

126. SONGS OF THANKFULNESS AND PRAISE

1. Songs of thank-ful-ness and praise, Je-sus, Lord to you we raise,
2. Man-i-fest at Jor-dan's stream, Pro-phet, Priest, and King su-preme;
3. Grant us, Lord, your gifts of grace. Faith to see your sa-cred face.
4. Grant us grace to see you, Lord, Mir-rored in your ho-ly word;

Man-i-fest-ed by the star To the sa-ges from a-far;
And at Ca-na, wed-ding guest, In your God-head man-i-fest;
Still re-vealed in your true Church, Giv-ing life to those who search;
May we im-i-tate you here, Live as those who know no fear;

Branch of roy-al Da-vid's stem, In your birth at Beth-le-hem,
Man-i-fest in pow'r di-vine, Chang-ing wa-ter in-to wine.
That same face which we shall see In that great E-piph-a-ny,
That we like to you may be At your great E-piph-a-ny;

An-thems be to you ad-dressed, God in flesh made man-i-fest!
An-thems be to you ad-dressed, God in flesh made man-i-fest!
An-thems be to you ad-dressed, God in flesh made man-i-fest!
God in flesh made man-i-fest! God in flesh made man-i-fest!

Text: Christopher Wordsworth, 1807–1885, vv. 1, 2, & 4 alt; Irvin Udulutsch, O.F.M., Cap., b. 1920, v. 3, ©
Music: SALZBURG, 77 77 77 77, Jacob Hintze, 1622–1702; adapt. J. S. Bach, 1685–1750

127. When John Baptized by Jordan

1. When John bap-tized by Jor-dan's riv - er In faith and hope the peo - ple came,
2. There as the Lord, bap-tized and pray - ing, Rose for the stream, the sin - less one,
3. O Son of Man, our na-ture shar - ing, In whose o - be-dience all are blest,

That John and Jor-dan might de - liv - er Their trou-bled souls from sin and shame.
A voice was heard from heav - en say - ing, "This is my own be - lov - ed son."
Sav - ior, our sins and sor - row bear - ing, Hear us and grant us this re - quest:

They came to seek a new be - gin - ning, The hu - man spir - it's age - less quest,
There as the Fa - ther's word was spo - ken, Not in the pow'r of wind and flame,
Dai - ly to grow by grace de - fend - ed, Filled with the Spir - it from a - bove;

Re - pent-ance, and an end of sin - ning. Re - nounc-ing ev - 'ry wrong con - fessed.
But of his love and peace the to - ken, Seen as a dove, the Spir - it came.
In Christ bap-tized, be - loved, be - friend - ed, Chil - dren of God in peace and love.

Text: Timothy Dudley-Smith, b. 1962, © 1984, Hope Publishing Co., Carol Stream, IL
Music: RENDEZ A DIEU, 98 98 98 98, Louis Bourgeois, c. 1510–1561, attr.

128. HAVE MERCY, LORD, ON US

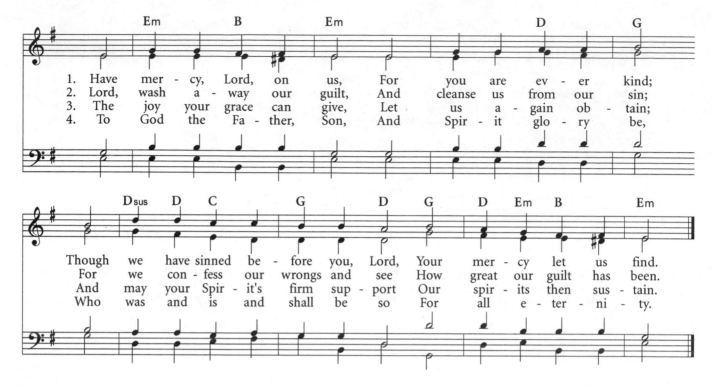

1. Have mercy, Lord, on us, For you are ever kind;
2. Lord, wash away our guilt, And cleanse us from our sin;
3. The joy your grace can give, Let us again obtain;
4. To God the Father, Son, And Spirit glory be,

Though we have sinned before you, Lord, Your mercy let us find.
For we confess our wrongs and see How great our guilt has been.
And may your Spirit's firm support Our spirits then sustain.
Who was and is and shall be so For all eternity.

Text: Nahum Tate, 1652–1715, and Nicholas Brady, 1659–1726
Music: SOUTHWELL, 66 86, William Damon, c. 1550–1593

129. O CROSS OF CHRIST

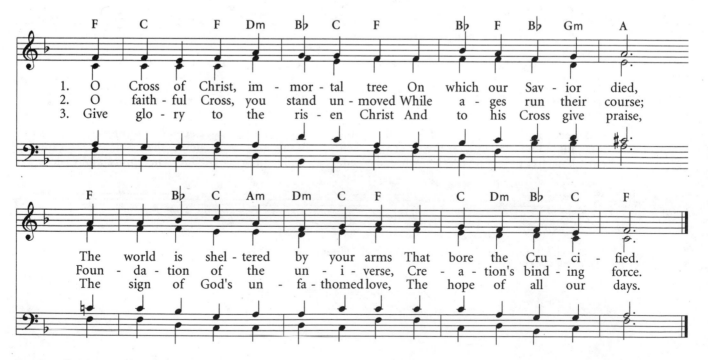

1. O Cross of Christ, immortal tree On which our Savior died,
2. O faithful Cross, you stand unmoved While ages run their course;
3. Give glory to the risen Christ And to his Cross give praise,

The world is sheltered by your arms That bore the Crucified.
Foundation of the universe, Creation's binding force.
The sign of God's unfathomed love, The hope of all our days.

Text: Benedictine Nuns of Stanbrook Abbey, ©
Music: ST. FLAVIAN, 86 86

130. As the Sun with Longer Journey

1. As the sun with long-er jour-ney Melts the win-ter's snow and ice,
2. Through the days of wait-ing, watch-ing, In the des-ert of our sin,
3. Praise be giv-en to the mak-er Of the sea-son's year-ly change,

With its slow-ly grow-ing ra-diance Warms the seed be-neath the earth, May the sun of
Search-ing on the far ho-ri-zon For a sign of cloud or wind, We a-wait the
To the Fa-ther, his Be-lov-ed, In their liv-ing u-ni-ty, As the ev-er

Christ's up-ris-ing Gen-tly bring our hearts to life.
heal-ing wa-ters Of our Sav-ior's vic-to-ry.
turn-ing a-ges Roll to their e-ter-nal rest.

Text: John Patrick Earls, O.S.B., b. 1935, ©
Music: SUN JOURNEY, 87 87 87, Henry Bryan Hays, O.S.B., b. 1920, ©

131. WHEN FROM BONDAGE

1. When from bon-dage we are sum-moned Out of dark-ness in-to light,
2. When our God names us his peo - ple, Then he leads us by the hand
3. At all sta-ges of the jour-ney God is with us, night and day,

We must go in hope and pa-tience, Walk by faith and not by sight,
Through a lone - ly, bar - ren des - ert, To a great and glo-rious land.
With com-pas - sion for our weak-ness Ev-'ry step a - long the way.

Let us throw off all that hin - ders; Let us run the race to win!

Let us has - ten to our home - land And, re - joic - ing, en - ter in.

Text: Sr. Delores Dufner, O.S.B., b. 1939, ©
Music: Jay F. Hunstiger, b. 1950, ©

132. BELOVED SON AND DAUGHTER

1. Be - lov - ed son and daugh - ter dear, I call you by your name. My
2. O turn to me with all your heart; With joy ap - proach my hall. From
3. Now blow the trum - pet, call a fast, As - sem - ble in my name, And

peo - ple, lis - ten to my voice: Your heart's love now I claim.
far and wide I gath - er you. My peo - ple, hear my call!
wel - come to your ban - quet hall My poor and blind and lame.

O come, let us re - turn to him, For gra - cious is the Lord. He
More faith - ful than the ris - ing sun, More gen - tle than the breeze; More
A - rise and let us come to him Who knows our fears and needs. With

knows our pain and heals our wounds; Our life in him re - stored!
lav - ish than the green - ing spring, Our God who saves and frees!
love may we re - spond to love, And fol - low where he leads.

Text: Sr. Delores Dufner, O.S.B., b. 1939, ©
Music: ST. CLOUD, 86 86 86 86, Jay F. Hunstiger, b. 1950, ©

259

133. IN THE CROSS OF CHRIST I GLORY

1. In the Cross of Christ I glory, Tow'r-ing o'er the wrecks of time;
2. When the woes of life o'er-take me, Hopes de-ceive and fears an-noy,
3. When the sun of bliss is beam-ing Light and love up-on my way,
4. Bane and bless-ing, pain and plea-sure, By the Cross are sanc-ti-fied;

All the light of sa-cred sto-ry Ga-thers round its head sub-lime.
Nev-er shall the Cross for-sake me, Lo! it glows with peace and joy.
From the Cross the ra-diance stream-ing, Adds more lus-ter to the day.
Peace is there that knows no mea-sure, Joys that through all time a-bide.

All the light of sa-cred sto-ry Ga-thers round its head sub-lime.
Nev-er shall the Cross for-sake me, Lo! it glows with peace and joy.
From the Cross the ra-diance stream-ing Adds more lus-ter to the day.
Peace is there that knows no mea-sure, Joys that through all time a-bide.

Text: Sir J. Bowring, 1792–1872
Music: RICHARD'S SHOP, 87 87, Henry Bryan Hays, O.S.B., b. 1920, ©

134. Lord Jesus, As We Turn from Sin

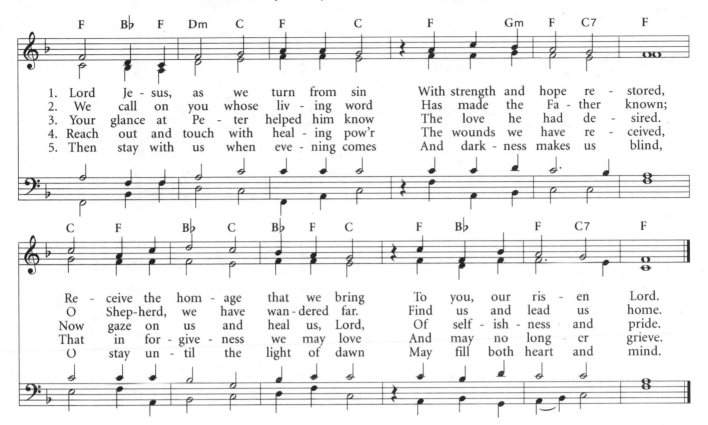

1. Lord Jesus, as we turn from sin With strength and hope restored,
Receive the homage that we bring To you, our risen Lord.

2. We call on you whose living word Has made the Father known;
O Shepherd, we have wandered far. Find us and lead us home.

3. Your glance at Peter helped him know The love he had desired.
Now gaze on us and heal us, Lord, Of selfishness and pride.

4. Reach out and touch with healing pow'r The wounds we have received,
That in forgiveness we may love And may no longer grieve.

5. Then stay with us when evening comes And darkness makes us blind,
O stay until the light of dawn May fill both heart and mind.

Text: Ralph Wright, O.S.B., b. 1938, ©
Music: GRAEFENBERG, 86 86, Johann Cruger, 1598–1662

135. O Merciful Redeemer, Hear

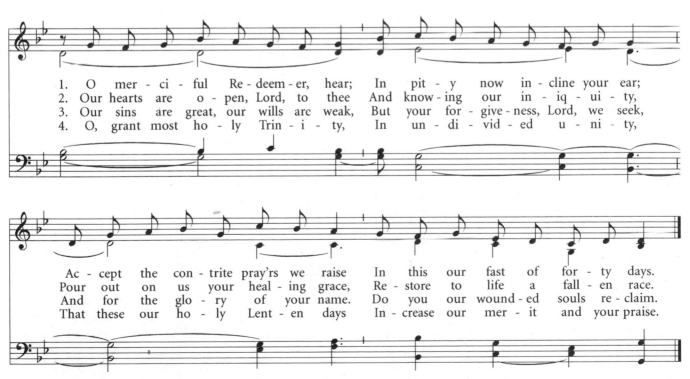

1. O merciful Redeemer, hear; In pity now incline your ear;
Accept the contrite pray'rs we raise In this our fast of forty days.

2. Our hearts are open, Lord, to thee And knowing our iniquity,
Pour out on us your healing grace, Restore to life a fallen race.

3. Our sins are great, our wills are weak, But your forgiveness, Lord, we seek,
And for the glory of your name. Do you our wounded souls reclaim.

4. O, grant most holy Trinity, In undivided unity,
That these our holy Lenten days Increase our merit and your praise.

Text: St. Gregory the Great, 540–604; tr. Irvin Udulutsch, O.S.F., Cap., b. 1920, ©
Music: AUDI REDEMPTOR, 88 88, *Plainchant, Mode II*; acc. Irvin Udulutsch, O.S.F., Cap., b. 1920, ©

136. FORTY DAYS AND FORTY NIGHTS

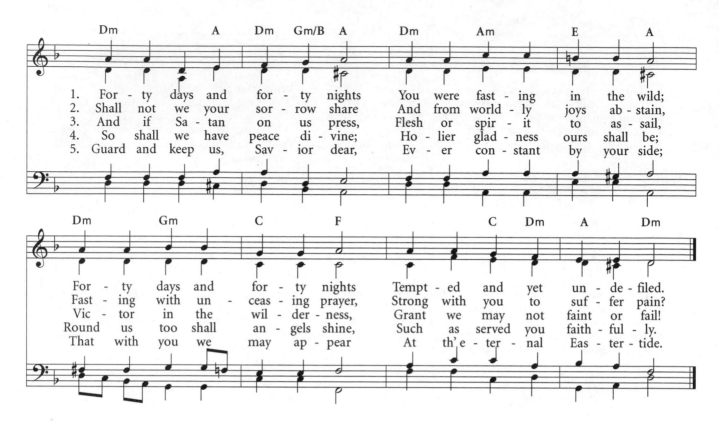

1. Forty days and forty nights You were fasting in the wild;
2. Shall not we your sorrow share And from worldly joys abstain,
3. And if Satan on us press, Flesh or spirit to assail,
4. So shall we have peace divine; Holier gladness ours shall be;
5. Guard and keep us, Savior dear, Ever constant by your side;

Forty days and forty nights Tempted and yet undefiled.
Fasting with unceasing prayer, Strong with you to suffer pain?
Victor in the wilderness, Grant we may not faint or fail!
Round us too shall angels shine, Such as served you faithfully.
That with you we may appear At th'eternal Eastertide.

Text: George Hunt Smyttan, 1822–1870; tr. Francis Pott, 1832–1909, alt.
Music: HEINLEIN, 77 77, Martin Herbst, 1654–1681, attr.

137. THE GLORY OF THESE FORTY DAYS

1. The glo-ry of these for-ty days We cel - e - brate with songs of praise;
2. A - lone and fast - ing, Mo - ses saw The lov - ing God who gave the law;
3. So Dan - iel trained his mys - tic sight, De - liv - ered from the li - on's might;
4. Then grant that we like them be true, Con - sumed in fast and prayer with you;

For Christ, by whom all things were made, Him - self has fast - ed and has prayed.
And to E - li - jah, fast - ing came The steeds and char - i - ots of flame.
And John, the Bride - groom's friend, be - came The her - ald of Mes - si - ah's name.
Our spir - its strength - en with your grace, And give us joy to see your face.

Text: *Clarum decus jejunii;* ascr. to Gregory the Great, c. 540–604; tr. Maurice F. Bell, 1862–1947, © Oxford University Press
Tune: ERHALT UNS HERR, LM, Klug's *Geistliche Lieder,* 1543; harm. J. S. Bach, 1685–1750

138. HEAR OUR ENTREATIES, LORD
139. ATTENDE, DOMINE

Hear our en-treat-ies, Lord, and show us mer-cy, For we are sin-ners be-fore you.
At-tén-de, Do-mi-ne, et mi-se-ré-re, Qui-a pec-cá-vi-mus ti-bi.

1. King high ex-alt-ed, all the world's Re-deem-er, To you your chil-dren
2. Right hand of God-head, head-stone of the cor-ner, Path of sal-va-tion,
3. We, your e-ter-nal maj-es-ty en-treat-ing, Make lam-en-ta-tion

1. Ad te Rex sum-me, óm-ni-um Re-dém-ptor, Ó-cu-los nó-stros
2. Déx-te-ra Pa-tris, la-pis an-gu-lá-ris, Vi-a sa-lú-tis,
3. Ro-gá-mus, De-us, tu-am ma-jes-tá-tem: Áu-ri-bus sa-cris

lift their eyes with weep - ing; Christ, we im-plore you, hear our sup-pli-ca - tion.
gate of heav-en's king - dom, Lord, cleanse your peo-ple, stained with much trans-gres - sion.
in your ho-ly hear - ing. Gra-cious-ly grant, Lord, to our sins for-give - ness.
sub-le-vá-mus flen - tes; Ex-aú-di, Chri-ste, sup-pli-cán-tum pre - ces.
já-nu-a cae - lé-stis, Áb-lu-e no-stri má-cu-las de-lí - ge.
gé-mi-tus ex-aú - di: Crí-mi-na no-stra plá-ci-dus in-dú - ge.

4. Humbly confessing all our sins against you,
   All our misdoings, hidden now no longer;
   Lord, our Redeemer, by your love grant pardon.

5. Led away captive, guiltless, unresisting,
   Brought by false witness unto death for sinners,
   Christ Jesus, keep us whom your blood has ransomed.

4. Tibi fatémur crímina admíssa:
   Contríto corde pándimus occúlta:
   Tua, Redémptor, piétas ignóscat.

5. Ínnocens captus, nec repúgnans ductus;
   Téstibus falsis pro impiis damnatús;
   Quos redemísti, tu consérva, Christe.

Text: Ancient Mozarabic Litany; Irvin Udulutsch, O.F.M., Cap., b. 1920, ©
Music: ATTENDE DOMINE, 11 11 11 with Refrain, *Mode V*; acc. Roger Nachtwey, b. 1930, ©

264

140. THROUGHOUT THESE FORTY DAYS, O LORD

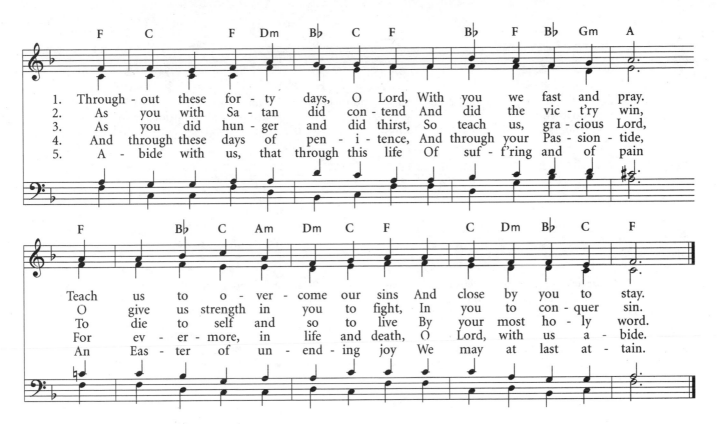

1. Through-out these for-ty days, O Lord, With you we fast and pray.
2. As you with Sa-tan did con-tend And did the vic-t'ry win,
3. As you did hun-ger and did thirst, So teach us, gra-cious Lord,
4. And through these days of pen-i-tence, And through your Pas-sion-tide,
5. A-bide with us, that through this life Of suf-f'ring and of pain

Teach us to o-ver-come our sins And close by you to stay.
O give us strength in you to fight, In you to con-quer sin.
To die to self and so to live By your most ho-ly word.
For ev-er-more, in life and death, O Lord, with us a-bide.
An Eas-ter of un-end-ing joy We may at last at-tain.

Text: Claudia F. Hernaman, 1838–1898, alt.
Music: ST. FLAVIAN, 86 86, adapt. from John Day's *Psalter*, 1562

141. GOD OF MERCY AND COMPASSION

1. God of mer-cy and com-pas-sion, Lord of life and blind-ing light.
2. God most ho-ly and for-giv-ing, Pen-e-trate our pride and sloth;
3. Lord, who out of love con-sent-ed To the worst that we could do;

Truth whom crea-tures would re-fas-ion, Place on us the gift of sight.
On a peo-ple part-ly liv-ing, Place the gift of life and growth.
Lord, a-ban-doned and tor-ment-ed, Let us love and suf-fer too.

REFRAIN

Truth in-sis-tent and de-mand-ing, Love re-sent-ed and ig-nored,

Life be-yond all un-der-stand-ing, Give us peace and par-don, Lord.

Text: Michael Hodgetts, alt., ©
Music: AU SANG QU'UN DIEU, 87 87 87 87, Traditional French Melody; arr. Rev. Percy Jones, ©

142. OUR FATHER, WE HAVE WANDERED

1. Our Father, we have wandered And hidden from your face; In foolishness have squandered Your legacy of grace. But now, in exile dwelling, We rise with fear and shame, As distant but compelling, We hear you call our name.

2. And now at length discerning The evil that we do, Behold us Lord, returning With hope and trust to you. In haste you come to meet us And home rejoicing bring, In gladness there to greet us With calf and robe and ring.

3. O Lord of all the living, Both banished and restored, Compassionate, forgiving And ever-caring Lord, Grant now that our transgressing, Our faithlessness may cease. Stretch out your hand in blessing In pardon and in peace.

Text: Msgr. Kevin Nichols, b. 1929, ©
Music: NESHANIC, 76 76 76 76

267

143. Our Father, We Have Wandered

1. Our Father, we have wandered And hidden from your face;
2. And now at length discerning The evil that we do,
3. O Lord of all the living, Both banished and restored,

In foolishness have squandered Your legacy of grace.
Behold us Lord, returning With hope and trust to you.
Compassionate, forgiving And ever-caring Lord,

But now, in exile dwelling, We rise with fear and shame,
In haste you come to meet us And home rejoicing bring,
Grant now that our transgressing, Our faithlessness may cease.

As distant but compelling, We hear you call our name.
In gladness there to greet us With calf and robe and ring.
Stretch out your hand in blessing In pardon and in peace.

Text: Msgr. Kevin Nichols, b. 1929, ©
Music: PASSION CHORALE, 76 76 D, Hans Leo Hassler, 1564–1612; harm. J. S. Bach, 1658–1750

144. ALL GLORY, LAUD, AND HONOR

All glo-ry, laud, and hon - or To you, Re-deem-er, King!

To whom the lips of chil - dren Made sweet ho-san-nas ring.

1. You are the King of Is - ra - el, And Da - vid's roy - al Son,
2. The com-pa - ny of an - gels Are prais - ing you on high;
3. The peo-ple of the He - brews With palms be - fore you went:
4. To you be - fore your pas - sion They sang their hymns of praise:
5. Their prais - es you ac - cept - ed, Ac-cept the prayers we bring,

Now in the Lord's Name com - ing, Our King and Bless - ed One.
And mor - tals, joined with all things Cre - a - ted, make re - ply.
Our praise and prayers and an - thems Be - fore you we pre - sent.
To you, now high ex - alt - ed, our mel - o - dy we raise.
Great source of love and good - ness, Our Sav - ior and our King.

Text: *Gloria, laus et honor;* Theodulph of Orleans, c. 760–821; tr. John M. Neale, 1818–1866, alt.
Tune: ST. THEODULPH, 76 76 D, Melchior Teschner, 1584–1635

145. A Prayer for the Elect

We praise and thank you, Lord, this day. Now with our cat-e-chu-mens stay. With-in their hearts, O Lord, a-bide, And their bap-tis-mal jour-ney guide.

VERSES

1. Your Spir-it send, whose breeze has blown On these whom you have al-ways known.
2. You call them now to love you more; On them your gra-ces you out-pour.
3. Their new life will be re-a-lized When in you, Lord, they are bap-tized

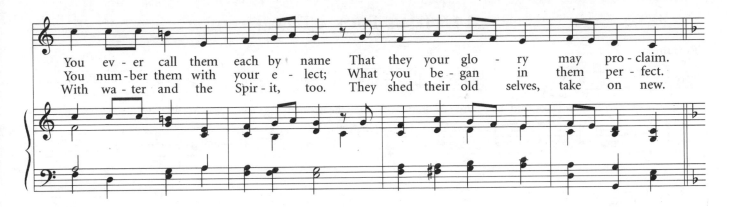

You ev-er call them each by name That they your glo-ry may pro-claim.
You num-ber them with your e-lect; What you be-gan in them per-fect.
With wa-ter and the Spir-it, too. They shed their old selves, take on new.

Text: Omer Westendorf, b. 1916, ©
Music: ENGLERT, 88 88 with Refrain, Eugene E. Englert, b. 1931, ©

146. WERE YOU THERE?

1. Were you there when they cru-ci-fied my Lord? Were you there when they cru-ci-
2. Were you there when they nailed him to the tree? Were you there when they nailed him
3. Were you there when they laid him in the tomb? Were you there when they laid him

fied my Lord? Oh, Some-times it caus-es me to trem-ble,
to the tree? Oh, Some-times it caus-es me to trem-ble,
in the tomb? Oh, Some-times it caus-es me to trem-ble,

trem-ble, trem-ble. Were you there when they cru-ci-fied my Lord?
trem-ble, trem-ble. Were you there when they nailed him to the tree?
trem-ble, trem-ble. Were you there when they laid him in the tomb?

Text: Afro-American Spiritual
Music: WERE YOU THERE, Irregular, Afro-American Spiritual

147. JESUS TOOK A TOWEL

Refrain

Je-sus took a tow-el and he gird-ed him-self, Then he washed my feet, yes, he washed my feet,

Je-sus took a ba-sin and he knelt him-self down, And he washed, yes, he washed my feet.

Verse 1

The hour had come, the Pasch was near; Je-sus loved his own, loved them to the end. O

Lord, let me see, let me un-der-stand Why you stooped and washed my feet.

Verse 2

Je-sus came to Pe-ter; Pe-ter said to him, "Do you wash my feet? Lord, do you wash my feet?"

Je-sus knelt down, but Pe-ter cried out, "Lord, you'll nev-er wash my feet!"

272

Verse 3

Je-sus said to Pe-ter, "Don't you un-der-stand? If you want to be mine, I must wash your feet." "Then not just my feet, but my head and my hands! O Lord, I want to be yours."

Verse 4

"Do you know, lit-tle chil-dren, what I've done for you? You call me Mas-ter, and you call me Lord. If I am your Mas-ter, and if I am your Lord, Then, what I've done, you must do."

Verse 5

Now friends, let's be glad, let our joy be full, For God is love, and God a-bides in us. He washed our feet, he wash-es them still When we do what he once did,

Verse 6

Who is like you, Lord, now en-throned on high, Where you look up-on the heav-ens and the earth be-low? Be-fore your face the earth trem-bles and quakes, Yet you stoop to wash my feet!

Verse 7

O the path is rug-ged, and the go-ing is rough, The jour-ney is long to our heav'n-ly home, Our feet are wea-ry and cov-ered with mud, So the Lord still wash-es our feet.

Text: *John 13;* Chrysogonus Waddell, O.S.C.O., b. 1930
Music: JESUS TOOK A TOWEL, Irregular, Chrysogonus Waddell, O.S.C.O., b. 1930, © Gethsemani Abbey

148. WHERE CHARITY AND LOVE PREVAIL

REFRAIN: Cantor/Choir; All repeat

Where char-i-ty and love are found, there is God.

VERSES: Cantor/Choir

V. The love of Christ has gath-ered us to-geth-er in-to one. Let us re-joice and be glad in him.

To Refrain

Let us fear and love the liv-ing God. and love each oth-er from the depths of our heart.

V. There-fore when we are to-geth-er, let us take heed not to be di-vid-ed in mind.

To Refrain

Let there be an end to bit-ter-ness and quar-rels, an end to strife, and in our midst be Christ our God.

V. And, in com-pa-ny with the bless-ed, may we see your face in glo-ry, Christ our God,

To Refrain

pure and un-bound-ed joy for ev-er and for ev-er.

Text: Anon.
Music: UBI CARITAS, *Plainchant, Mode VI*

274

149. O Sacred Head Surrounded

1. O Sacred Head, surrounded By crown of piercing thorn,
O bleeding Head, so wounded Reviled and put to scorn.
Our sins have marred the glory Of your most holy face,
Yet angel hosts adore thee, And tremble as they gaze.

2. The Lord of every nation Was hung upon a tree;
His death was our salvation Our sins, his agony.
O Jesus, by your passion, Your Life in us increase;
Your death for us did fashion Our pardon and our peace.

3. In this, your bitter passion, Good Shepherd think of me
With your most kind compassion, Unworthy though I be:
Beneath your cross abiding Forever would I rest,
In your dear love confiding, And with your presence blest.

Text: St. Bernard of Clairvaux, c. 1091–1153, attr.; tr. Henry Williams Baker, 1821–1977, v. 1; Melvin Farrell, S.S., b. 1930, v. 2; Arthur Russell, 1806–1874, alt. v. 3
Music: PASSION CHORALE, 76 76 D, Hans Leo Hassler, 1564–1612; harm. J. S. Bach, 1685–1750; tr. v. 2, © 1961, World Library Publications, Inc.

275

150. ADORAMUS TE CHRISTE

Ad - o - ra - mus te Chri - ste, et be - ne - di - ci - mus ti - bi: Ad - o - ra - mus te Chri - ste,

et be - ne - di - ci - mus ti - bi: qui - a per san - ctam cru - cem tu - am red - e - mi - sti mun - dum.

Ad - o - ra - mus te Chri - ste, et be - ne - di - ci - mus - ti - bi: Ad - o - ra - mus te Chri - ste.

151. DRINKING EARTH'S PURE WATER

1. Drink-ing earth's pure wa - ter, na - ture springs a - live. Sprin - kled with this
2. O'er the flood's deep wa - ters, No - ah rode se - cure. Sail - ing on this
3. In the Red Sea wa - ters, Pha - raoh's hosts were slain. Drowned now in this
4. Saved from death's dark wa - ters, Christ the Lord now lives. Bap - tized in this
5. In this sa - cred wa - ter, Christ - ians come to birth. Blest now with this

First ending, 1 - 4

wa - ter, wea - ry souls re - vive. We share a - new God's good - ness from a - bove:
wa - ter, ours a pas - sage sure. We share a - new God's fa - vor from a - bove:
wa - ter, pow'r of sin is vain. We share a - new God's free - dom from a - bove:
wa - ter, ours the life he gives. We share a - new God's like - ness from a - bove:
wa - ter, ours a god - ly worth. We share a - new God's *(glo - ry from a - bove:)*

Christ has won sal - va - tion, ev - er - last - ing love!

Final ending, 5

glo - ry from a - bove: Christ has won sal - va - tion, ev - er - last - ing love!

Text: Michael Kwatera, O.S.B., and David Klingeman, O.S.B., © 1991 St. John's Abbey, Collegeville, Minnesota
Music: NOEL NOUVELET, 11 10 10 11, French Carol; arr. Martin Shaw, 1875–1958, ©

152. SPRINGS OF WATER

REFRAIN:

Springs of wa-ter, Bless the Lord, Give God glo - ry, glo-ry and praise. For ev - er and ev - er, Al-le - lu-ia! Al-le - lu - ia! ia!

1.-4. (to Verses)   Last Time

VERSE 1:
I saw wa-ter flow-ing from the tem-ple, Al -

VERSE 2:
Give thanks for the good-ness of the Lord whose

VERSE 3:
The right hand of the Lord has tri-umphed, the

VERSE 4:
That stone which was re - ject-ed, has be-

le - lu - ia! It brought God's life and sal -

mer - cy en - dures for - ev - er. Let Is - ra - el now pro -

Lord's right hand is ex - al - ted. I shall not die, I shall

come the cor - ner - stone. It is the Lord's own

va - tion, and the peo - ple sang in joy - ful praise. Springs of

claim, "The mer - cy of the Lord is for - ev - er!" Springs of

live, de - clar - ing the works of the Lord! Springs of

work, It is won - der - ful in our eyes, Springs of

Text: Vidi Aquam and *Psalm 118;* tr. Eric Holland, b. 1960, ©
Music: Eric Holland, b. 1960, ©

279

153. ALL CREATURES OF OUR GOD AND KING

1. All crea-tures of our God and King, Lift up your voice and with us
2. O rush-ing wind and breez-es soft, O clouds that ride the winds a-
3. O flow-ing wa-ters, pure and clear, Make mu-sic for your Lord to
4. Dear moth-er earth, who day by day Un-folds rich bless-ings on our

sing: Al-le-lu-ia! Al-le-lu-ia! O burn-ing sun with gold-en
loft: O praise him! Al-le-lu-ia! O ris-ing morn, in praise re-
hear. O praise him! Al-le-lu-ia! O fire so mas-ter-ful and
way, O praise him! Al-le-lu-ia! The fruits and flow'rs that ver-dant

beam, And sil-ver moon with soft-er gleam:
joice, O lights of eve-ning, find a voice.
bright, Pro-vid-ing us with warmth and light.
grow, Let them his praise a-bun-dant show.

O praise him! O praise him! Al-le-lu-ia, al-le-lu-ia, al-le-lu-ia!

5.
O ev'ry one of tender heart,
Forgiving others, take your part,
O praise him! Alleluia!
All you who pain and sorrow bear,
praise God and lay on him your care.
O praise him! O praise him!
Allcluia, alleluia, alleluia!

6.
And you, most kind and gentle death,
Waiting to hush our final breath,
O praise him! Alleluia!
You lead to heav'n the child of God,
Where Christ our Lord the way has trod.
O praise him! O praise him!
Alleluia, alleluia, alleluia!

7.
Let all things their Creator bless,
And worship him in humbleness,
O praise him! Alleluia!
O praise the Father, praise the Son,
And praise the Spirit, Three in One!
O praise him! O praise him!
Alleluia, alleluia, alleluia!

Text: St. Francis of Assisi, 1182–1226; tr. William Henry Draper, 1855–1933, ©
Music: LASST UNS ERFREUEN, 88 44 88 with Refrain, Ralph Vaughan Williams, 1872–1958

154. Let Hymns of Grief to Joy Succeed

1. Let hymns of grief to joy succeed. We know that Christ is ris'n in-deed. Alleluia, Alleluia! We hear his white-robed angel's voice, And in our risen Lord rejoice.

2. The morn has spread her crimson rays, When rang the skies with shouts of praise: Alleluia, Alleluia! Earth joined the joyful hymn to swell, That brought despair to vanquished hell.

3. The days of mourning now are past, The pains of death are loosed at last; Alleluia, Alleluia! An angel robed in light has said: "The Lord is risen from the dead."

4. To God the Father let us sing; To God the Son, our risen King: Alleluia, Alleluia! And equally let us adore, The Holy Spirit evermore.

Alleluia, Alleluia, Alleluia, Alleluia, Alleluia!

Text: *Aurora caelum purpurat;* tr. R. Campbell, 1868, alt.
Music: LASST UNS ERFREUEN, 88 44 88 with Alleluias, *Geistliche Kirchengesange, Cologne,* 1623; harm. Ralph Vaughan Williams, 1872–1958, ©

155. SING WE TRIUMPHANT HYMNS OF PRAISE

1. Sing we tri-um-phant hymns of praise To greet our Lord these fes-tive days, Al-le-lu - ia, Al-le-lu - ia; Who by a road be-fore un-trod As - cend-ed to the throne of God, Al-le-lu - ia, Al-le-lu - ia, Al-le-lu - ia, Al-le-lu - ia, Al-le-lu - ia!

2. In wond'r-ing awe his faith-ful band Up - on the Mount of Ol - ives stand. Al-le-lu - ia, Al-le-lu - ia! And with the Vir - gin Moth-er see Their Lord as - cend in maj - es - ty.

3. O ris - en Christ, as - cend - ed Lord, All praise to you let earth ac-cord, Al-le-lu - ia, Al-le-lu - ia! Who are, while end-less a - ges run, With Fa - ther and with Spir - it One.

4. To God the Fa - ther let us sing; To God the Son, our ris - en King: Al-le-lu - ia, Al-le-lu - ia! And e - qual-ly let us a-dore, The Ho - ly Spir - it ev - er - more.

Text: The Venerable Bede, c. 673–735; tr. John David Chambers, 1805–1893, vv. 1, 2, & 4; Benjamin Webb, 1819–1885, v. 3
Music: LASST UNS ERFREUEN, 88 44 88 with Alleluias

156. Come, You Faithful, Raise the Strain

1. Come, you faith - ful, raise the strain Of tri - um - phant glad - ness;
God has brought his Is - ra - el In - to joy from sad - ness;
Loosed from Pha - roah's bit - ter yoke Ja - cob's sons and daugh - ters
Led them with un - mois - tened foot Through the Red Sea wa - ters.

2. Now the spring of souls has come; Christ has burst his pris - on,
And from three days' sleep in death As a sun has ris - en;
All the win - ter of our sins, Long and dark is fly - ing
From his light, to whom we sing Songs of praise un - dy - ing.

3. Now the bright - ness of the spring With the day of splen - dor,
With the roy - al feast of feasts, Comes its joy to ren - der.
Comes to glad Je - ru - sa - lem, And with true af - fec - tion
Wel - comes in un - wea - ried strains Je - sus' res - ur - rec - tion.

4. Nei - ther might the gates of death, Nor the tomb's dark por - tal,
Nor the watch - ers, nor the seal Hold you as a mor - tal;
But to - day a - mong the twelve You ap - peared be - stow - ing
Bless - ed peace which ev - er - more Pass - es hu - man know - ing.

Text: St. John of Damascus, 8th cent.; tr. John Mason Neale, 1818–1866, alt.
Music: GAUDEAMUS PARITUR, 76 76 76 76, Johann Horn, c. 1495–1547

157. JESUS CHRIST IS RIS'N TODAY

1. Jesus Christ is ris'n to-day, Alleluia!
2. Hymns of praise then let us sing, Alleluia!
3. But the pains which he en-dured, Alleluia!
4. Sing we to our God a-bove, Alleluia!

Our tri-um-phant ho-ly day, Alleluia!
Un-to Christ, our heav'n-ly King, Alleluia!
Our sal-va-tion have pro-cured; Alleluia!
Praise e-ter-nal as his love; Alleluia!

Who did once up-on the cross, Alleluia!
Who en-dured the cross and grave, Alleluia!
Now ex-alt-ed he is king, Alleluia!
Praise him, all you heav'n-ly host, Alleluia!

Suf-fer to re-deem our loss, Alleluia!
Sin-ners to re-deem and save. Alleluia!
Where the an-gels ev-er sing. Alleluia!
Fa-ther, Son and Ho-ly Ghost. Alleluia!

Text: Latin Carol, 14th cent., vv. 1–3; Charles Wesley, 1707–1788, v. 4
Music: EASTER HYMN, 77 77 with Alleluias, *Lyra Davidica*, 1708

158. THAT EASTER DAY WITH JOY WAS BRIGHT

1. That Eas - ter day with joy was bright, The sun shone out with fair - er light,
2. His ris - en flesh with ra - diance glowed; His wound - ed hands and feet he showed;
3. O Je - sus, King of gen - tle - ness, Do thou thy - self our hearts pos - sess
4. O Lord of all, with us a - bide In this our joy - ful Eas - ter - tide;
5. All praise, O ris - en Lord, we give To thee, who, dead, a - gain dost live;

When to their long - ing eyes re - stored, The a - pos - tles saw their ris - en Lord.
Those scars their sol - emn wit - ness gave That Christ was ris - en from the grave.
That we may give thee all our days The will - ing tri - bute of our praise.
From ev - 'ry wea - pon death can wield Thine own re - deemed for ev - er shield.
To God the Fa - ther e - qual praise, And God the Ho - ly Ghost, we raise.

Text: Latin, 5th cent.; tr. John M. Neale, 1818–1866, alt.
Music: PUER NOBIS, 88 88, Michael Praetorius, 1571–1621, adapt.; harm. *Hymns Ancient & Modern, Revised*, 1950, ©

159. O Sons and Daughters

Al - le - lu - ia, al - le - lu - ia, al - le - lu - ia.

1. O sons and daugh - ters, let us sing! The King of heav'n the
2. That Eas - ter morn, at break of day, The faith - ful wom - en
3. An an - gel clad in white they see, Who sat and spoke un -
4. That night th'a - pos - tles met in fear; A - mong them came their

glo - rious King, O'er death to - day rose tri - umph - ing. Al - le - lu - ia!
went their way To seek the tomb where Je - sus lay. Al - le - lu - ia!
to the three, "Your Lord has gone to Gal - i - lee." Al - le - lu - ia!
Lord most dear, And said, "My peace be with you here." Al - le - lu - ia!

Text: Jean Tisserand, 16th cent.; tr. John Mason Neale, 1818–1866
Music: O FILII ET FILAE, 888 with Alleluias, *Plainchant, Mode II;* acc. Rev. Percy Jones, ©

160. THE DAY OF RESURRECTION

1. The day of res-ur-rec - tion! Earth, spread the news a - broad;
2. Our hearts be free from e - vil That we may see a - right
3. His love is ev-er-last - ing; His mer - cies nev - er cease;
4. Now let the heav'ns be joy - ful, And earth her song be - gin;

The Pas - chal feast of glad - ness, The Pas - chal feast of God,
The Sav - ior res - ur - rect - ed In his e - ter - nal light,
The res - ur - rect - ed Sav - ior, Will all our joys in - crease.
The whole world keep high tri - umph And all that is there - in;

From death to life e - ter - nal, From earth to heav - en's height
And hear his mes - sage plain - ly, De - liv - ered calm and clear:
He'll keep us in his fa - vor, Sup - ply - ing ho - ly grace,
Let all things in cre - a - tion Their notes of glad - ness blend,

Our Sav - ior Christ has brought us, The glo - rious Lord of Light.
"Re - joice with me in tri - umph, Be glad and do not fear."
To all his pil - grim peo - ple Who seek his heav'n - ly place.
For Christ the Lord has ris - en, Our joy that has no end.

Text: St. John of Damascus, c. 696–754; tr. John Mason Neale, 1818–1866, alt. vv. 1, 2, 4; John Dunn, v. 3, ©
Music: ELLACOMBE, 76 76 76 76, *Würtemburg Gesangbuch*, 1784

161. Christ Is Alive

1. Christ is a-live! Let Chris-tians sing. His cross stands emp - ty to the sky.
2. Christ is a-live! No long - er bound To dis - tant years in Pal - es - tine,
3. Not throned a - bove, re - mote - ly high, Un-touched, un - moved by hu - man pains,
4. In ev - 'ry in - sult, rift, and war Where co - lor, scorn or wealth di - vide,
5. Christ is a-live! His Spir - it burns Through this and ev' - ry fu - ture age,

Let streets and homes with prais - es ring. His love in death shall nev - er die.
He comes to claim the here and now And con - quer ev - 'ry place and time.
But dai - ly, in the midst of life, Our Sav - ior with the Fa - ther reigns.
He suf - fers still, yet loves the more, And lives, though ev - er cru - ci - fied.
Till all cre - a - tion lives and learns His joy, his jus - tice, love, and praise.

Text: Brian A. Wren, b. 1936, rev., © 1975 by Hope Publishing Co.
Music: TRURO, 88 88, *Psalmodia Evangelica, Part II,* 1789; harm. Lowell Mason, 1792–1872, alt.

162. The Strife Is O'er, the Battle Done

REFRAIN

Al - le - lu - ia! Al - le - lu - ia! Al - le - lu - ia!

VERSES

1. The strife is o'er, the bat - tle done. The vic - to - ry of life is
2. The pow'rs of death have done their worst, But Christ their le - gions has dis -
3. On the third morn he rose a - gain Glo - rious in maj - es - ty to
4. He closed the yawn - ing gates of hell, The bars from heav'n's high por - tals

Repeat Refrain

won; The song of tri - umph has be - gun;
persed; Let shouts of praise and joy out - burst:
reign; O let us swell the joy - ful strain: Al - le - lu - ia!
fell; Let hymns of praise his tri - umphs tell:

Text: Anon.; tr. Francis Pott, 1832–1909, alt.
Music: VICTORY, 888 with Alleluias, Giovanni Pierluigi da Palestrina, c. 1525–1594; adapt. with alleluias William Henry Monk, 1823–1889

163. CHRIST THE LORD IS RIS'N TODAY

1. Christ the Lord is ris'n to-day; Chris-tians, haste your vows to pay;
2. Christ, the vic-tim un-de-filed, God and sin-ners rec-on-ciled;
3. Say, O wond-'ring Mar-y, say What you saw a-long the way.
4. Christ, who once for sin-ners bled, Now the first-born from the dead,

Of-fer now your prais-es meet At the Pas-chal Vic-tim's feet;
When in strange and aw-ful strife Met to-geth-er death and life;
"I be-held, where Christ had lain, Emp-ty tomb and an-gels twain;
Throned in end-less might and pow'r, Lives and reigns for ev-er-more.

For the sheep the Lamb has bled, Sin-less in the sin-ner's stead.
Chris-tians, on this hap-py day, Haste with joy your vows to pay.
I be-held the glo-ry bright Of the ris-ing Lord of light.
Hail, e-ter-nal hope on high! Hail, our King of vic-to-ry!

Christ the Lord is ris'n on high; Now he lives, no more to die.
Christ the Lord is ris'n on high; Now he lives, no more to die.
Christ my hope is ris'n a-gain; Now he lives, and lives to reign."
Hail, our Prince of life a-dored! Help and save us, gra-cious Lord!

Text: Wipo of Burgundy, c. 10th cent., attr.; tr. Jane Elizabeth Leeson, 1809–1881
Music: VICTIMAE PASCHALI, 77 77 77 77, *Wurth's Katholisches Gesangbuch*, 1859

164. THESE THINGS DID THOMAS COUNT AS REAL

1. These things did Thom-as count as real: The warmth of blood, the chill of steel, The grain of wood, the heft of stone, The last frail twitch of flesh and bone.

2. The vi-sion of his skep-tic mind Was keen e-nough to make him blind To an-y un-ex-pect-ed act Too large for his small world of fact.

3. His rea-soned cer-tain-ties de-nied That one could live when one had died, Un-til his fin-gers read like Braille The mark-ings of the spear and nail.

4. May we, O God, by grace be-lieve And thus the ris-en Christ re-ceive, Whose raw im-print-ed palms reached out And beck-oned Thom-as from his doubt.

Text: Thomas H. Troeger, b. 1945, ©
Music: MERLE MARIE, 88 88, Carol Doran, b. 1936, ©

165. ALLELUIA! ALLELUIA! LET THE HOLY ANTHEM RISE

Text: Edward Caswall, 1814–1878, vv. 1–3; Edward J. McKenna, b. 1939, v. 4, ©
Music: HOLY ANTHEM, 87 87 87 87, Traditional Melody

166. ALLELUIA! ALLELUIA! LET THE HOLY ANTHEM RISE

1. Al - le - lu - ia, al - le - lu - ia, Let the ho - ly an - them rise! And the choirs of heav - en chant it In the tem - ple of the skies. Let the moun - tains skip with glad - ness And the joy - ful val - leys ring, With ho - san - nas in the high - est To our Sav - ior and our King: With ho - san - nas in the high - est To our Sav - ior and our King.

2. Al - le - lu - ia, al - le - lu - ia, Like the sun from out the wave, He has ris - en up in tri - umph From the dark - ness of the grave. He, the splen - dor of the na - tions, He, the lamp of end - less day, It is he, the Lord of glo - ry, Who is ris - en up to - day. It is he, the Lord of glo - ry, Who is ris - en up to - day.

3. Al - le - lu - ia, al - le - lu - ia, Bless - ed Je - sus, make us rise From the life of this cor - rup - tion To the life that nev - er dies. May we share with thee thy glo - ry When the days of time are past, And the dead shall be a - wak - ened By the trum - pet's might - y blast. And the dead shall be a - wak - ened By the trum - pet's might - y blast.

Text: Edward Caswall, 1841–1878
Music: ECCLESIA, 87 87 87 87, Richard R. Terry, 1865–1938, ©

167. CHRISTIANS, LIFT UP YOUR HEARTS

REFRAIN

Chris - tians, lift up your hearts, and make this a day of re - joic - ing;

God is our strength and song; glo - ry and praise to his name! name!

First time only | *2.*

VERSES

1. This is the house of the Lord, where seek - ers and find - ers are wel - come;
3. Praise that his love o - ver - flowed in the hearts of all who re - ceived him,
5. Come, Ho - ly Spir - it, to us, who live by your pres - ence with - in us,

En - ter its gates with your praise, fill all its courts with your song:
Join - ing to - geth - er in peace those once di - vid - ed by sin:
Come to di - rect our course, give us your life and your pow'r:

Repeat Refrain once after each stanza

294

Repeat Refrain once after each stanza

2. Strong and a - lert in his grace, God's peo - ple are one in their wor - ship:
4. Those who are bur - dened with sin find here the joy of for - give - ness,
6. Al - might - y God, send us out to live to your praise and your glo - ry;

Kept by his peace they de - part, read - y for serv - ing their Lord:
Lay - ing their sins be - fore Christ, par - don and peace their re - ward:
Yours is the pow'r and the might, ours be the cour - age and faith:

Text: John E. Bowers, alt., © Canon John E. Bowers
Music: SALVE, FESTA DIES, Irregular with Refrain, Ralph Vaughan Williams, 1872–1958, © Oxford University Press

168. HAIL THEE, FESTIVAL DAY!

REFRAIN

(Easter) Hail thee, fes - ti - val day! Blest day to be hal-lowed for - ev - er;
(Ascension) Hail thee, fes - ti - val day! Blest day to be hal-lowed for - ev - er;
(Pentecost) Hail thee, fes - ti - val day! Blest day to be hal-lowed for - ev - er;

First time only | *2.*

Day when our Lord was raised, break-ing the king - dom of death. death.
Day when our ris - en Lord rose in the heav - ens to reign. reign.
Day when the Ho - ly Ghost shone in the world with God's grace. grace.

VERSES

(Easter) All the fair beau - ty of earth from the death of the win - ter a - ris - ing!
(Ascension) He who was nailed to the cross is rul - er and Lord of all peo - ple.
(Pentecost) Bright and in like - ness of fire, on those who a - wait his ap - pear - ing,
3. God the Al - might - y, the Lord, the rul - er of earth and the heav - ens
5. Spir - it of life and of pow'r now flow in us, fount of our be - ing,

Ev - 'ry good gift of the year now with its mas - ter re - turns:
All things cre - at - ed on earth sing to the glo - ry of God:
He whom the Lord had fore - told sud - den - ly, swift - ly de - scends:
Guard us from harm with - out; cleanse us from e - vil with - in:
Light that en - light - ens us all, life that in all may a - bide:

(Easter) Rise from the grave now, O Lord, the au - thor of life and cre - a - tion.
(Ascension) Dai - ly the love - li - ness grows, a - dorned with the glo - ry of blos - som;
(Pentecost) Forth from the Fa - ther he comes with sev - en - fold mys - ti - cal of - f'ring,
4. Je - sus, the health of the world, en - light - en our minds, great Re - deem - er,
6. Praise to the giv - er of good! O Lov - er and Au - thor of con - cord,

Repeat Refrain once after each stanza

Tread - ing the path - way of death, new life you give to us all:
Heav - en her gates un - bars, fling - ing her in - crease of light:
Pour - ing on all hu - man souls in - fi - nite rich - es of God:
Son of the Fa - ther su - preme, on - ly be - got - ten of God:
Pour out your balm on our days; or - der our ways in your peace.

Text: Venantius Fortunatus, c. 530–609; tr. *English Hymnal*, 1906, alt. ©
Music: SALVE, FESTA DIES, Irregular with Refrain, Ralph Vaughan Williams, 1872–1958, © Oxford University Press

297

169. Good Christians All, Rejoice and Sing!

1. Good Chris-tians all, re-joice and sing! Now is the tri - umph of our King! To all the world glad news we bring: Al - le - lu - ia, al - le - lu - ia, al - le - lu - ia!
2. The Lord of life is ris'n to - day! Sing songs of praise a - long the way; Let all the earth re - joice and say:
3. Praise we in songs of vic - to - ry That love, that life which can - not die, And sing with hearts up - lift - ed high:
4. Your Name we bless, O ris - en Lord, And sing to - day with one ac - cord The life laid down, the life re - stored:

Text: Cyril A. Arlington, 1872–1955, alt., ©
Music: GELOBT SEI GOTT, 888 with Alleluias, Melchior Vulpius, 1560?–1616

170. HAIL THE DAY THAT SEES HIM RISE

1. Hail the day that sees him rise, Al - le - lu - ia!
2. There for him high tri - umph waits; Al - le - lu - ia!
3. High - est heav'n its Lord re - ceives, Al - le - lu - ia!
4. See, he lifts his hands a - bove; Al - le - lu - ia!

To his throne a - bove the skies; Al - le - lu - ia!
Lift your heads, e - ter - nal gates; Al - le - lu - ia!
Yet he loves the earth he leaves: Al - le - lu - ia!
See, he shows the prints of love; Al - le - lu - ia!

Christ, a - while to mor - tals giv'n, Al - le - lu - ia!
He has con - quered death and sin; Al - le - lu - ia!
Though re - turn - ing to his throne, Al - le - lu - ia!
Hark, his gra - cious lips be - stow Al - le - lu - ia!

Re - as - cends his na - tive heav'n, Al - le - lu - ia!
Take the King of glo - ry in. Al - le - lu - ia!
Still he calls us all his own. Al - le - lu - ia!
Bless - ing on his Church be - low. Al - le - lu - ia!

Text: Charles Wesley, 1707–1788
Music: LLANFAIR, 77 77 with Alleluias, Robert Williams, 1781–1821; harm. John Roberts, 1822–1877

171. COME AND LET US DRINK OF THAT NEW RIVER

1. Come and let us drink of that new riv - er, Not from bar-ren rock di - vine - ly poured,
2. Now the world has bright il - lu - mi - na - tion, Heav - en and all things up - on the earth;
3. Yes - ter - day with you in bur - ial ly - ing Now with you in tri - umph I a - rise,

But the fount of life that springs for - ev - er From the sa - cred bod - y of our Lord.
Ris - en is the God of all cre - a - tion, Christ the Lord who gave cre - a - tion birth.
Yes - ter - day the part - ner of your dy - ing, Raise me with you far be - yond the skies.

Text: John of Damascus, c. 675–746; tr. John Mason Neale, 1818–1866; adapt. Anthony G. Petti, 1932–1985, ©
Music: NEW RIVER, 10 9 10 9, Kenneth D. Smith, b. 1928, ©

172. HE IS RISEN, HE IS RISEN

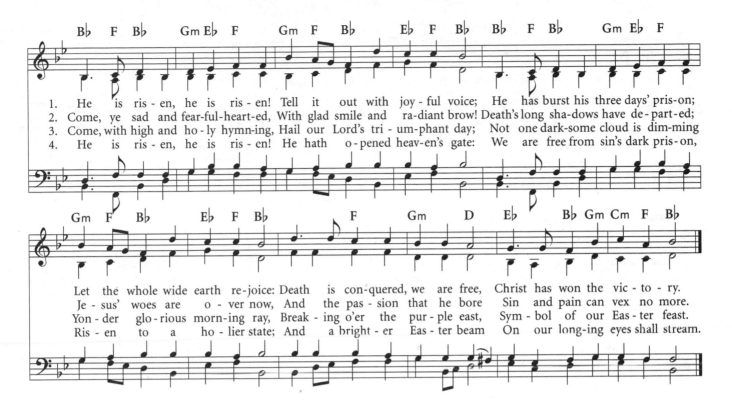

1. He is ris-en, he is ris-en! Tell it out with joy-ful voice; He has burst his three days' pris-on;
2. Come, ye sad and fear-ful-heart-ed, With glad smile and ra-diant brow! Death's long sha-dows have de-part-ed;
3. Come, with high and ho-ly hymn-ing, Hail our Lord's tri-um-phant day; Not one dark-some cloud is dim-ming
4. He is ris-en, he is ris-en! He hath o-pened heav-en's gate: We are free from sin's dark pris-on,

Let the whole wide earth re-joice: Death is con-quered, we are free, Christ has won the vic-to-ry.
Je-sus' woes are o-ver now, And the pas-sion that he bore Sin and pain can vex no more.
Yon-der glo-rious morn-ing ray, Break-ing o'er the pur-ple east, Sym-bol of our Eas-ter feast.
Ris-en to a ho-lier state; And a bright-er Eas-ter beam On our long-ing eyes shall stream.

Text: Cecil Frances Alexander, 1818–1895, alt.
Music: UNSER HERRSCHER, 87 87 77, Joachim Neander, 1650–1680

173. ALLELUIA, ALLELUIA, GIVE THANKS TO THE RISEN LORD

Al-le-lu-ia, al-le-lu-ia, give thanks to the ris-en Lord, Al-le-lu-ia, al-le-lu-ia, give praise to his name. name.

1. Je - sus is Lord of all the earth, He is the King of cre - a - tion.
2. Spread the good news o'er all the earth, Je - sus has died and has ris - en.
3. We have been cru - ci - fied with Christ. Now we shall live for - ev - er. Al-le-
4. God has pro - claimed the just re - ward, Life for all, al - le - lu - ia.
5. Come let us praise the liv - ing God, Joy - ful - ly sing to our Sav - ior.

Text: Donald Fishel, b. 1950; © 1973, The Word of God
Music: ALLELUIA NO. 1, 8 8 with Refrain, Donald Fishel, b. 1950; harm. Betty Carr Pulkingham, b. 1929; © 1973, The Word of God

302

174. COME, HOLY GHOST, CREATOR BLEST

1. Come, Holy Ghost, Creator blest, And in our hearts take up your rest; Come with your grace and heav'n-ly aid To fill the hearts which you have made, To fill the hearts which you have made.

2. O Comfort-er, to you we cry, The heav'n-ly gift of God most high. The font of life and fire of love, And sweet a-noint-ing from a-bove, And sweet a-noint-ing from a-bove.

3. To ev-'ry sense your light im-part And shed your love in ev-'ry heart. To our weak flesh, your strength sup-ply: Un-fail-ing cour-age from on high, Un-fail-ing cour-age from on high.

4. O grant that we through you may come To know the Fa-ther and the Son, And hold with firm, un-chang-ing faith, That you are Spir-it of them both, That you are Spir-it of them both.

5. Praise we the Fa-ther and the Son, And Ho-ly Spir-it, with them one; And may the Son on us be-stow The gifts that from the Spir-it flow, The gifts that from the Spir-it flow.

Text: Anon.; tr. Edward Caswall, 1814–1878
Music: HOLY SPIRIT, 88 888, Louis Lambillotte, S.J., 1796–1855; acc. Sr. Theophane Hytrek, O.S.F., b. 1915, ©

175. Come, O Come, Life-Giving Spirit

1. Come, O come, life-giv-ing Spir-it, God be-fore the dawn of time!
2. Grant our hearts in full-est meas-ure Wis-dom, coun-sel, pu-ri-ty,
3. Ho-ly Spir-it, strong and might-y, Thou who mak-est all things new,

Fire our hearts with ho-ly ar-dor, Bless-ed Com-fort-er sub-lime!
That they ev-er may be seek-ing On-ly that which pleas-eth thee.
Make thy work with-in us per-fect And the e-vil foe sub-due.

Let thy ra-diance fill our night, Turn-ing dark-ness in-to light.
Let thy knowl-edge spread and grow, Work-ing er-ror's o-ver-throw.
Grant us weap-ons for the strife And with vic-t'ry crown our life.

Text: Heinrich Held, c. 1659; tr. Edward T. Horn III, b. 1909, alt. v. 1; Charles W. Schaeffer, 1813–1896, alt. v. 2, 3
Music: KOMM, O KOMM, DU GEIST DES LEBENS, 87 87 77, *Neu-vermehrtes Gesangbuch, Meiningen*, 1693

176. O Breathe on Me

1. O breathe on me, Thou breath of God, Fill me with life a-new;
2. O breathe on me, Thou breath of God, Un-til my heart is pure;
3. O breathe on me, Thou breath of God, So shall I nev-er die,

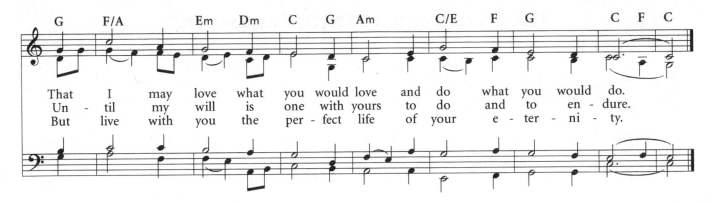

That I may love what you would love and do what you would do.
Un- til my will is one with yours to do and to en- dure.
But live with you the per- fect life of your e- ter- ni- ty.

Text: Edwin Hatch, 1878, alt.
Music: ST. COLUMBA (ERIN), 87 87, Traditional Irish Hymn Melody; acc. Russell Woollen, b. 1923, ©

177. FIRE OF GOD, UNDYING FLAME

1. Fire of God, un- dy- ing flame, Spir- it who in splen- dor came,
2. Breath of God, that swept in pow'r In the Pen- te- cos- tal hour,
3. Strength of God, your might with- in Con- quers sor- row, pain and sin;
4. Truth of God, your pierc- ing rays Pen- e- trate my se- cret ways,
5. Love of God, your grace pro- found Knows not ei- ther age or bound;

Let your heat my soul re- fine, Till it glows with love di- vine.
Ho- ly breath, be now in me Source of vi- tal en- er- gy.
For- ti- fy from e- vil art All the gate- ways of my heart.
May the light that shames my sin Guide me ho- lier paths to win.
Come, my heart's own guest to be, Dwell for ev- er- more in me.

Text: Albert F. Bayly, 1901–1984, alt., © Oxford University Press
Music: NUN KOMM DER HEIDEN HEILAND, 77 77, *Geystliche Gesangk Buchleyn, Wittenberg*, 1524; harm. Melchior Vulpius, c. 1560–1616

178. COME, GRACIOUS SPIRIT, HEAVENLY DOVE

1. Come, gra - cious Spir - it, heav'n - ly dove, With light and com - fort from a - bove.
2. The light of truth to us dis - play And make us know and choose your way;
3. Lead us to Christ, the liv - ing way, Nor let us from his pas - tures stray;
4. Lead us to heav'n, that we may share Full - ness of joy for - ev - er there;

Come, be our guard - ian and our guide; O'er ev - 'ry thought and step pre - side.
Plant ho - ly fear in ev - 'ry heart, That we from God may ne'er de - part.
Lead us to ho - li - ness, the road That we must take to dwell with God.
Lead us to our e - ter - nal rest, To be with God for - ev - er blest.

Text: Simon Browne, 1680–1732, alt.
Music: WAREHAM, 88 88, William Knapp, 1698–1768

179. FOR THE BEAUTY OF THE EARTH

1. For the beau-ty of the earth, For the beau-ty of the skies,
2. For the beau-ty of each hour, Of the day and of the night,
3. For the joy of ear and eye, For the heart and mind's de-light,
4. For the joy of hu-man love, Broth-er, sis-ter, par-ent, child,

For the love which from our birth O-ver and a-round us lies,
Hill and vale, and tree and flow'r, Sun and moon and stars of light,
For the mys-tic har-mo-ny Link-ing sense to sound and sight,
Friends on earth and friend's a-bove, For all gen-tle thoughts and mild,

Christ, our God, to thee we raise This our hymn of thank-ful praise.

5. For each perfect gift of thine
To this world so freely giv'n,
Graces human and divine,
Flow'rs of earth and buds of heav'n,
Refrain

6. For your Church, that evermore
Lifts its holy hands above,
Off'ring up on ev'ry shore
Its pure sacrifice of love,
Refrain

Text: Folliot Sandford Pierpoint, 1835–1917
Music: DIX, 77 77 77, Conrad Kocher, 1786–1872; arr. William Henry Monk, 1823–1889

180. CROWN HIM WITH MANY CROWNS

1. Crown him with man-y crowns, The Lamb up-on his throne;
2. Crown him the Lord of life, Who tri-umphed o'er the grave,
3. Crown him the Lord of love, Be-hold his hands and side,
4. Crown him the Lord of peace, Whose pow'r a scep-ter sways

Hark! How the heav'n-ly an-them drowns All mu-sic but its own.
And rose vic-to-rious in the strife For those he came to save.
Rich wounds yet vis-i-ble a-bove In beau-ty glo-ri-fied.
From pole to pole, that wars may cease, Ab-sorbed in prayer and praise.

A-wake, my soul, and sing Of him who set us free,
His glo-ries now we sing, Who died and rose on high,
No an-gel in the sky Can ful-ly bear that sight,
His reign shall know no end, And 'round his pierc-ed feet

And hail him as your heav'n-ly King Through all e-ter-ni-ty.
Who died, e-ter-nal life to bring, And lives that death may die.
But down-ward bends his burn-ing eye At mys-ter-ies so bright.
Fair flow'rs of par-a-dise ex-tend Their fra-grance ev-er sweet.

Text: Matthew Bridges, 1800–1894, vv. 1, 3–5; Godfrey Thring, 1823–1903, v. 2
Music: DIADEMATA, 66 86 66 86, George Job Elvey, 1816–1893

181. ALL PEOPLE THAT ON EARTH DO DWELL
182. PRAISE GOD, FROM WHOM ALL BLESSINGS FLOW

1. All peo-ple that on earth do dwell, Sing to the Lord with cheer-ful voice;
2. Know that the Lord is God in - deed; With - out our aid he did us make;
3. O en - ter then his gates with praise; Ap - proach with joy his courts un - to;
4. For why? the Lord our God is good: His mer - cy is for - ev - er sure;
5. To Fa - ther, Son, and Ho - ly Ghost, The God whom heaven and earth a - dore,
* Praise God, from whom all bless - ings flow; Praise him, all crea - tures here be - low;

Him serve with mirth, his praise forth tell, Come we be - fore him, and re - joice.
We are his folk, he does us feed, And for his sheep he does us take.
Praise, laud, and bless his Name al - ways, For it is seem - ly so to do.
His truth at all times firm - ly stood, And shall from age to age en - dure.
From us and from the an - gel host Be praise and glo - ry ev - er - more.
Praise him a - bove, you heav'n - ly host: Praise Fa - ther, Son and Ho - ly Ghost.

* This stanza may be sung alone or used as an alternate to stanza 5.

Text: *Psalm (99) 100;* William Kethe, d. c. 1593; Doxology, Thomas Ken, 1637–1711
Music: OLD 100TH, LM, Louis Bourgeois, c. 1510–1561

183. How Can I Keep from Singing?

1. My life flows on in end-less song; — A-bove earth's lam-en-ta-tion. I
2. Through all the tu-mult and the strife, I hear that mu-sic ring-ing; It
3. What though the tem-pest 'round me roar, I hear the truth it liv-eth. What
4. The peace of Christ makes fresh my heart, A foun-tain ev-er spring-ing. All

hear the real though far-off hymn That hails a new cre-a-tion.
sounds and ech-oes in my soul; How can I keep from sing-ing?
though the dark-ness 'round me close, Songs in the night it giv-eth.
things are mine since I am his; How can I keep from sing-ing?

No storm can shake my in-most calm, While to that rock I'm cling-ing. Since

Christ is Lord of heav-en and earth, How can I keep from sing-ing?

Text: Robert Lowry, 1826–1899
Music: Traditional Quaker Melody, 8 7 8 7 with Refrain, Robert Lowry, 1826–1899

184. ALLELUIA! SING TO JESUS

1. Al - le - lu - ia! Sing to Je - sus! His the scep - ter, his the throne;
2. Al - le - lu - ia! Not as or - phans Are we left in sor - row now;
3. Al - le - lu - ia! Bread of heav - en, Here on earth our food, our stay!
4. Al - le - lu - ia! King e - ter - nal, You the Lord of lords we own:

Al - le - lu - ia! his the tri - umph, His the vic - to - ry a - lone:
Al - le - lu - ia! he is near us, Faith be - lieves, nor ques - tions how;
Al - le - lu - ia! here the sin - ful Flee to you from day to day;
Al - le - lu - ia! born of Mar - y, Earth your foot - stool, heav'n your throne:

Hark! The songs of peace - ful Zi - on Thun - der like a might - y flood;
Though the cloud from sight re - ceived him, When the for - ty days were o'er,
In - ter - ces - sor, friend of sin - ners, Earth's Re - deem - er, plead for me,
You with - in the veil have en - tered, Robed in flesh, our great High Priest:

Je - sus out of ev - 'ry na - tion Has re - deemed us by his blood.
Shall our hearts for - get his prom - ise, "I am with you ev - er - more"?
Where the songs of all the sin - less Sweep a - cross the crys - tal sea.
Here on earth both Priest and Vic - tim In the eu - cha - ris - tic feast.

Text: William Chatterton Dix, 1837–1898, alt.
Music: HYFRYDOL, 87 87 87 87, Rowland H. Prichard, 1811–1887

311

185. LOVE DIVINE, ALL LOVES EXCELLING

1. Love di-vine, all loves ex-cel-ling, Joy of heav'n, to earth come down,
2. Breathe, oh, breathe thy lov-ing Spir-it In-to ev-'ry trou-bled breast;
3. Come, al-might-y to de-liv-er, Let us all thy life re-ceive;
4. Fin-ish then thy new cre-a-tion; Pure and spot-less let us be;

Fix in us thy hum-ble dwell-ing, All thy faith-ful mer-cies crown.
Let us all in thee in-her-it; Let us find thy prom-ised rest.
Sud-den-ly re-turn, and nev-er, Nev-er-more thy tem-ples leave.
Let us see thy great sal-va-tion Per-fect-ly re-stored in thee:

Je-sus, thou art all com-pas-sion, Pure, un-bound-ed love thou art;
Take a-way the love of sin-ning; Al-pha and O-me-ga be;
Thee we would be al-ways bless-ing, Serve thee as thy hosts a-bove,
Changed from glo-ry in-to glo-ry, Till in heav'n we take our place,

Vis-it us with thy sal-va-tion, En-ter ev-'ry trem-bling heart.
End of faith, as its be-gin-ning, Set our hearts at lib-er-ty.
Pray, and praise thee with-out ceas-ing, Glo-ry in thy per-fect love.
Till we cast our crowns be-fore thee, Lost in won-der, love, and praise.

Text: Charles Wesley, 1707–1788
Music: HYFRYDOL, 87 87 87 87, Rowland H. Prichard, 1811–1887

312

186. ON THIS DAY, THE FIRST OF DAYS

1. On this day, the first of days, God the Fa-ther's name we praise;
2. On this day the e-ter-nal Son O - ver death his tri - umph won;
3. Fa - ther, who did fash - ion all God-like by your lov - ing call,
4. Word - made - flesh, all hail to thee, Who from sin has set us free;

Who, cre - a - tion's Lord and spring, Did the world from dark - ness bring.
On this day the Spir - it came With his gifts of liv - ing flame.
Fill us with that love di - vine And our wills to yours in - cline.
And in you we die and rise Un - to God in sac - ri - fice.

5. Holy Spirit, you impart
   Gifts of love to ev'ry heart;
   Give us light and grace, we pray;
   Fill our hearts this holy day.

6. God, the blessed Three-in-One,
   May your holy will be done;
   In your word our souls are blest,
   As with you this day we rest.

Text: *Carcassonne Breviary,* 1745; tr. Henry W. Baker, 1821-1877, alt.
Music: LUBECK, 77 77, J. A. Freylinghausen, 1670–1739; adapt. and harm. William Henry Havergal, 1793–1870, and William Henry Monk, 1823–1889

187. SING WITH ALL THE SAINTS IN GLORY

1. Sing with all the saints in glory, sing the res-ur-rec-tion song!
2. O what glory, far ex-ceed-ing all the eye has yet per-ceived!
3. Life e-ter-nal! heav'n re-joic-es; Je-sus lives who once was dead;
4. Life e-ter-nal! O what won-ders crowd on faith, what joy un-known.

Death and sor-row, earth's dark sto-ry, to the for-mer days be-long.
Ho-liest hearts for a-ges plead-ing, ne-ver that full joy con-ceived.
Join with all the heav'n-ly voic-es; child of God, lift up your head!
When, a-mid earth's clos-ing thun-ders, saints shall stand be-fore the throne!

All a-round the clouds are break-ing, soon the storms of time shall cease;
God has prom-ised, Christ pre-pares it, there on high our wel-come waits;
Pa-triarchs from the dis-tant a-ges, saints all long-ing for their heav'n.
O to en-ter that bright por-tal, see that glow-ing fir-ma-ment.

In God's like-ness, peo-ple wak-ing, know the ev-er-last-ing peace.
Ev-'ry hum-ble spir-it shares it, Christ has passed the e-ter-nal gates.
Proph-ets, psalm-ists, seers, and sag-es, all a-wait the glo-ry giv'n.
Know, with you O God, im-mor-tal, Je-sus Christ whom you have sent!

Text: *1 Corinthians 15:20;* William J. Irons, 1812–1883, alt.
Music: HYMN TO JOY, 87 87 87 87, Ludwig van Beethoven, 1770–1827; adapt. Edward Hodges, 1796–1867

188. JOYFUL, JOYFUL, WE ADORE THEE

1. Joy-ful, joy-ful, we a-dore thee, God of glo-ry, Lord of love;
2. All thy works with joy sur-round thee, Earth and heav'n re-flect thy rays,
3. Thou art giv-ing and for-giv-ing, Ev-er bless-ing, ev-er blest,
4. Mor-tals, join the might-y cho-rus Which the morn-ing stars be-gan;

Hearts un-fold like flow'rs be-fore thee, Prais-ing thee, their sun a-bove.
Stars and an-gels sing a-round thee, Cen-ter of un-bro-ken praise;
Well-spring of the joy of liv-ing, O-cean-depth of hap-py rest!
Love di-vine is reign-ing o'er us, Hu-man love, God's ho-ly plan.

Melt the clouds of sin and sad-ness; Drive the dark of doubt a-way;
Field and for-est, vale and moun-tain, Bloom-ing mead-ow, flash-ing sea,
Thou our Fa-ther, Christ our broth-er, All who live in love are thine;
Ev-er sing-ing, march we on-ward, Vic-tor's in the midst of strife;

Giv-er of im-mor-tal glad-ness, Fill us with the light of day!
Chant-ing bird and flow-ing foun-tain, Call us to re-joice in thee.
Teach us how to love each oth-er, Lift us to the joy di-vine.
Joy-ful mu-sic lifts us sun-ward In the tri-umph song of life.

Text: Henry van Dyke, 1852–1933, alt., ©
Music: HYMN TO JOY, 87 87 87 87, Ludwig van Beethoven, 1770–1827; adapt. Edward Hodges, 1796–1867

189. I Sing the Almighty Power of God

1. I sing the al-might-y power of God, That made the moun-tains rise,
That spread the flow-ing seas a-broad And built the loft-y skies.
I sing the wis-dom that or-dained The sun to rule the day;
The moon shines full at his com-mand, And all the stars o-bey.

2. I sing the good-ness of the Lord, That filled the earth with food;
He formed the crea-tures with his word, And then pro-nounced them good.
Lord, how thy won-ders are dis-played, Wher-e'er I turn my eye,
If I sur-vey the ground I tread, Or gaze up-on the sky!

3. There's not a plant or flow-er be-low, But makes thy glo-ries known;
And clouds a-rise, and tem-pests blow, By or-der from thy throne;
While all that bor-rows life from thee Is ev-er in thy care,
And ev-'ry-where that I could be, Thou, God, art pres-ent there.

Text: Isaac Watts, 1674–1748, alt.
Music: FOREST GREEN, 86 86 86 86, English Folk Song; harm. Ralph Vaughan Williams, 1872–1958, ©

316

190. THIS DAY GOD GIVES ME

1. This day God gives me Strength of high heav - en, Sun and moon shin - ing, Flame in my hearth, Flash - ing of light - ning, Wind in its swift - ness, Deeps of the o - cean, Firm - ness of earth.

2. This day God sends me Strength as my steers - man, Might to up - hold me, Wis - dom as guide. Your eyes are watch - ful, Your ears are list'n - ing, Your lips are speak - ing, Friend at my side.

3. God's way is my way, God's shield is 'round me, God's host de - fends me, Sav - ing from ill. An - gels of heav - en, Drive from me al - ways All that would harm me, Stand by me still.

4. Ris - ing, I thank you Might - y and strong One, King of cre - a - tion, Giv - er of rest, Firm - ly con - fess - ing Three - ness of Per - sons, One - ness of God - head, Trin - i - ty blest.

Text: St. Patrick, 372–466, attr.; tr. James Quinn, S.J., b. 1919, © 1969
Music: BUNESSAN, 55 54 55 54, Scots Gaelic Melody

191. O GOD, ALMIGHTY FATHER

1. O God, al-might-y Fa - ther, Cre - a - tor of all things,
2. O Je - sus, Word in-car - nate, Re-deem - er most a - dored,
3. O God, the Ho - ly Spir - it, Who lives with-in our soul,

The heav-ens stand in won - der, While earth your glo - ry sings.
All glo - ry, praise, and hon - or Be yours, O sov-'reign Lord.
Send forth your light and lead us To our e - ter - nal goal.

REFRAIN

O most ho - ly Trin - i - ty, Un - di - vid - ed u - ni - ty,

Ho - ly God, might - y God, God im - mor - tal be a - dored!

Text: Anon.; tr. Irvin Udulutsch, O.F.M., Cap., b. 1920, ©
Music: GOTT VATER, SEI GEPRIESEN, 76 76 with Refrain, *Limburg Gesangbuch,* 1838; acc. Sr. Mary Sylvestra, O.S.F., ©

192. PRAISE AND THANKSGIVING

1. Praise and thanks-giv - ing, Fa - ther, we of - fer, For all things
2. Lord, bless the la - bor We bring to serve you, That with our
3. Fa - ther, pro - vid - ing Food for your chil - dren, Your wis - dom
4. Then will your bless - ing Reach ev - 'ry peo - ple, Free - ly con -

liv - ing You have made good. Har - vest of sown fields, Fruits of the
neigh - bor We may be fed. Sow - ing or till - ing, We would work
guid - ing Teach - es us share One with an - oth - er, So that re -
fess - ing Your gra - cious hand. Where you are reign - ing No one will

or - chard, Hay from the mown fields, Blos - som and wood.
with you, Har - vest - ing, mill - ing, For dai - ly bread.
joic - ing With us, all oth - ers May know your care.
hun - ger, Your love sus - tain - ing, Fruit - ful the land.

Text: Albert F. Bayly, © Oxford University Press
Music: BUNESSAN, 55 54 55 54, Scots Gaelic Melody

319

193. HOW GREAT THOU ART

1. O Lord my God, when I in awe-some won-der, Con-sid-er
2. When through the woods and for-est glades I wan-der, I hear the
3. But when I think that God, his Son not spar-ing, Sent him to
4. When Christ shall come, with shout of ac-cla-ma-tion, And take me

all the works thy hand hath made, I see the stars, I hear the might-y
birds sing sweet-ly in the trees; When I look down from loft-y moun-tain
die, I scarce can take it in, That on the cross my bur-den glad-ly
home, what joy shall fill my heart! Then I shall bow in hum-ble ad-o-

thun-der, Thy pow'r through-out the u-ni-verse dis-played;
gran-deur And hear the brook and feel the gen-tle breeze;
bear-ing He bled and died to take a-way my sin;
ra-tion And there pro-claim, "My God, how great thou art!"

REFRAIN

Then sings my soul, my Sav-ior God, to thee, How great thou art! How great thou art!

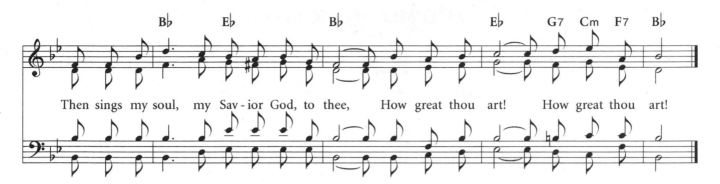

Then sings my soul, my Sav-ior God, to thee, How great thou art! How great thou art!

Text: Stuart K. Hine, b. 1899
Music: O STORE GUD, 11 10 11 10 with Refrain, Stuart K. Hine, b. 1899

194. TO JESUS CHRIST, OUR SOV'REIGN KING

1. To Je-sus Christ, our sov-'reign King Who is the world's sal-va-tion,
2. Your reign ex-tend, O King be-nign, To ev-'ry land and na-tion;
3. To you and to your Church, great King, We pledge our hearts' ob-la-tion;

All praise and hom-age do we bring And thanks and ad-o-ra-tion.
For in your king-dom, Lord di-vine, A-lone we find sal-va-tion.
Un-til be-fore your throne we sing In end-less ju-bi-la-tion.

Christ Je-sus, Vic-tor! Christ Je-sus, Rul-er! Christ Je-sus, Lord and Re-deem-er!

Text: Martin B. Hellriegel, 1890–1981, ©
Music: ICH GLAUB AN GOTT, 87 87 with Refrain, Godfrey Ridout, b. 1918

321

195. O Merciful Redeemer

1. O merciful Redeemer, Whom yet unseen we love; O name of might and favor, All other names above. O bringer of salvation, Who wondrously hast wrought, Thyself the revelation Of love beyond all thought: We worship thee and bless thee; To thee alone we sing; We praise thee and confess thee; Our gracious Lord and King.

2. In thee all fullness dwelleth, All grace and pow'r divine; The glory that excelleth, O Son of God is thine. O grant the consummation Of this our song above, In endless adoration And everlasting love; Then shall we praise and bless thee; Where perfect praises ring, And evermore confess thee, Our Savior and our King.

Text: Frances R. Havergal, 1836–1879, alt.
Music: THAXTED, 13 13 13 13 13 13, Gustav Holst, 1874–1934, alt., ©

196. PRAISE TO THE LORD, THE ALMIGHTY

1. Praise to the Lord, the Al - might - y, the King of cre - a - tion!
2. Praise to the Lord, let us of - fer our gifts at the al - tar.
3. Praise to the Lord, who will pros - per our work and de - fend us;
4. Praise to the Lord! O let all that is in us a - dore him!

O my soul, praise him for he is your health and sal - va - tion.
Let not our sins and trans - gres - sions now cause us to fal - ter.
Sure - ly his good - ness and mer - cy here dai - ly at - tend us;
All that has life and breath, come now in prais - es be - fore him!

All you who hear, Now to his al - tar draw near; Join in pro - found a - do - ra - tion.
Christ the high priest Bids us all join in his feast, Vic - tims with him on the al - tar.
Pon - der a - new What the Al - might - y can do, Who with his love will be - friend us.
Let the A - men Sound from his peo - ple a - gain, Now as we wor - ship be - fore him.

Text: Joachim Neander, 1650–1680; tr. Catherine Winkworth, 1827–1878, et al.
Music: LOBE DEN HERREN, 14 14 4 7 8, *Erneuerten Gesangbuch*, 1665

197. On Eagle's Wings

VERSES 1-3

1. You who dwell in the shel-ter of the Lord, who a-bide in his shad-ow for
(2.) snare of the fowl-er will nev-er cap-ture you, and fam-ine will bring you no
3. You need not fear the ter-ror of the night, nor the ar-row that flies by

life,   say to the Lord: "My ref-uge, my rock   in whom I   trust!"

fear: un-der his wings your ref-uge, his faith-ful-ness   your shield.

day;   though thou-sands fall a-bout you,   near   you it shall not come.

DMaj7/F♯   F   Dm   F   Gm   Asus4

REFRAIN

Descant:

And he will raise you up on ea-gle's wings,   bear   you on   the

Melody

And he will raise you up on ea-gle's wings,   bear   you on   the

A7   D   Em

breath of dawn,   make you to shine like the sun,   and

breath of dawn,   make you to shine like the sun,   and

A7   D   D7/F♯   G   Em   A

Text: *Psalm 91;* Michael Joncas, b. 1951
Music: © 1979, New Dawn Music, Michael Joncas, b. 1951

198. In Christ There Is No East or West

1. In Christ there is no east or west, In him no south or north,
2. Join hands, dis-ci-ples of the faith, What-e'er your race may be!
3. In Christ now meet both east and west, In him meet south and north,

But one great fel-low-ship of love, Through-out the whole wide earth.
Who serves my Fa-ther as his child Is sure-ly kin to me.
All Christ-ly souls are one in him, Through-out the whole wide earth.

Text: John Oxenham, 1852–1941, alt., ©
Music: MCKEE, 86 86, Afro-American Spiritual; adapt. and arr. Harry T. Burleigh, 1866–1949, ©

199. BE THOU MY VISION

1. Be thou my vi - sion, O Lord of my heart; All else be nought to me, save that thou art. Thou my best thought, by day or by night, Wak - ing or sleep - ing, thy pres - ence my light.

2. Be thou my wis - dom, and thou my true word; I ev - er with thee and thou with me, Lord; Thou my great Fa - ther; thine own may I be; Thou in me dwell - ing, and I one with thee.

3. High King of heav - en, when vic - tory is won, May I reach heav - en's joys, bright heav - en's Sun! Heart of my heart, what - ev - er be - fall, Still be my vi - sion, O Rul - er of all.

Text: Irish, c. 700, versified by Mary Elizabeth Byrne, 1880–1931; tr. Eleanor H. Hull, 1860–1935, alt.
Music: SLANE, 10 10 9 10, Irish Ballad Melody; adapt. *The Church Hymnary,* 1927; harm. David Evans, 1874–1948, ©

328

200. O CHRIST THE GREAT FOUNDATION

1. O Christ the great foundation
   On which your people stand
   To preach your true salvation
   In ev'ry age and land:
   Pour out your Holy Spirit
   To make us strong and pure,
   To keep the faith unbroken
   As long as worlds endure.

2. Baptized in one confession,
   One Church in all the earth,
   We bear our Lord's impression,
   The sign of second birth:
   One holy people gathered
   In love beyond our own,
   By grace we were invited,
   By grace we make you known.

3. Where tyrants' hold is tightened,
   Where strong devour the weak,
   Where innocents are frightened
   The righteous fear to speak,
   There let your Church awaking
   Attack the pow'rs of sin
   And, all their ramparts breaking,
   With you the vic'try win.

4. This is the moment glorious
   When he who once was dead
   Shall lead his Church victorious,
   Their champion and their head.
   The Lord of all creation
   his heav'nly kingdom brings
   The final consummation,
   The glory of all things.

Text: Timothy Tingfang Lew, 1891–1947, alt.
Music: AURELIA, 76 76 76 76, Samuel S. Wesley, 1810–1876

201. Christ Is Made the Sure Foundation

1. Christ is made the sure foun-da-tion, Christ the head and cor-ner-stone;
2. To this tem-ple, where we call you, Come, O Lord of hosts, to-day;
3. Grant, we pray, to all your peo-ple, All the grace they ask to gain;

Cho-sen of the Lord, and pre-cious, Bind-ing all the Church in one;
With your wont-ed lov-ing-kind-ness Hear your ser-vants as they pray,
What they gain from you for-ev-er With the bless-ed to re-tain,

Ho-ly Zi-on's help for-ev-er, And her con-fi-dence a-lone.
And your full-est ben-e-dic-tion Shed in all its bright ar-ray.
And here-af-ter in your glo-ry Ev-er-more with you to reign.

Text: Latin, 7th cent.; tr. John Mason Neale, 1818–1866, alt.
Music: WESTMINSTER ABBEY, 87 87 87, Henry Purcell, 1659–1695, adapt.

202. Blest Are the Pure in Heart

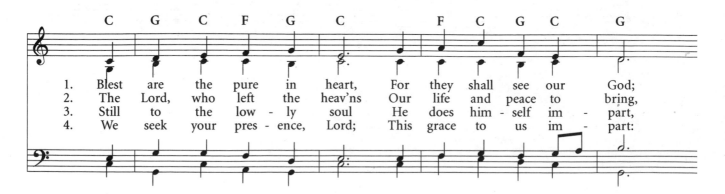

1. Blest are the pure in heart, For they shall see our God;
2. The Lord, who left the heav'ns Our life and peace to bring,
3. Still to the low-ly soul He does him-self im-part,
4. We seek your pres-ence, Lord; This grace to us im-part:

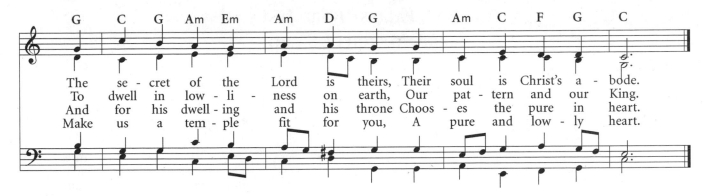

The se-cret of the Lord is theirs, Their soul is Christ's a-bode.
To dwell in low-li-ness on earth, Our pat-tern and our King.
And for his dwell-ing and his throne Choos-es the pure in heart.
Make us a tem-ple fit for you, A pure and low-ly heart.

Text: John Keble, 1792–1866, vv. 1 & 3; Wm. John Hall, 1793–1861, vv. 2 & 4
Music: FRANCONIA, 66 86, Johann B. Konig, 1691–1758, from his *Chorale;* adapt. and harm. Wm. Henry Havergal, 1793–1870

203. COME, MY WAY, MY TRUTH, MY LIFE

1. Come, my Way, my Truth, my Life: Such a way as gives us breath; Such a
2. Come, my Light, my Feast, my Strength: Such a light as shows a feast; Such a
3. Come, my Joy, my Love, my Heart: Such a joy as none can move; Such a

truth as ends all strife; Such a life as kill - eth death.
feast as mends in length; Such a strength as makes his guest.
love as none can part; Such a heart as joys in love.

Text: George Herbert, 1593–1632
Music: THE CALL, 77 77, Ralph Vaughan Williams, 1872–1958, ©

331

204. Fairest Lord Jesus
205. Merciful Savior

1. Fair - est Lord Je - sus, Ru - ler of all na - ture,
2. Fair are the mea - dows, fair - er still the wood - lands,
3. Fair is the sun - shine, fair - er still the moon - light,

O thou of God and man the Son; thee will I cher - ish,
robed in the bloom - ing garb of spring: Je - sus is fair - er,
and all the twink - ling star - ry host: Je - sus shines bright - er,

thee will I hon - or, thou, my soul's glo - ry, joy, and crown.
Je - sus is pur - er, who makes my woe - ful heart to sing.
Je - sus shines pur - er, than all the an - gels heav'n can boast.

1. Merciful Savior, Lord of Creation,
    Son of God and Son of Man!
    Jesus, we love you, serve and obey you,
    Light of the soul, our joy and peace.

2. Merciful Savior, King of the nations,
    Son of God and Son of Man!
    Glory and honor,
    praise adoration, ever be yours from all mankind!

Text: German composite; tr. pub. New York, 1850, alt.
Music: ST. ELIZABETH, 11 8 10 8, Melody from *Schlesische Volkslieder,* 1842; harm. Thomas Tertius Noble, 1867–1953

206. Holy, Holy, Holy!

1. Ho-ly, Ho-ly, Ho-ly! Lord God Al-might-y! Ear-ly in the morn-ing our song shall rise to thee: Ho-ly, Ho-ly, Ho-ly! mer-ci-ful and might-y, God in three Per-sons, bless-ed Trin-i-ty.

2. Ho-ly, Ho-ly, Ho-ly! all the saints a-dore thee, Cast-ing down their gold-en crowns a-round the glass-y sea; Cher-u-bim and ser-a-phim fall-ing down be-fore thee, God ev-er-last-ing through e-ter-ni-ty.

3. Ho-ly, Ho-ly, Ho-ly! though the dark-ness hide thee, Though the eye made blind by sin thy glo-ry may not see, On-ly thou art ho-ly; there is none be-side thee, Per-fect in pow'r, in love, and pu-ri-ty.

4. Ho-ly, Ho-ly, Ho-ly! Lord God Al-might-y! All thy works shall praise thy Name, in earth, and sky, and sea; Ho-ly, Ho-ly, Ho-ly! mer-ci-ful and might-y, God in three Per-sons, bless-ed Trin-i-ty.

Text: Reginald Heber, 1783–1826
Music: NICAEA, 11 12 12 10, John Bacchus Dykes, 1823–1876

333

207. O JESUS, JOY OF LOVING HEARTS

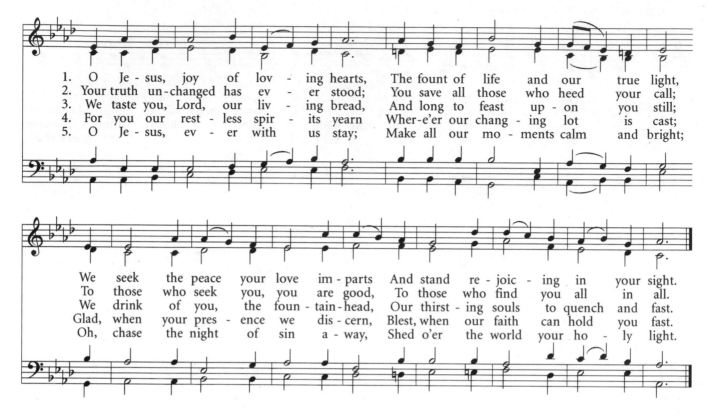

1. O Jesus, joy of lov - ing hearts, The fount of life and our true light,
2. Your truth un-changed has ev - er stood; You save all those who heed your call;
3. We taste you, Lord, our liv - ing bread, And long to feast up - on you still;
4. For you our rest - less spir - its yearn Wher-e'er our chang - ing lot is cast;
5. O Je - sus, ev - er with us stay; Make all our mo - ments calm and bright;

We seek the peace your love im-parts And stand re - joic - ing in your sight.
To those who seek you, you are good, To those who find you all in all.
We drink of you, the foun - tain-head, Our thirst - ing souls to quench and fast.
Glad, when your pres - ence we dis - cern, Blest, when our faith can hold you fast.
Oh, chase the night of sin a - way, Shed o'er the world your ho - ly light.

Text: St. Bernard Clairvaux, 1091–1153, attr.; tr. Ray Palmer, 1808–1887, alt.
Music: FULDA (WALTON), 88 88, William Gardiner, 1770–1853, attr.

208. I COME WITH JOY

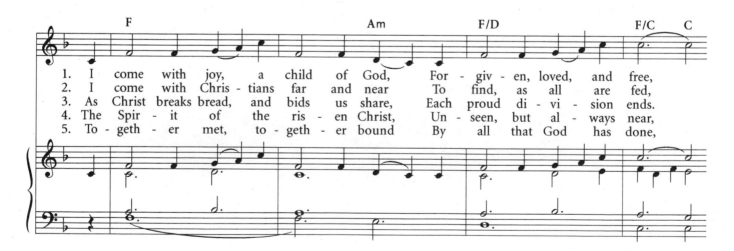

1. I come with joy, a child of God, For - giv - en, loved, and free,
2. I come with Chris - tians far and near To find, as all are fed,
3. As Christ breaks bread, and bids us share, Each proud di - vi - sion ends.
4. The Spir - it of the ris - en Christ, Un - seen, but al - ways near,
5. To - geth - er met, to - geth - er bound By all that God has done,

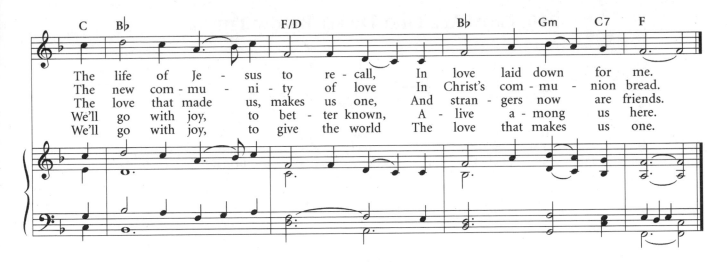

The life of Je - sus to re - call, In love laid down for me.
The new com - mu - ni - ty of love In Christ's com - mu - nion bread.
The love that made us, makes us one, And stran - gers now are friends.
We'll go with joy, to bet - ter known, A - live a - mong us here.
We'll go with joy, to give the world The love that makes us one.

Text: Brian Wren, © 1971
Music: LAND OF REST, 86 86, Scottish-American Folk Melody; adapt. and arr. Annabel Morris Buchanan, 1889–1983, ©

209. THE KING OF LOVE

1. The King of love my Shep - herd is, Whose good - ness fails me nev - er;
2. Where streams of liv - ing wa - ter flow, My ran - somed soul he's lead - ing,
3. Con - fused and fool - ish oft I strayed, But yet in love he sought me,
4. In death's dark vale I fear no ill With you, dear Lord, be - side me;

I noth - ing lack if I am his, And he is mine for - ev - er.
And where the ver - dant pas - tures grow, With food ce - les - tial feed - ing.
And on his shoul - der gent - ly laid, And home re - joic - ing brought me.
Your rod and staff my com - fort still, Your cross be - fore to guide me.

5. You spread a table in my sight;
   Your grace so rich bestowing;
   And, oh, what transport of delight,
   From your pure cup is flowing.

6. And so through all the length of days
   Your goodness fails me never;
   Good Shepherd, may I sing your praise
   Within your house forever.

Text: Henry W. Baker, 1821–1877
Music: ST. COLUMBA, 87 87, Ancient Irish Melody

210. FROM ALL THAT DWELL BELOW THE SKIES

1. From all that dwell be - low the skies, Let the Cre -
2. E - ter - nal are your mer - cies, Lord; E - ter - nal
3. Your loft - y themes, all mor - tals, bring; In songs of
4. In ev - 'ry land be - gin the song; To ev - 'ry

a - tor's praise a - rise; Let the Re - deem - er's
truth at - tends your word: Your praise shall sound from
praise di - vine - ly sing; The great sal - va - tion
land the strains be - long; In cheer - ful sounds all

name be sung, Through ev - 'ry land by ev - 'ry tongue.
shore to shore, Till suns shall rise and set no more.
loud pro - claim, And shout for joy the Sav - ior's name.
voic - es raise, And fill the world with loud - est praise.

Text: Isaac Watts, 1674–1748, vv. 1 & 2; anon., vv. 3 & 4; para. *Psalm 117*
Music: DUKE STREET, 88 88, John Hatton, c. 1710–1793

211. FAITH OF OUR FATHERS

1. Faith of our fa - thers! liv - ing still In spite of dun - geon, fire, and sword; Oh, how our hearts beat high with joy When-e'er we hear that glo - rious word:
2. Our fa - thers, chained in pris - ons dark, Were still in heart and con - science free: And how blest would be their chil - dren's fate, If we, like them, should die for thee!
3. Faith of our fa - thers! Mar - y's prayers Shall win our coun - try un - to thee; And through the truth that comes from God Our peo - ple shall be tru - ly free:
4. Faith of our fa - thers! we will love Both friend and foe in all our strife; And preach thee, too, as love knows how, By kind - ly deeds and vir - tuous life:

Faith of our fa - thers, ho - ly faith! We will be true to thee till death.

Text: Frederick Wm. Faber, C.O., 1814–1868, alt.
Music: ST. CATHERINE (TYNEMOUTH), 88 88 88, Henry Frederick Hemy, 1818–1888; adapt. and arr. James George Walton

212. O My Soul, Bless God the Father

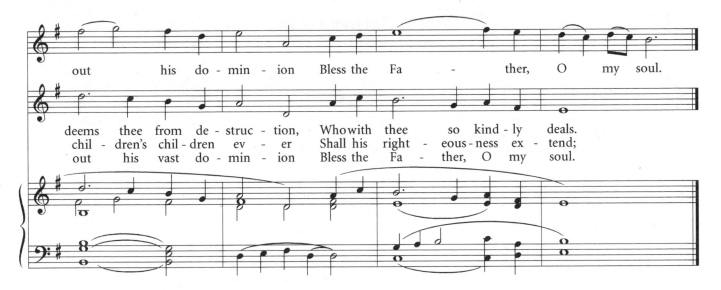

out his do-min-ion Bless the Fa - ther, O my soul.

deems thee from de-struc-tion, Who with thee so kind-ly deals.
chil - dren's chil-dren ev - er Shall his right - eous-ness ex - tend;
out his vast do-min-ion Bless the Fa - ther, O my soul.

Text: Adapt. in *Hymns Ancient & Modern*, 1861
Music: SABINE CROSSROADS, 87 87 87 87, Henry Bryan Hayes, O.S.B., b. 1920, ©

213. WE WALK BY FAITH

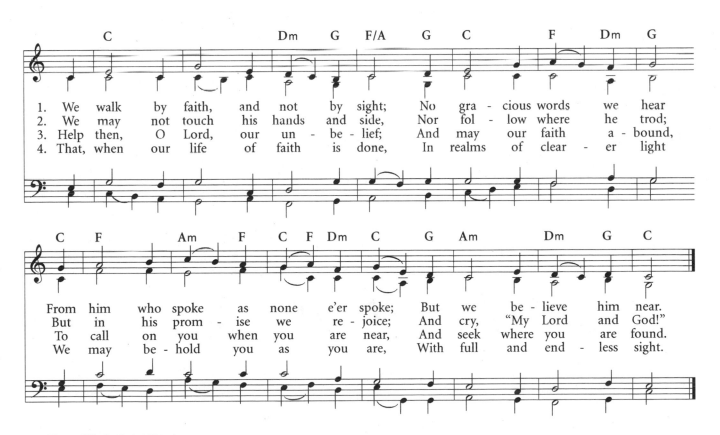

1. We walk by faith, and not by sight; No gra - cious words we hear
2. We may not touch his hands and side, Nor fol - low where he trod;
3. Help then, O Lord, our un - be-lief; And may our faith a - bound,
4. That, when our life of faith is done, In realms of clear - er light

From him who spoke as none e'er spoke; But we be - lieve him near.
But in his prom - ise we re - joice; And cry, "My Lord and God!"
To call on you when you are near, And seek where you are found.
We may be - hold you as you are, With full and end - less sight.

Text: Henry Alford, 1810–1871, alt.
Music: ST. BOTOLPH, 86 86, Gordon Slater, 1896–1979, ©

214. GATHER US IN

1. Here in this place, new light is stream-ing, now is the dark-ness
2. We are the young, our lives are a mys-t'ry, we are the old who
3. Here we will take the wine and the wa-ter, here we will take the
4. Not in the dark of build-ings con-fin-ing, not in some heav-en,

van-ished a - way, See, in this space, our fears and our dream-ings,
yearn for your face, We have been sung through-out all of his-t'ry,
bread of new birth, Here you shall call your sons and your daugh-ters,
light years a - way, but here in this place, the new light is shin-ing,

brought here to you in the light of this day. Ga-ther us in, the
called to be light to the whole hu-man race. Ga-ther us in, the
call us a-new to be salt for the earth. Give us to drink the
now is the king-dom, now is the day. Ga-ther us in and

lost and for - sa - ken, Ga - ther us in, the blind and the lame; Call to us now, and
rich and the haugh - ty, Ga - ther us in, the proud and the strong; Give us a heart so
wine of com - pas - sion, Give us to eat the bread that is you; Nour - ish us well, and
hold us for - ev - er, Ga - ther us in and make us your own; Ga - ther us in, all

we shall a - wak - en, we shall a - rise at the sound of our name.
meek and so low - ly, give us the cour - age to en - ter the song.
teach us to fash - ion lives that are ho - ly and hearts that are true.
peo - ples to - geth - er, fire of love in our flesh and our bone.

Text: Marty Haugen, b. 1952, ©
Music: Marty Haugen, b. 1952, ©

215. LET THERE BE PEACE ON EARTH

1. Let there be peace on earth And let it be-gin with me;
2. Let peace be - gin with me, Let this be the mo - ment now.

Let there be peace on earth, The peace that was meant to be. With
With ev - 'ry step I take, Let this be my sol - emn vow: To

God as our Fa - ther, Chil - dren all are we.

Let us walk with each oth - er In per - fect har - mo - ny.

take each mo - ment and live each mo - ment in peace e - ter - nal - ly.

216. LORD, YOUR ALMIGHTY WORD

1. Lord, your al-might-y word Cha-os and dark-ness heard, And took their flight; Hear us, we hum-bly pray, And where the gos-pel day Sheds not its glo-rious ray, Let there be light!
2. Sav-ior, you came to give Those who in dark-ness live Heal-ing and sight, Health to the sick in mind, Sight to the in-ly blind, Now to all hu-man-kind Let there be light!
3. Spir-it of truth and love, Life-giv-ing, ho-ly dove, Speed forth your flight! Move on the wa-ter's face Bear-ing the lamp of grace, And in earth's dark-est place Let there be light!
4. Ho-ly and bless-ed Three, Glo-ri-ous Trin-i-ty, Wis-dom, love, might; Bound-less as o-cean's tide, Roll-ing in full-est pride, Through the world far and wide, Let there be light!

343

217. BLEST ARE THEY

Blest are they, full of sor-row, they shall be con-soled.

Blest are they who hun-ger and thirst, they shall have their fill.

Blest are they, the pure of heart, they shall see God!

Blest are they who suf-fer in faith, the glo-ry of God is theirs.

To Final Refrain

Re-joice and be glad, yours is the king-dom; shine for all to see.

G   Gsus4   G   D/F#   C   Dsus4   D   C/G
Ab   Absus4   Ab   Eb/G   Db   Ebsus4 Eb   Db/Ab

Refrain following verses 1, 2, 3, 4

Re-joice and be glad! Bless-ed are

G   C   D7   G   D/F#   Em   G/D   C
Ab   Db   Db7   Ab   Eb/G   Fm   Ab/Eb Db

345

you,   ho - ly are you! Re - joice   and be

glad!   Yours is the king-dom of God!

First ending

D.S.   *Final Refrain*

Re - joice   and be glad!

Re - joice and be glad!

Text: *Matthew 5:3-12*; David Haas, b. 1957
Music: David Haas, b. 1957; vocal arr. by David Haas, b. 1957, Michael Joncas, b. 1951
© 1985, GIA Publications, Inc.

218. LORD, WHOSE LOVE IN HUMBLE SERVICE

1. Lord, whose love in hum-ble serv-ice Bore the weight of hu-man need,
2. Still your chil-dren wan-der home-less; Still the hun-gry cry for bread;
3. As we wor-ship, grant us vi-sion, Till your love's re-veal-ing light,
4. Called from wor-ship in-to serv-ice, Forth in your great name we go,

Who did on the cross, for-sak-en, Show us mer-cy's per-fect deed;
Still the cap-tives long for free-dom; Still in grief we mourn our dead.
In its height and depth and great-ness Dawns up-on our hu-man sight:
To the child, the youth, the a-ged, Love in liv-ing deeds to show;

We, your serv-ants, bring the wor-ship Not of voice a-lone, but heart:
As, O Lord, your deep com-pas-sion Healed the sick and freed the soul,
Mak-ing known the needs and bur-dens Your com-pas-sion bids us bear,
Hope and health, good-will and com-fort, Coun-sel, aid, and peace we give,

Con - se - crat - ing to your pur - pose Ev - 'ry gift which you im - part.
Use the love your Spir - it kin - dles Still to save and make us whole.
Stir - ring us to faith - ful serv - ice. Your a - bun - dant life to share.
That your chil - dren, Lord, in free - dom, May your mer - cy know and live.

Text: Albert F. Bayly, 1901–1984, alt., ©
Music: IN BABILONE, 87 87 87 87, Traditional Dutch Melody; harm. Charles Winfred Douglas, 1867–1944, ©

219. O God, Our Help in Ages Past

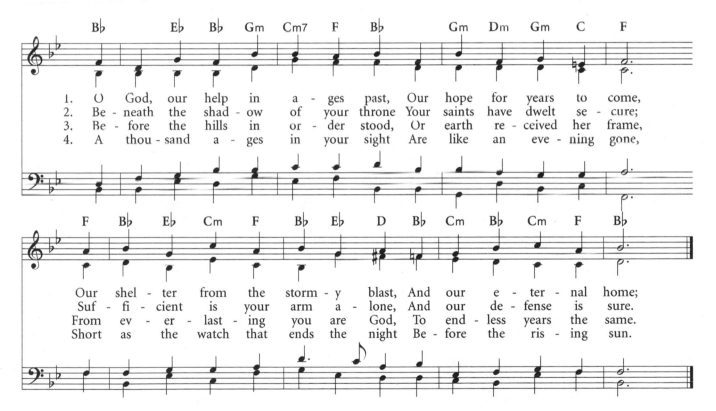

1. O God, our help in a - ges past, Our hope for years to come,
2. Be - neath the shad - ow of your throne Your saints have dwelt se - cure;
3. Be - fore the hills in or - der stood, Or earth re - ceived her frame,
4. A thou - sand a - ges in your sight Are like an eve - ning gone,

Our shel - ter from the storm - y blast, And our e - ter - nal home;
Suf - fi - cient is your arm a - lone, And our de - fense is sure.
From ev - er - last - ing you are God, To end - less years the same.
Short as the watch that ends the night Be - fore the ris - ing sun.

5. Time, like an ever-rolling stream,
Bears all our lives away;
They fly forgotten, as a dream
Dies at the op'ning day.

6. O God, our help in ages past,
Our hope for years to come,
Be now our guard while troubles last,
And our eternal home.

Text: Isaac Watts, 1674–1748, alt.
Music: ST. ANNE, 86 86, William Croft, 1678–1727, alt.; harm. William Henry Monk, 1823–1889

220. We're Called to Be Disciples

1. We're called to be dis-ci-ples of Je-sus Christ, our King; We have a no-ble rea-son to cel-e-brate and sing. We're called to spread his king-dom, that is our no-ble call, our call, To tell an anx-ious peo-ple that

2. He came to bring his free-dom to all who sit in chains; He brings the sick and wound-ed an oint-ment for their pains; His words can mean sal-va-tion, the words that we re-peat, re-peat, And give us hope for mer-cy be-

3. He gave to us a gos-pel, a won-drous thing to speak, Re-fresh-ment for the wear-y and cour-age for the weak; The sad will have true glad-ness, the cap-tive a re-lease, re-lease, To walk a-gain in free-dom and

Je - sus died for all! To tell an anx-ious peo - ple that Je - sus died for all!
fore the judg-ment seat, And give us hope for mer - cy be - fore the judg-ment seat.
fol - low ways of peace. To walk a - gain in free - dom and fol - low ways of peace.

Text: Willard F. Jabusch, b. 1930, ©
Music: 76 76 76 76, German Melody; acc. S. R. Rudcki, b. 1928, ©

221. O Christ Our True and Only Light

1. O Christ our true and on - ly light, Il - lu - mine those who sit in
2. And all those who have strayed from thee O gent - ly seek; thy heal - ing
3. O make the deaf to hear thy word, And teach the dumb to speak, dear
4. Shine on the dark - ened and the cold, Re - call the wan - d'rers from thy
5. So they with us may ev - er - more Such grace with won - d'ring thanks a -

night; Let those a - far now hear thy voice, And in thy fold with us re - joice.
be, To ev - 'ry wound - ed con-science giv'n, And let them al - so share thy heav'n.
Lord, Who dare not yet the faith a - vow, Though se - cret - ly they hold it now.
fold, Those now u - nite who walk a - part, Con-firm the weak and doubt-ing heart.
dore; And end - less praise to thee be giv'n By all thy Church in earth and heav'n.

Text: Johann Heermann, 1585–1647; tr. Catherine Winkworth, 1827–1878
Music: O WALY WALY, 98 98, English Traditional Melody

222. You Are Mine

1. I will come to you in the si - lence, I will lift you from all your fear. You will hear my voice, I claim you as my choice, be still and know I am here. *(To verse 2)*

2. I am hope for all who are hope - less, I am eyes for all who long to see. In the shad - ows of the night, I will be your light, come and rest in me. *(To refrain)*

3. I am strength for all the des - pair - ing, heal - ing for the ones who dwell in shame. All the blind will see, the lame will all run free, and all will know my name. *(To refrain)*

4. am the Word that leads all to free - dom, I am the peace the world can - not give. I will call your name, em - brac - ing all your pain, stand up, now walk, and live! *(To refrain)*

Capo 3: G / C/G / G / D/F# / Em7
Bb / Eb/Bb / Bb / F/A / Gm7

C / Dsus4 / D / G / C/G
Eb / Fsus4 / F / Bb / Eb/Bb

B / B/D# / Em / Am / G/B / C / Dsus4 / D / Dsus4 / D
D / D/F# / Gm / Cm / Bb/D / Eb / Fsus4 / F / Fsus4 / F

Do not be a-fraid, I am with you. I have called you each by name.

Come and fol-low me, I will bring you home; I love you and you are

mine.

D.C. *Final ending*

4. I

223. THOSE WHO LOVE AND THOSE WHO LABOR

1. Those who love and those who la-bor Fol-low in the way of Christ;
2. Where the man-y work to-geth-er They with Christ him-self a-bide,
3. Let the seek-er nev-er fal-ter Till the truth is found a-far

Thus the first dis-ci-ples found him, Thus the gift of love suf-ficed.
But the lone-ly work-ers al-so Find him ev-er at their side.
With the wis-dom of the a-ges un-der-neath a gi-ant star.

Je-sus says to those who seek him, I will nev-er pass you by;
Lo, the Prince of com-mon wel-fare Dwells with-in the mar-ket strife;
With the rich-est and the poor-est, Of the sum of things pos-sessed.

Raise the stone and you shall find me; Cleave the wood and there am I.
Lo, the bread of heav'n is bro-ken In the sac-ra-ment of life.
Like a child at first to won-der, Like a king at last to rest.

Text: Geoffrey Dearmer, b. 1893, ©
Music: DOMHNACH TRIONOIDE, 87 87 87 87, Gaelic; acc. Edward Currie

224. IMMORTAL, INVISIBLE, GOD ONLY WISE

1. Im - mor - tal, in - vis - i - ble, God on - ly wise, In light in - ac -
2. Un - rest - ing, un - hast - ing, and si - lent as light, Nor want - ing, nor
3. To all life thou giv - est, to both great and small; In all life thou
4. Great Fa - ther of glo - ry, pure Fa - ther of light, Thine an - gels a -

ces - si - ble hid from our eyes, Most bless - ed, most glo - rious, the
wast - ing, thou rul - est in might; Thy jus - tice like moun - tains high
liv - est, the true life of all; We blos - som and flour - ish as
dore thee, all veil - ing their sight; Of all thy rich grac - es this

An - cient of Days, Al - might - y, vic - to - rious, thy great name we praise.
soar - ing a - bove, Thy clouds which are foun - tains of good - ness and love.
leaves on a tree, And with - er and per - ish: but nought chang - eth thee.
grace, Lord, im - part: Take the veil from our fac - es, the veil from our heart.

Text: Walter Chalmers Smith, 1824–1908
Music: ST. DENIO, 11 11 11 11, Welsh Melody

225. SHEPHERD ME, O GOD

Refrain

Shep-herd me, O God, be - yond my wants, be - yond my fears, from

Capo 1: Em   C   G   D   Bm7   C
Fm   Db   Ab   Eb   Cm7   Db

To verses 1, 2, 3, 5   *To verse 4*

death in - to life.   life.

Am7   Bm7   Em   Am/E   Em7   A/E   Em   D/F# G
Bbm7 Cm7   Fm   Bbm/F Fm7 Bb/F   Fm   Eb/G Ab

Verses 1, 2, 3,

1. God is my shep-herd, so noth-ing shall I want, I rest in the mead-ows of
2. Gent - ly you raise me and heal my wea - ry soul, you lead me by path-ways of
3. Though I should wan-der the val - ley of death, I fear no e - vil, for

Em   Am/E   Em7   A/E   Em   Am/E
Fm   Bbm/F   Fm7   Bb/F   Fm   Bbm/F

faith - ful - ness and love,   I walk by the qui - et wa - ters of
right - eous - ness and truth,   my spir - it shall sing the mu - sic of your
you are at my side,   your rod and your staff,   my com - fort and my

Em7   A/E   Am7   Bm7   Am/C   D
Fm7   B♭/F   B♭m7   Cm7   B♭m/D♭   E♭

D.C.   Verse 4

peace.
name.
hope.

4. You have set me a ban-quet of love

Em   Am/E   Em7   A/E   Am   D
Fm   B♭m/F   Fm7   B♭/F   B♭m   E♭

in the face of ha - tred,   crown-ing me with love be - yond my

G   C   Am   Am7/G   F♯m7-5
A♭   D♭   B♭m   B♭m7/A♭   Gm7-5

357

Text: *Psalm 23*, Marty Haugen, ©
Music: Marty Haugen, ©

226. Lord of All Hopefulness

1. Lord of all hope-ful-ness, Lord of all joy, Whose trust, ev - er child - like, no care could de - stroy: Be there at our wak - ing, and give us, we pray, Your bliss in our hearts, Lord, at the break of the day.

2. Lord of all ea - ger-ness, Lord of all faith, Whose strong hands were skilled at the plane and the lathe: Be there at our la - bors, and give us, we pray, Your strength in our hearts, Lord, at the noon of the day.

3. Lord of all kind - li - ness, Lord of all grace, Your hands swift to wel - come, your arms to em - brace: Be there at our hom - ing, and give us, we pray, Your love in out hearts, Lord, at the eve of the day.

4. Lord of all gen - tle - ness, Lord of all calm, Whose voice is con - tent - ment, whose pres - ence is balm: Be there at our sleep - ing, and give us, we pray, Your peace in our hearts, Lord, at the end of the day.

Text: Jan Struther, 1901–1953, ©
Music: SLANE, 10 11 11 12, Irish Folk Tune; acc. Erik Routley, 1917–1982, ©

227. BE NOT AFRAID

way.   You shall speak your words in for-eign lands and all will un-der-

harmed.   If you stand be-fore the pow'r of hell and death is at your

stand.   You shall see the face of God and live.

side,   know that I am with you through it all.

Refrain
Melody:
Be not a-fraid.   I go be-fore you al-ways.

Harmony:
Be not a-fraid.   I go be-fore you al-ways.

Come, fol-low me, and I will give you rest.

Come, fol-low me, I will give you rest.

C   G/B   Bm   Em   Am   D   G Gsus4   G   Gsus4   G   Gsus4

Last time

G

Verse 3

Descant:

Ooh   king-dom shall be

3. Bless-ed are your poor,   for the king-dom shall be

G   Gsus4   G   Gsus4   G   Gsus4

theirs.   Bless - ed are the ones who

theirs.   Blest are you that weep and mourn, for one day you shall

G   D/F#   C   Csus2   C   C/B   Am   Am7/C

mourn. If they hate you all be-cause of

laugh. And if wick-ed tongues in-sult and hate you all be-cause of

me, bless-ed, bless-ed are you!

me, bless-ed, bless-ed are you!

Text: *Isaiah 43:2-3, Luke 6:20ff.;* Bob Dufford, S.J., b. 1943
Music: Bob Dufford, S.J., b. 1943; acc. Sr. Theophane Hytrek, O.S.F., 1915–1992
© 1975, Robert J. Dufford, S.J., and New Dawn Music

228. Lord, When You Came / Pescador De Hombres

INTRODUCTION

VERSES

1. Lord, when you came to the
2. Lord, you knew what my boat
1. Tú has ve - ni - do a la o -
2. Tú sa - bes bien lo que

sea - shore You weren't seek - ing the wise or the wealth - y,
car - ried; Nei - ther mon - ey nor weap - ons for fight - ing,
ri - lla, no has bus - ca - do ni a sa - bios, ni a ri - cos,
ten - go, en mi bar - ca no hay o - ro ni es - pa - das,

But on - ly ask - ing that I might fol - low.
But nets for fish - ing, my dai - ly la - bor.
tan só - lo quie - res que yo te si - ga.
tan só - lo re - des y mi tra - ba - jo.

REFRAIN

O Lord, in my eyes you were gaz - ing, Kind - ly
Se - ñor, me has mi - ra - do a los o - jos, son - ri -

smil - ing, my name you were say - ing; All I treas - ured,
en - do has di - cho mi nom - bre, en la a - re - na

I have left on the sand there; Close to you, I will find oth - er seas.
he de - ja - do mi bar - ca, jun - to a tí bus - ca - ré o - tro - mar.

3. Lord, have you need of my labor,
   Hands for service, a heart made for loving,
   My arms for lifting the poor and broken? *Refrain*

4. Lord, send me where you would have me,
   To a village, or heart of the city;
   I will remember that you are with me. *Refrain*

3. Tú necesitas mis manos,
   mi cansancio que a otros descanse,
   amor que quiera seguir amando. *Refrain*

4. Tú pescadore de otros mares,
   ansia eterna, almas que esperan.
   Amigo bueno, que así me llamas. *Refrain*

Text: Cesareo Gabarain (Spanish), Willard F. Jabusch, b. 1930 (English), ©
Music: Cesareo Gabarain, arr. Robert E. Kreutz, b. 1922 ©

229. Lift High the Cross

Descant

Lift high the cross, the love of Christ proclaim

Lift high the cross, the love of Christ proclaim

till all the world a - dore his sa - cred name.

till all the world a - dore his sa - cred name.

1. Led on their way by this tri - um - phant sign,
2. Each new - born ser - vant of the Cru - ci - fied
3. O Lord, once lift - ed on the glo - rious tree,
4. So shall our song of tri - umph ev - er be:

The hosts of God in con - quering ranks com - bine.
Bears on the brow the seal of him who died.
As thou hast prom - ised, draw the world to thee.
Praise to the Cru - ci - fied for vic - to - ry.

Text: Geo. W. Kitchin, 1827–1912; M. R. Newbolt, 1874–1956, alt., ©
Music: CRUCIFER, 10 10 with Refrain, Sydney H. Nicholson, 1875–1947; desc. Richard Proulx, b. 1937, ©

230. WORD OF GOD, COME DOWN ON EARTH

1. Word of God, come down on earth, Liv-ing rain from heav'n de-scend-ing;
2. Word e-ter-nal, throned on high, Word that brought to life cre-a-tion,
3. Word that caused blind eyes to see, Speak and heal our mor-tal blind-ness;
4. Word that speaks God's ten-der love, One with God be-yond all tell-ing,

Touch our hearts and bring to birth Faith and hope and love un-end-ing.
Word that came from heav'n to die, Cru-ci-fied for our sal-va-tion,
Deaf we are: our heal-er be; Lose our tongues to tell your kind-ness.
Word that sends us from a-bove, God the Spir-it, with us dwell-ing,

Word al-might-y, we re-vere you; Word made flesh, we long to hear you.
Sav-ing Word, the world re-stor-ing, Speak to us, your love out-pour-ing.
be our Word in pit-y spo-ken, Heal the world, by our sin bro-ken.
Word of truth, to all truth lead us, Word of life, with one Bread feed us.

Text: James Quinn, S.J., b. 1919, © 1969
Music: LIEBSTER JESU, 78 78 88, Johann R. Ahle, 1625–1673; arr. George H. Palmer, 1846–1926

231. Blessed Jesus, at Thy Word

1. Bless-ed Jesus, at thy word We are gath-ered all to hear thee;
   Let our hearts and souls be stirred Now to seek and love and fear thee;
   By thy teach-ings pure and ho - ly, Drawn from earth to love thee sole - ly.

2. All our know-ledge, sense, and sight Lie in deep-est dark-ness shroud - ed,
   Till thy Spir - it breaks our night With the beams of truth un - cloud - ed;
   Thou a - lone to God canst win us; Thou must work all good with - in us.

3. Gra - cious Lord, thy - self im - part! Light of Light, from God pro - ceed - ing,
   O - pen thou our ears and heart, help us by thy Spir - it's plead - ing,
   Hear the cry thy Church up - rais - es; Hear, and bless our prayers and prais - es.

Text: Benjamin Schmolck, 1672–1737; tr. Catherine Winkworth, 1827–1878, alt.
Music: LIEBSTER JESU, 78 78 88, Johann R. Ahle, 1625–1673; arr. George H. Palmer, 1846–1926

232. Come Before Him Singing

1. Come be-fore him singing, thanks and prais-es bring Shout that he's our safety, he's our Rock and King. Depths of earth are his: high-est moun-tains his! He made land and sea and all things that live.

2. Come and bow be-fore him, to him bend your knee, We're his flock and surely he'll our Shep-herd be. Hard-en not your hearts, like your el-ders' hearts; For-ty years they wan-dered so far a-stray.

3. Praise the Lord for-ever in his ho-ly house; Praise him for his wonders in his ho-ly house. Let the horns re-sound; let the flutes all sound; Drums and crash-ing cym-bals sing praise to God.

Text: Willard F. Jabusch, b. 1930; *Psalm 95*, para., ©
Music: Robert E. Kreutz, b. 1922

233. HOLY GOD, WE PRAISE THY NAME

1. Ho - ly God, we praise thy name. Lord of all we
2. Hark the loud ce - les - tial hymn; An - gel choirs a -
3. Lo! the ap - os - tol - ic train Join, the sa - cred
4. Ho - ly Fath - er, Ho - ly Son, Ho - ly Spir - it,

bow be - fore thee. All on earth thy scep - ter claim.
bove are rais - ing, Cher - u - bim and ser - a - phim,
name to hal - low; Proph - ets swell the loud re - frain,
Three we name thee; While in es - sence on - ly One,

All in heav'n a - bove a - dore thee. In - fi -
In un - ceas - ing chor - us prais - ing; Fill the
And the white - robed mar - tyrs fol - low: And from
Un - di - vid - ed God we claim thee; And a -

nite thy vast do - main, Ev - er - last - ing is thy
heav'ns with sweet ac - cord: Ho - ly, ho - ly, ho - ly
morn to set of sun, Through the Church the song goes
dor - ing bend the knee, While we own the mys - ter -

reign. / Lord. / on. / y.

In - fi - nite thy vast do - main,
Fill the heav'ns with sweet ac - cord:
And from morn to set of sun,
And a - dor - ing bend the knee,

Ev - er - last - ing is thy reign.
Ho - ly, ho - ly, ho - ly Lord.
Through the Church the song goes on.
While we own the mys - ter - y.

Text: Ignaz Franz, 1719–1790, attr.; tr. Clarence Augustus Walworth, 1820–1900
Music: TE DEUM (GROSSER GOTT), 78 78 77 77, *Katholisches Gesangbuch,* 1686; alt. *Cantate,* 1851; arr. Sr. Theophane Hytrek, O.S.F., ©

234. AMAZING GRACE

1. A - maz - ing grace! How sweet the sound, That saved and strength - ened me!
2. 'Twas grace that taught my heart to fear, And grace my fears re - lieved;
3. The Lord has prom - ised good to me, His word my hope se - cures;
4. Through man - y dan - gers, toils, and snares, I have al - read - y come;
5. When we've been there ten thou - sand years, Bright shin - ing as the sun,

I once was lost, but now am found, Was blind, but now I see.
How pre - cious did that grace ap - pear The hour I first be - lieved!
He will my shield and por - tion be As long as life en - dures.
'Tis grace that brought me safe thus far, And grace will lead me home.
We've no less days to sing God's praise Than when we'd first be - gun.

Text: John Newton, 1725–1807, alt., vv. 1–4; John Rees, fl. 1859, v. 5
Music: NEW BRITAIN, 86 86, Early American Melody, 1831; adapt. Edwin Othello Excell, 1851–1921

235. MY SHEPHERD WILL SUPPLY MY NEED

1. My Shepherd will supply my need; The Lord God is his name.
2. When I walk through the shades of death, Thy presence is my stay;
3. The sure provisions of my God Attend me all my days;

In pastures green he makes me feed, Beside the living stream.
One word of thy supporting breath Drives all my fears away.
O may thy house be my abode, And all my work be praise!

He brings my wan-d'ring spirit back, When I forsake his ways;
Thy hand, in sight of all my foes, Does still my table spread;
There would I find a settled rest, While others go and come,

And leads me for his mer - cy's sake, In paths of truth and grace.
My cup with bless - ings o - ver - flows, Thine oil a - noints my head.
No more a stran - ger nor a guest; But like a child at home.

Text: Isaac Watts, 1674–1748, alt.
Music: RESIGNATION, 86 86 86 86, *Southern Harmony*, 1835

236. Shepherd of Souls

1. Shep - herd of souls, re - fresh and bless Your cho - sen pil - grim flock
2. We would not live by bread a - lone, But by your word of grace,
3. Be known to us in break - ing bread, But do not then de - part;
4. Lord, sup with us in love di - vine; Your Bod - y and your Blood,

With man - na in the wil - der - ness, With wa - ter from the rock.
In strength of which we trav - el on To our a - bid - ing place.
Sav - ior, a - bide with us, and spread Your ta - ble in our heart.
That liv - ing bread, that heav'n - ly wine, Be our im - mor - tal food.

Text: Vv. 1 & 2, James Montgomery, 1771–1854; vv. 3 & 4, anon.
Music: ST. AGNES, 86 86, John Bacchus Dykes, 1823–1876

237. I Heard the Voice of Jesus Say

1. I heard the voice of Je-sus say, "Come un-to me and rest;
2. I heard the voice of Je-sus say, "Be-hold, I free-ly give
3. I heard the voice of Je-sus say, "I am this dark world's light;

And in your wea-ri-ness lay down Your head up-on my breast."
The liv-ing wa-ter; thirst-y one, Stoop down and drink, and live."
Look un-to me, your morn shall rise, And all your day be bright."

I came to Je-sus as I was, So wea-ry, worn, and sad;
I came to Je-sus, and I drank Of that life-giv-ing stream;
I looked to Je-sus, and I found In him my Star, my Sun;

I found in him a rest-ing place, And he has made me glad.
My thirst was quenched, my soul re-vived, And now I live in him.
And in that light of life I'll walk Till pil-grim days are done.

Text: Horatius Bonar, 1808–1889
Music: THIRD MODE MELODY, 86 86 86 86, Thomas Tallis, c. 1505–1585; harm. John Wilson, b. 1905, ©

374

238. I Heard the Voice of Jesus Say

1. I heard the voice of Je-sus say, "Come un-to me and rest; And in your wear-i-ness lay down Your head up-on my breast." I came to Je-sus as I was, So wear-y, worn, and sad; I found in him a rest-ing place, And he has made me glad.

2. I heard the voice of Je-sus say, "Be-hold, I free-ly give The liv-ing wa-ter, thirst-y one: Stoop down and drink and live." I came to Je-sus and I drank Of that life-giv-ing stream; My thirst was quenched, my soul re-vived, And now I live in him.

3. I heard the voice of Je-sus say, "I am this dark world's light; Look un-to me, your morn shall rise, And all your day be bright." I looked to Je-sus and I found In him my star, my sun; And in that light of life I'll walk Till pil-grim days are done.

Text: Horatius Bonar, 1808–1889
Music: KINGSFOLD, CMD, English Tune; harm. Ralph Vaughan Williams, 1872–1959

239. THERE'S A WIDENESS IN GOD'S MERCY

1. There's a wide-ness in God's mer - cy, Like the wide-ness of the sea;
2. For the love of God is broad - er Than the mea - sure of our mind;

There's a kind - ness in his jus - tice, Which is more than lib - er - ty.
And the heart of the E - ter - nal Is most won - der - ful - ly kind.

There is wel - come for the sin - ner, And more bless - ings for the good;
There is plen - ti - ful re - demp - tion In the blood that has been shed;

There is mer - cy with the Sav - ior; There is heal - ing in his blood.
There is joy for all the mem - bers Now at one with Christ our Head.

Text: Frederick William Faber, 1814–1863, alt.
Music: 87 87 87 87, Gerard Wojchowski, O.S.B., 1925–1997, ©

240. THERE IS A BALM IN GILEAD

REFRAIN

There is a balm in Gil - e - ad To make the wound - ed whole,
There is a balm in Gil - e - ad To heal the sin - sick soul.

VERSES

1. Some - times I feel dis - cour - aged And think my work's in vain,
2. If you can - not preach like Pe - ter, If you can - not pray like Paul,
3. Don't ev - er feel dis - cour - aged, For Je - sus is your friend;

To Refrain

But then the Ho - ly Spir - it Re - vives my soul a - gain.
You can tell the love of Je - sus, And say, "He died for all!"
And if you lack for knowl - edge He'll ne'er re - fuse to lend.

Text: *Jeremiah 8:22*
Music: BALM IN GILEAD, Irregular with Refrain, Spiritual

241. Come, Our Almighty King

1. Come, our almighty King, Help us your name to sing; Help us to praise: Father, all glorious, Ever victorious, Come and reign over us, Ancient of Days.

2. Come, O incarnate Word, By heav'n and earth adored; Our prayer attend: Come and your people bless, And give your word success; Spirit of holiness, On us descend.

3. Come, holy Comforter, Your sacred witness bear In this glad hour! Your grace to us impart, Now rule in every heart, Never from us depart, Spirit of pow'r.

4. To the great One in Three, Eternal praises be Hence evermore! Your sovereign majesty May we in glory see, And to eternity Love and adore.

Text: Anon., c. 1757, alt.
Music: ITALIAN HYMN, 664 6664, Felice de Giardini, 1716–1796

378

242. God, Who Stretched the Spangled Heavens

1. God, who stretched the span-gled heav-ens In - fi - nite in time and place,
2. We have ven - tured worlds un - dreamed of Since the child-hood of our race;
3. As each far ho - ri - zon beck - ons, May it chal - lenge us a - new:

Flung the suns in burn-ing ra - diance Through the si - lent fields of space:
Known the ec - sta - sy of wing - ing Through un - trav - eled realms of space;
Chil - dren of cre - a - tive pur - pose, Serv - ing oth - ers, hon - 'ring you.

We your chil - dren in your like - ness, Share in - ven - tive pow'rs with you;
Probed the se - crets of the at - om, yield - ing un - i - mag - ined pow'r,
May our dreams prove rich with prom - ise; Each en - deav - or well be - gun;

Great Cre - a - tor, still cre - at - ing, Show us what we yet may do.
Fac - ing us with life's de - struc - tion Or our most tri - um - phant hour.
Great Cre - a - tor, give us guid - ance Till our goals and yours are one.

Text: Catherine Cameron, b. 1927
Music: HOLY MANNA, 87 87 87 87, William Moore, 1835; harm. Charles Anders, b. 1929, ©

243. If Anyone Would Follow Me

1. "If an-y-one would fol-low me, then come and take the
2. "The last shall be ac-count-ed first, the first will come in
3. How strange, yet good, sound Je-sus' words, what wis-dom they con-

cross, And if you gain the whole wide world, then count it as a
last; The poor will eat at heav-en's feast, the rich will have to
tain; They touch our souls all parched and bleak like sum-mer's heal-ing

loss." His words are hard, a-gainst the grain and yet they still com-
fast." Who give their lives for Je-sus' sake will live to share his
rain. No eas-y grace he of-fers us to lull a la-zy

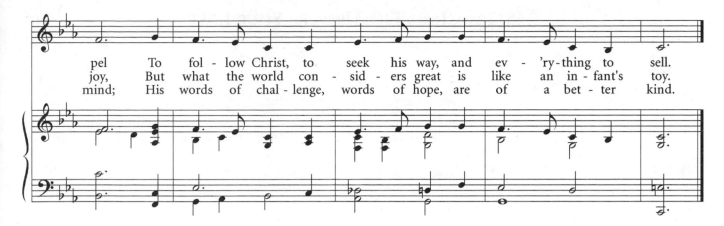

pel To fol - low Christ, to seek his way, and ev - 'ry-thing to sell.
joy, But what the world con - sid - ers great is like an in - fant's toy.
mind; His words of chal - lenge, words of hope, are of a bet - ter kind.

Text: Willard F. Jabusch, b. 1930, ©
Music: 86 86 86 86, American Melody; acc. S. R. Rudcki, b. 1928, ©

244. SING A NEW SONG TO THE LORD

1. Sing a new song to the Lord, He to whom won - ders be -
2. Now to the ends of the earth See His sal - va - tion is
3. Sing a new song and re - joice, Pub - lish His prais - es a -
4. Join with the hills and the sea Thun - ders of praise to pro -

long! Re - joice in His tri - umph and tell of His
shown; And still He re - mem - bers His mer - cy and
broad! Let voic - es in cho - rus, with trum - pet and
long! In judg - ment and jus - tice He comes to the

pow'r, O sing to the Lord a new song!
truth, Un - chang - ing in love to his own.
horn, Re - sound for the joy of the Lord!
earth. O sing to the Lord a new song!

Text: Based on *Psalm 98,* Timothy Dudley-Smith, ©
Music: David G. Wilson, ©

245. Jesu, Jesu, Fill Us with Your Love

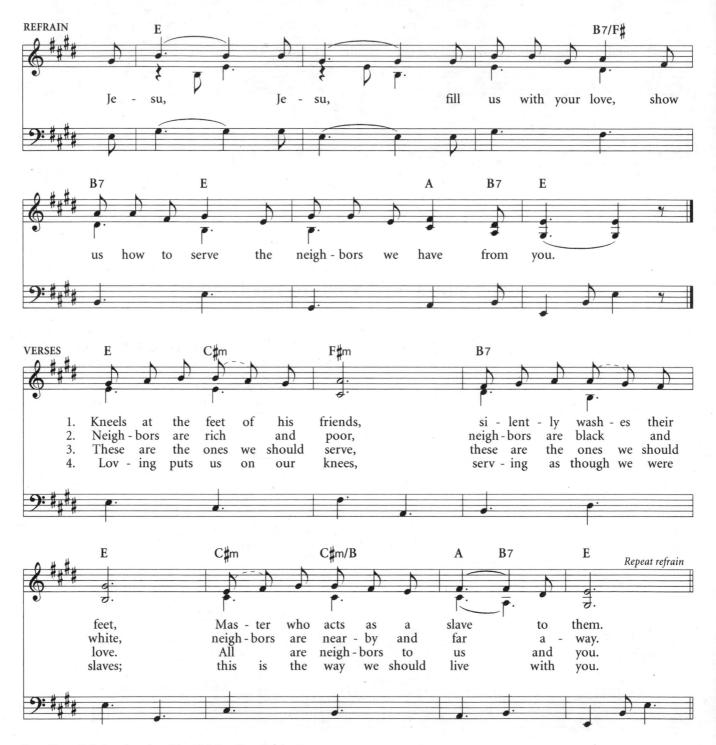

REFRAIN
E
B7/F♯
Je - su, Je - su, fill us with your love, show
B7
E
A
B7
E
us how to serve the neigh - bors we have from you.
VERSES
E
C♯m
F♯m
B7
1. Kneels at the feet of his friends, si - lent - ly wash - es their
2. Neigh - bors are rich and poor, neigh - bors are black and
3. These are the ones we should serve, these are the ones we should
4. Lov - ing puts us on our knees, serv - ing as though we were
E
C♯m
C♯m/B
A
B7
E
Repeat refrain
feet, Mas - ter who acts as a slave to them.
white, neigh - bors are near - by and far a - way.
love. All are neigh - bors to us and you.
slaves; this is the way we should live with you.

Text: Ghana Folk Song based on *John 13:3-5;* tr. Tom Colvin, ©
Music: CHEREPONI, Irregular, Ghana Folk Song; acc. Jane M. Marshall, ©

246. How Lovely Is Your Dwelling Place

REFRAIN

How love-ly is your dwell-ing place, O Lord of hosts!

VERSES

1. My soul longs and pines for the courts of the Lord.
2. Yes, e-ven the spar-row finds a home,
3. For all your peo-ple, O Lord my God,
4. How hap-py are they who dwell in your house,
5. The Lord bless-es all who walk in the truth.

My heart and my flesh cry for God, the liv-ing God.
and the swal-low a nest to shel-ter her young.
your al-tars are shel-ter, your pres-ence is peace.
they tru-ly are strong who find strength in the Lord.
How hap-py are they who trust in the Lord.

Text: Based on *Psalm 84*
Music: Eugene E. Englert, ©

247. SHEPHERD AND TEACHER

384

Text: Omer Westendorf, ©
Music: Robert E. Kreutz, ©

385

248. Sing Ye Praises to the Father

1. Sing ye prais-es to the Fa - ther, Sing ye prais-es to the
2. Join the praise of ev - 'ry crea - ture, Sing with sing-ing birds of
3. Praise our God on days of glad - ness For a sum-mons to re -

Son, Sing ye prais-es to the Spir - it, Liv-ing and e-ter-nal
dawn; When the stars shine forth at night - fall, Hear their heav'n-ly an-ti-
joice; Praise God in our times of sad - ness For the com-fort of God's

One. God has made us, God has blessed us, God has called us to be
phon. Praise God for the light of Sum - mer, Au-tumn glo-ries, Win-ter
voice. God our Fa - ther, strong and lov - ing, Christ our Sav - ior, Lead-er,

true; God is Lord of all cre - a - tion, Dai - ly
snows, For the com - ing of the Spring - time, And the
Lord, Liv - ing God, Cre - a - tor Spir - it, Be your

mak - ing all things new, Dai - ly mak - ing all things new.
life of all that grows, And the life of all that grows.
ho - ly name a - dored, Be your ho - ly name a - dored.

Text: Robert B. Y. Scott, b. 1899
Music: Robert E. Kreutz, ©

387

249. THE GOD OF ABRAHAM PRAISE

1. The God of A-braham praise, Who reigns en-throned a - bove;
2. The Lord, our God has sworn: I on that oath de - pend;
3. There dwells the Lord, our King, The Lord, our Right-eous - ness,
4. The God who reigns on high The great arch - an - gels sing,

The an - cient of e - ter - nal days, And God of love;
I shall, on ea - gle - wings up-borne, To heav'n as - cend;
Tri - umph-ant o'er the world and sin, The Prince of Peace;
And "Ho - ly, Ho - ly, Ho - ly," cry, "Al - might - y King!

The Lord, the great I AM, By earth and heav'n con - fessed
I shall be - hold God's face, I shall God's pow'r a - dore,
On Zi - on's sa - cred height The king - dom God main - tains,
Who was, and is, the same, For all e - ter - ni - ty,

We bow and bless the sa - cred name For ev - er blest.
And sing the won - ders of God's grace For ev - er - more.
And, glo - rious with the saints in light, For ev - er reigns.
Im - mor - tal God, the great I AM, All glo - ry be."

Text: *Yigdal Elohim Hai;* ascr. to Daniel ben Judah Dayyan, fl. 1400; para. by Thomas Olivers, 1725–1799, alt.
Music: LEONI, 6 6 8 4 D, from the *Yigdal;* transcribed by Meyer Lyon, c. 1751–1797

250. LORD OF LIGHT

1. Lord of light, your name out-shin-ing, All the stars and suns of space,
2. By the toil of faith-ful work-ers In some far out-ly-ing field,
3. Grant that knowl-edge, still in-creas-ing, At your feet may low-ly kneel;
4. By the prayers of faith-ful watch-ers, Nev-er si-lent day or night;

Use our tal-ents in your king-dom As the serv-ants of your grace;
By the cour-age where the ra-diance Of the cross is still re-vealed,
With your grace our tri-umphs hal-low, With your char-i-ty our zeal;
By the cross of Je-sus, bring-ing Peace to all and heal-ing light;

use us to ful-fill your pur-pose In the gift of Christ your Son:
By the vic-to-ries of meek-ness, Through re-proach and suf-f'ring won:
Lift the na-tions from the shad-ows To the glad-ness of the sun:
By the love that pass-es knowl-edge, Mak-ing all your chil-dren one:

1.-4. Fa-ther, as in high-est heav-en, So on earth your will be done.

Text: Howell E. Lewis, 1860–1953, alt. ©
Music: ABBOTT'S LEIGH, 87 87 87 87, Cyril V. Taylor, b. 1907, ©

251. Lord, You Give the Great Commission

1. Lord, you give the great com-mis-sion: "Heal the sick and preach the word."
2. Lord, you call us to your serv-ice: "In my name bap-tize and teach."
3. Lord, you make the com-mon ho-ly: "This my bod-y, this my blood."
4. Lord, you show us love's true meas-ure; "Fa-ther, what they do, for-give."
5. Lord, you bless with words as-sur-ing: "I am with you to the end."

Lest the Church ne-glect its mis-sion, And the Gos-pel go un-heard,
That the world may trust your pro-mise, Life a-bun-dant meant for each,
Let us all, for earth's true glo-ry, Dai-ly lift life heav-en-ward,
Yet we hoard as pri-vate treas-ure All that you so free-ly give.
Faith and hope and love re-stor-ing, May we serve as you in-tend,

Help us wit-ness to your pur-pose With re-newed in-teg-ri-ty;
Give us all new fer-vor, draw us Clos-er in com-mu-ni-ty;
Ask-ing that the world a-round us Share your chil-dren's lib-er-ty;
May your care and mer-cy lead us To a just so-ci-e-ty;
And, a-mid the cares that claim us, Hold in mind e-ter-ni-ty:

1.-4. With the Spir-it's gifts em-pow'r us For the work of min-is-try.

Text: Jeffrey Rowthorn, b. 1934, ©
Music: ABBOT'S LEIGH, 87 87 87 87, Cyril V. Taylor, b. 1907, ©

390

252. How Firm a Foundation

1. How firm a foun - da - tion, you saints of the Lord, Is laid for your
2. Fear not, he is with you, O be not dis - mayed, For he is your
3. When through the deep wa - ters he calls you to go, The riv - ers of
4. When through fi - 'ry tri - als your path - way shall lie His grace all - suf -

faith in his ex - cel - lent word; What more can he say than to you he has
God, and will still give you aid: He'll strength - en you, help you, and cause you to
grief shall not you o - ver - flow; The Lord will be with you in trou - ble to
fi - cient shall be your sup - ply; The flame shall not hurt you, his on - ly de -

said, To all who for ref - uge to Je - sus have fled?
stand, Up - held by his right - eous, om - ni - po - tent hand.
bless, And sanc - ti - fy you in your deep - est dis - tress.
sign Your dross to con - sume and your gold to re - fine.

Text: Richard Keen, c. 1787, attr.
Music: FOUNDATION, 11 11 11 11, *The Sacred Harp*, 1844; arr. Russell Woollen, b. 1923

253. FOR ALL THE SAINTS

1. For all the saints who from their la - bors rest, Who thee by
2. Thou wast their rock, their for - tress and their might; Thou, Lord, their
3. O may thy sol - diers, faith - ful, true and bold, Fight as the
4. O blest com - mun - ion, fel - low-ship di - vine! We fee - bly
5. But lo! there breaks a yet more glo - rious day; The saints tri -
6. From earth's wide bounds, from o - cean's far - thest coast, Through gates of

faith be - fore the world con - fessed, Thy name, O Je - sus,
cap - tain in the well-fought fight: Thou, in the dark - ness
saints who no - bly fought of old, And win, with them, the
strug - gle, they in glo - ry shine; Yet all are one in
um - phant rise in bright ar - ray; The King of glo - ry
pearl streams in the count - less host, Sing - ing to Fa - ther,

be for - ev - er blest.
drear, their one true light.
vic - tor's crown of gold. Al - le - lu - ia! Al - le - lu - ia!
thee, for all are thine.
pass - es on his way.
Son and Ho - ly Ghost.

Text: William Walsham How, 1823–1897
Music: SINE NOMINE, Ralph Vaughan Williams, 1872–1958, ©

254. THE VOICE OF GOD SPEAKS BUT OF PEACE

1. The voice of God speaks but of peace; Peace for all his friends,
2. Mer - cy and faith - ful - ness have met, Jus - tice and peace em - braced.
3. The Lord shall bless our dai - ly work; Earth shall yield its fruit.

For those who turn to him their heart, His help is al - ways near.
God's love smile up from earth be - low, His jus - tice down from heav'n.
Jus - tice shall march be - fore the Lord, And peace be - hind his steps.

REFRAIN

Re - store a - gain our life, O Lord, May we re - joice in you!

Your mer - cy let us see, O Lord, Give us your sav - ing help.

Text: *Psalm 85;* adapt. Henry Bryan Hayes, O.S.B., b. 1920, ©
Music: SHALOM, 85 85 with Refrain, Henry Bryan Hayes, O.S.B., b. 1920, ©

255. What Wondrous Love Is This?

1. What won-drous love is this, O my soul, O my soul? What won-drous love is this, O my soul? What won-drous love is this That caused the Lord of bliss To bear the dread-ful curse for my

2. To God and to the Lamb I will sing, I will sing; To God and to the Lamb I will sing; To God and to the Lamb Who is the great I AM, While mil-lions join the theme, I will

3. And when from death I'm free, I'll sing on, I'll sing on; And when from death I'm free, I'll sing on; And when from death I'm free, I'll sing and joy-ful be, And through e-ter-ni-ty I'll sing

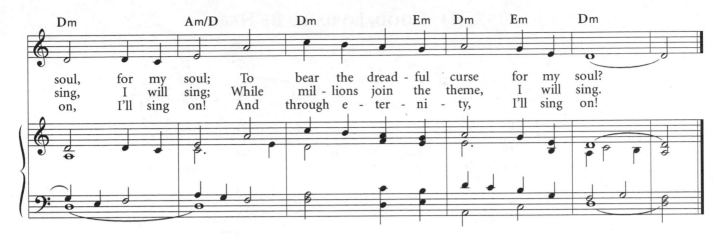

soul, for my soul; To bear the dread - ful curse for my soul?
sing, I will sing; While mil - lions join the theme, I will sing.
on, I'll sing on! And through e - ter - ni - ty, I'll sing on!

Text: Rev. Alexander Means, 1801–1853
Music: WONDROUS LOVE, 12 9 12 12 9, American Folk Hymn, c. 1835; arr. Sr. Theophane Hytrek, O.S.F., b. 1915, ©

256. TAKE UP YOUR CROSS

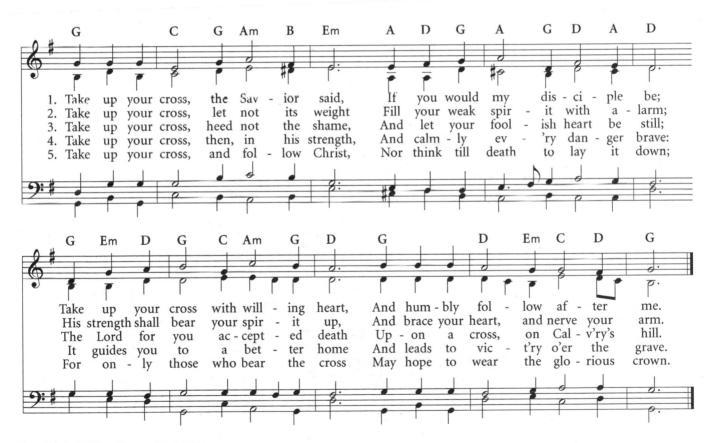

1. Take up your cross, the Sav - ior said, If you would my dis - ci - ple be;
2. Take up your cross, let not its weight Fill your weak spir - it with a - larm;
3. Take up your cross, heed not the shame, And let your fool - ish heart be still;
4. Take up your cross, then, in his strength, And calm - ly ev - 'ry dan - ger brave:
5. Take up your cross, and fol - low Christ, Nor think till death to lay it down;

Take up your cross with will - ing heart, And hum - bly fol - low af - ter me.
His strength shall bear your spir - it up, And brace your heart, and nerve your arm.
The Lord for you ac - cept - ed death Up - on a cross, on Cal - v'ry's hill.
It guides you to a bet - ter home And leads to vic - t'ry o'er the grave.
For on - ly those who bear the cross May hope to wear the glo - rious crown.

Text: Charles William Everest, 1814–1877
Music: BRESLAU, 88 88, Felix Mendelssohn-Bartholdy, 1809–1847, attr.

257. 'TIS GOOD, LORD, TO BE HERE

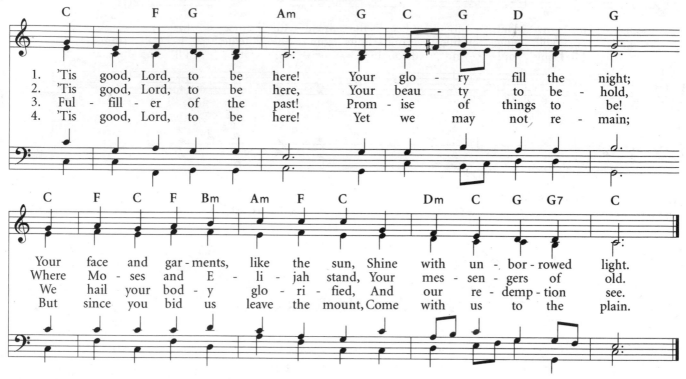

1. 'Tis good, Lord, to be here! Your glo - ry fill the night;
2. 'Tis good, Lord, to be here, Your beau - ty to be - hold,
3. Ful - fill - er of the past! Prom - ise of things to be!
4. 'Tis good, Lord, to be here! Yet we may not re - main;

Your face and gar - ments, like the sun, Shine with un - bor - rowed light.
Where Mo - ses and E - li - jah stand, Your mes - sen - gers of old.
We hail your bod - y glo - ri - fied, And our re - demp - tion see.
But since you bid us leave the mount, Come with us to the plain.

Text: Joseph A. Robinson, 1858–1933
Music: SWABIA, 66 86, Johann J. Speiss, 1715–1772; adapt. William H. Havergal, 1793–1870

258. PRAISE TO THE HOLIEST IN THE HEIGHT

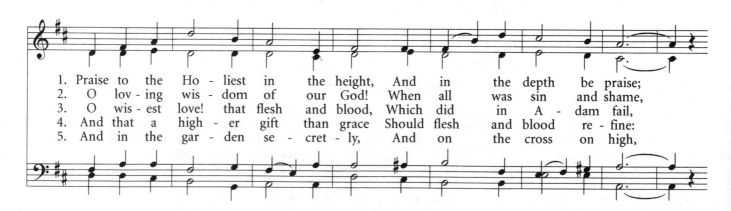

1. Praise to the Ho - liest in the height, And in the depth be praise;
2. O lov - ing wis - dom of our God! When all was sin and shame,
3. O wis - est love! that flesh and blood, Which did in A - dam fail,
4. And that a high - er gift than grace Should flesh and blood re - fine:
5. And in the gar - den se - cret - ly, And on the cross on high,

In all his words most won - der - ful, Most sure in all his ways!
A sec - ond A - dam to the fight And to the res - cue came.
Should strive a - fresh a - gainst the foe, Should strive, and should pre - vail;
God's pres - ence and his ver - y self, And es - sence all di - vine.
Should teach his breth - ren, and in - spire To suf - fer and to die.

Text: John Henry Newman, 1801–1890, alt.
Music: NEWMAN, 86 86, Richard Runciman Terry, 1865–1938

259. God Is My Strong Salvation

1. God is my strong sal - va - tion; What foe have I to fear?
2. Though hosts en - camp a - round me, Firm in the fight I stand;
3. Place on the Lord re - li - ance, My soul, with cour - age wait;
4. His might thy heart shall strength - en, His love thy joy in - crease;

In dark - ness and temp - ta - tion My light, my help is near.
What ter - ror can con - found me, With God at my right hand?
His truth be thine af - fi - ance, When faint and des - o - late.
Mer - cy thy days shall length - en; The Lord will give thee peace.

Text: James Montgomery, 1771–1854; *Psalm 27*, para.
Music: DINWIDDIE, Henry Bryan Hayes, O.S.B., b. 1920, ©

260. PRAISE WE OUR GOD WITH JOY

1. Praise we our God with joy
And gladness never ending;
Angels and saints with us
Their grateful voices blending.
He is our Shepherd true,
With watchful care and love;
His mercies without end
He showers from above.

2. He is our Shepherd true;
With watchful care unsleeping,
On us, his erring sheep,
An eye of pity keeping;
So with a mighty arm
The bonds of sin he breaks,
And to our burdened hearts
In words of peace he speaks.

3. Graces in copious stream
From that pure fount are welling,
Where, in our heart of hearts,
Our God has set his dwelling.
His word our lantern is,
His peace our comfort still,
His sweetness all our rest,
Our law, our life, his will.

4. All praise and thanks to God
The Father now be given,
The Son, and Holy Ghost
Enthroned in highest heaven;
The one, eternal God,
Whom earth and heav'n adore;
For thus it was, is now,
And shall be evermore.

Text: Frederick Oakeley, 1802–1880, et al.; tr. Catherine Winkworth, 1827–1878, alt.
Music: DARMSTADT, 67 67 66 66, Ahasuerus Fritsch, 1629–1701 (Melody); acc. J. S. Bach, 1685–1750

261. Let All Mortal Flesh Keep Silence

Let all mor-tal flesh keep si - lence, And with fear and trem - bling stand;
King of kings, yet born of Mar - y, As of old on earth he stood,
Rank on rank the host of heav - en Spreads its van-guard on the way,
At his feet the six - winged ser - aph; Cher - u - bim with sleep - less eye,

Pon - der noth-ing earth - ly mind - ed, For with bless-ing in his hand
Lord of lords in hu - man ves - ture, In the Bo - dy and the Blood
As the Light of Light de - scend - eth From the realms of end - less day,
Veil their fac - es to the Pres - ence, As with cease-less voice they cry,

Christ our God to earth de - scend - eth, Our full hom-age to de - mand.
He will give to all the faith - ful His own self for heav'n - ly food.
That the pow'rs of hell may van - ish As the dark-ness clears a - way.
"Al - le - lu - ia, Al - le - lu - ia, Al - le - lu - ia, Lord most high!"

Text: Liturgy of St. James; tr. Gerard Moultrie, 1829–1885
Music: PICARDY, 87 87 87, French Carol, 17th cent.

262. Go Make of All Disciples

1. "Go make of all dis-ci-ples": We hear the call, O Lord,
That comes from you, our Fa-ther, In your e-ter-nal Word.
In-spire our ways of learn-ing Through ear-nest, fer-vent prayer,
And let our dai-ly liv-ing Re-veal you ev-'ry-where.

2. "Go make of all dis-ci-ples": Bap-tiz-ing in the name
Of Fa-ther, Son, and Spir-it From age to age the same.
We call each new dis-ci-ple To fol-low you O Lord,
Re-deem-ing soul and bod-y. By wa-ter and the Word.

3. "Go make of all dis-ci-ples": We at your feet would stay
Un-til each life's vo-ca-tion Ac-cents your ho-ly way.
We cul-ti-vate the na-ture God plants in ev-'ry heart,
Re-veal-ing in our wit-ness The Mas-ter Teach-er's art.

4. "Go make of all dis-ci-ples": We wel-come your com-mand;
"Lo, I am with you al-ways": We take your guid-ing hand.
The task looms large be-fore us, We fol-low with-out fear.
In heav'n and earth your pow-er Shall bring God's king-dom here.

Text: Leon M. Adkins, b. 1896, alt., © 1955, 1964 Abingdon Press, from *The Book of Hymns*
Music: ELLACOMBE, 76 76 76 76, *Gesangbuch de Herzogl, Wirtemberg*, 1784

263. FORTH IN THE PEACE OF CHRIST

1. Forth in the peace of Christ we go; Christ to the world with
2. Priests of the world, Christ sends us forth The world of time to
3. Christ's are our lips, his word we speak; Proph - ets are we whose
4. We are the Church; Christ bids us show That in his Church all

joy we bring; Christ in our minds, Christ on our
con - se - crate, This world of sin by grace to
deeds pro - claim Christ's truth in love that we may
na - tions find Their hearth and home, where Christ re -

lips, Christ in our hearts, the world's true King.
heal, Christ's world in Christ to re - cre - ate.
be Christ in the world to spread Christ's name.
stores True peace, true love, to hu - man - kind.

Text: James Quinn, S.J., b. 1919, © 1969
Music: LLEDROD, 88 88, *Welsh Caniadan y Cyssegr*, 1893

401

264. Only Begotten, Word of God Eternal

1. Only begotten, Word of God eternal, Lord of creation, merciful and mighty, Hear now your servants, when their tuneful voices Rise to your presence.

2. Holy this temple where our Lord is dwelling, This is none other than the gate of heaven; Strangers and pilgrims, seeking homes eternal, Pass through its portals.

3. Lord, we beseech you, as we throng your temple, By your past blessings, by your present bounty, Smile on your children, and with tender mercy Hear our petitions.

4. God in Three Persons, Father ever-living, Son co-eternal, ever-blessed Spirit, Yours be the glory, praise and adoration, Now and forever.

Text: Anon., Latin, 9th cent.; tr. Maxwell J. Blacker, 1822–1888
Music: ISTE CONFESSOR, 11 11 11 5, Rouen Church Melody, *Processionale*, 1763; arr. Carl Schalk, b. 1929, ©

265. GREAT ARTIST OF THE UNIVERSE

1. Great art-ist of the u - ni - verse, Of land and sea and skies,
2. O gra-cious giv - er of all good, Of warmth and food and light,
3. Con-sol-ing pres - ence in our pain And shel - t'ring dusk of night,

Cre - a - tor God of all that is, Our source and fi - nal prize!
O ev-er-flow - ing stream of love, Our long - ing hearts' de - light!
Trans-form-ing ra - diance of the dawn, Our hope and fu - ture bright!

Re - ceive our hymns of grate - ful praise, Re - ceive our joy - ful song.
Re - ceive our psalms of joy - ful praise, The wor - ship of our song.
Re - ceive our psalms and hymns of praise, Re - joic - ing in our song.

O may we bless you all our days, Give thanks our whole life long!
O may we bless you all our days, Give thanks our whole life long!
O may we bless you all our days, Give thanks our whole life long!

Text: Sr. Delores Dufner, O.S.B., ©
Music: Sr. Terri Nehl, O.S.B.; acc. Sr. Ellen Cotone, O.S.B., ©

266. O HOLY CITY, SEEN OF JOHN

1. O ho-ly cit-y, seen of John, Where Christ, the Lamb, does reign,
2. O shame to us who rest con-tent While lust and greed for gain
3. Give us, O God, the strength to build The cit-y that has stood
4. Al-read-y in the mind of God That cit-y ris-es fair:

With-in those four-square walls shall come No night, nor need, nor pain,
In street and shop and ten-e-ment Wring gold from hu-man pain,
Too long a dream, whose laws are love, Whose ways, the com-mon good,
Lo, how its splen-dor chal-leng-es The souls that great-ly dare:

And where the tears are wiped from eyes That shall not weep a-gain.
And bit-ter lips in blind de-spair Cry, "Christ has died in vain."
And where the shin-ing sun be-comes God's grace for hu-man good.
Yea, bids us seize the whole of life And build its glo-ry there.

Text: Russell Bowie, 1882–1969, alt.
Music: MORNING SONG (CONSOLATION), 86 86 86, Elkanah Kelsay Dare, 1782–1826; acc. C. Winfred Douglas, 1867–1944, ©

267. PRAISE CHRIST JESUS, KING OF HEAVEN

1. Praise Christ Jesus, King of heaven; To his throne due tribute bring;
2. Praise him for his grace and favor To our forebears in distress;
3. Father-like he tends and spares us; Well our weaknesses he knows;
4. Angels, help us to adore him; You behold him face to face;

Ransomed, healed, restored, forgiven, Gratefully your love now sing:
Praise him truly who is ever, Slow to chide and swift to bless:
In his hands he gently bears us, Rescues us from all our foes,
Sun and moon, bow down before him, Dwellers all in time and space.

Alleluia! Alleluia! Praise the everlasting King.
Alleluia! Alleluia! Glorious in his faithfulness.
Alleluia! Alleluia! Widely yet his mercy flows.
Alleluia! Alleluia! Praise with us the God of grace.

Text: Henry F. Lyte, 1793–1847, alt.
Music: LAUDA ANIMA, 87 87 87, John Goss, 1800–1880

268. God Is Working His Purpose Out

1. God is work-ing his pur-pose out As year suc-ceeds to
2. From ut-most east to ut-most west, Wher - ev - er foot has
3. March we forth in the strength of God, With the ban-ner of Christ un-
4. All we can do is worth-less toil Un - less God bless-es the

year: God is work-ing his pur-pose out, And the
trod, By the mouth of man - y mes-sen - gers Goes
furled, That the light of the glo - rious gos-pel of truth May
deed; Vain - ly we hope for the har - vest - tide Till

time is draw-ing near; Near - er and near - er draws the time, The
forth the voice of God; Give ear to me, you con - ti - nents, You
shine through-out the world: Fight we the fight with sor - row and sin To
God gives life to the seed; Yet near - er and near - er draws the time, The

time that shall sure - ly be, When the earth shall be filled with the glo - ry of God As the
isles, give ear to me, That the earth may be filled with the glo - ry of God As the
set their cap - tives free, That the earth may be filled with the glo - ry of God As the
time that shall sure - ly be, When the earth shall be filled with the glo - ry of God As the

1. - 3. *4.*

wa - ters cov - er the sea.
wa - ters cov - er the sea.
wa - ters cov - er the sea.
wa - ters cov - er the sea.

Text: Arthur C. Ainger, 1841–1919, alt.
Music: PURPOSE, Irregular, Martin Shaw, 1875–1958, ©

269. A GRACIOUS GUIDE THE LORD

1. A gracious guide the Lord, the Shepherd strong who came To walk in valleys dark and call us each by name. A Shepherd always there, whose voice and accent known Brings out all that are his and claims them for his own.

2. His flock a wanderer's race, who thirst and hunger still For what they hardly dream to find beyond the hill, They look for one who knows where verdant pastures lie And tables spread, and cup, where gentle streams run by.

3. He knows the desert well, its silence and its dread, The hope of human-kind to turn its stones to bread. A desert man himself who knew the stars at sight, The lonely Shepherd he an *Ab-ba* cry by night.

4. O Shepherd of our souls be there where we can hear Your strong and constant voice that casts away our fear. And in that fold where you shall make your flocks be one. Then time shall be no more and all our work be done.

Text: Thomas P. O'Malley, S.J., b. 1930, ©
Music: GELUKKIG, 12 12 12 12, Old Dutch Melody, acc. Edward J. McKenna, b. 1939, ©

270. Praise the Lord! Ye Heavens, Adore Him

1. Praise the Lord! Ye heav'ns, a - dore him; Praise him, an - gels in the height;
2. Praise the Lord! For he is glo - rious; Nev - er shall his prom - ise fail;
3. Praise the Lord! His might con - fess - ing; Laud him ev - er; bless his name.
4. Wor - ship, hon - or, glo - ry, bless - ing, Lord, we of - fer un - to thee;

Sun and moon, re - joice be - fore him; Praise him, all ye stars of light.
God hath made his saints vic - to - rious; Sin and death shall not pre - vail.
An - gels, saints, his throne ad - dress - ing, Wor - ship him, his pow'r pro - claim.
Young and old, thy praise ex - press - ing, In glad hom - age bend the knee.

Praise the Lord! For he hath spo - ken; Worlds his might - y voice o - beyed;
Praise the God of our sal - va - tion! Hosts on high, his pow'r pro - claim;
Praise the Lord of all cre - a - tion, Praise the glo - rious King of might;
All the saints in heav'n a - dore thee; We would bow be - fore thy throne:

Laws which nev - er shall be bro - ken For their guid - ance he hath made.
Heav'n and earth and all cre - a - tion, Laud and mag - ni - fy his name.
Praise the God of our sal - va - tion; Praise him, praise him in the height.
As thine an - gels serve be - fore thee, So on earth thy will be done.

Text: From the *Foundling Hospital Collection*, 1796, vv. 1 & 2; Edward Osler, 1798–1863, v. 3; John Dunn, v. 4, ©
Music: AUSTRIA, Franz Josef Haydn, 1732–1809

271. As Those Who Serve

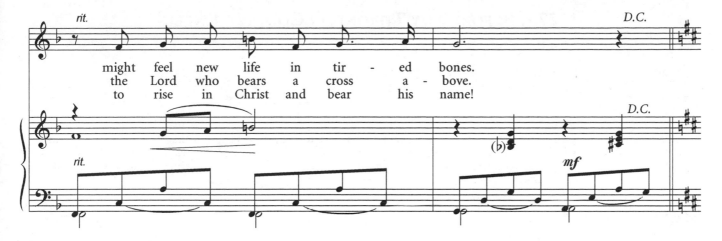

Text: Edward J. McKenna, b. 1939, ©
Music: BERNARDIN, Irregular, Edward J. McKenna, b. 1939, ©

272. Let My Heart Be Glad

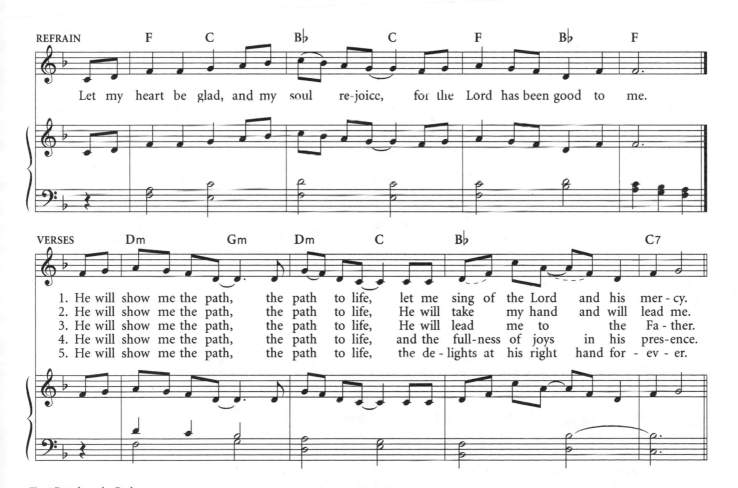

Text: Based on the Psalms
Music: LET MY HEART BE GLAD, Irregular, Eugene Englert, © 1989 Eugene Englert

273. Before Thy Throne, O God, We Kneel

1. Be - fore thy throne, O God, we kneel: Give us a con - science quick to feel, A read - y mind to un - der - stand The mean - ing of thy chas - t'ning hand; What - e'er the pain and shame may be; Bring us, O Fa - ther, near - er thee.

2. Search out our hearts and make us true; Help us to give to all their due. From love of plea - sure, lust of gold, From sins which make the heart grow cold, Wean us and train us with thy rod; Teach us to know our faults, O God.

3. For sins of heed - less word and deed, For pride am - bi - tious to suc - ceed, From craft - y trade and sub - tle snare, For lives be - reft of pur - pose high, For - give, for - give, O Lord, we cry.

4. Let the fierce fires which burn and try, Our in - most spir - its pu - ri - fy: Con - sume the ill; purge out the shame; O God, be with us in the flame; A new - born peo - ple may we rise, More pure, more true, more no - bly wise.

Text: William Boyd Carpenter, 1841–1918, alt.
Music: COLERAINE (LA SCALA SANTA), 88 88 88, *La Scala Santa*, 1681; harm. A. Gregory Murray, b. 1905, ©

412

274. ALL HAIL THE POWER OF JESUS' NAME

1. All hail the pow'r of Jesus' name! Let angels prostrate fall;
2. Crown him, you martyrs of our God, Who from his altar call:
3. Hail him, you heirs of David's line, Whom David Lord did call,
4. You chosen seed of Israel's race, A remnant weak and small,

Bring forth the royal diadem, And crown him Lord of all,
Praise him whose way of pain you trod, And crown him Lord of all,
The God incarnate, Man divine, And crown him Lord of all,
Hail him who saved you by his grace, And crown him Lord of all,

Bring forth the royal diadem, And crown him Lord of all.
Praise him whose way of pain you trod, And crown him Lord of all.
The God incarnate, Man divine, And crown him Lord of all.
Hail him who saved you by his grace, And crown him Lord of all.

5. As sinners let us not forget,
The wormwood and the gall;
We spread our trophies at his feet,
And crown him Lord of all,
We spread our trophies at his feet,
And crown him Lord of all.

6. Let ev'ry tribe and ev'ry tongue
Respond to Jesus' call,
Lift high the universal song,
And crown him Lord of all,
Lift high the universal song,
And crown him Lord of all.

Text: Edward Perronet, 1726–1792; tr. John Rippon, 1751–1836, alt.
Music: CORONATION, 86 86 86, Oliver Holden, 1765–1844

275. Rejoice, the Lord Is King

1. Re - joice, the Lord is King! Your Lord and King a - dore!
2. The Lord, our Sav - ior, reigns, The God of truth and love:
3. His king - dom can - not fail, He rules o'er earth and heav'n;
4. Re - joice in glo - rious hope! Our Lord the judge shall come

Re - joice, give thanks, and sing, And tri - umph ev - er - more:
When he had purged our stains, He took his seat a - bove:
The keys of death and hell Are to our Je - sus giv'n:
And take his serv - ants up To their e - ter - nal home:

Lift up your heart, lift up your voice! Re - joice, a - gain I say, re - joice!

Text: Charles Wesley, 1707–1788
Music: DARWALL'S 148TH, 66 66 88, John Darwall, 1731–1789 (Melody and Bass); acc. William Henry Monk, 1823–1889, alt.

276. O King of Might and Splendor

1. O King of might and splen - dor, Cre - a - tor most a - dored,
2. Thy bod - y thou hast giv - en, Thy blood thou hast out - poured

This sac - ri - fice we ren - der To thee as sov - 'reign Lord.
That sin might be for - giv - en, O Je - sus, lov - ing Lord.

May these our gifts be pleas - ing Un - to thy maj - es - ty.
As now with love most ten - der Thy death we cel - e - brate.

Man - kind from sin re - leas - ing Who have of - fend - ed thee.
Our lives in self - sur - ren - der To thee we con - se - crate.

Text: Tr. A. Gregory Murray, O.S.B., b. 1905, ©
Music: PASSION CHORALE, 76 76 76 76, Hans Leo Hassler, 1564–1612; acc. J. S. Bach, 1685–1750; adapt. Sr. Mary Teresine Hytrek, O.S.F., ©

277. ALL GOOD GIFTS

REFRAIN

All good gifts a - round us are sent from heav'n a - bove, so thank the Lord, O

thank the Lord for all his love.

First ending

Final ending

love, for all his love.

VERSES

1. We plow the fields and scat - ter the good seed on the land,
2. He sends the snow in win - ter, the warmth to swell the grain,
3. He on - ly is the mak - er of all things near and far;
4. The winds and waves o - bey him, by him the birds are fed;
5. We thank you, then, dear Fa - ther, for all things bright and good,
6. And all that we can of - fer your bound - less love im - parts,

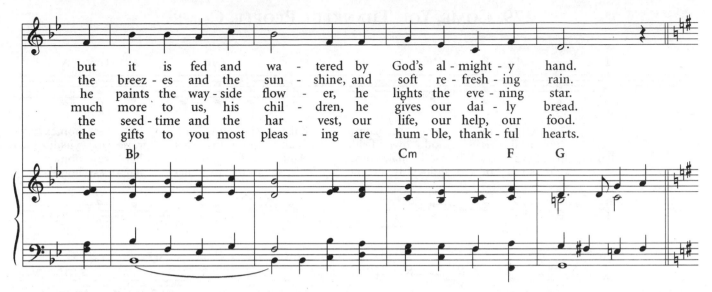

but it is fed and wa - tered by God's al - might - y hand.
the breez - es and the sun - shine, and soft re - fresh - ing rain.
he paints the way - side flow - er, he lights the eve - ning star.
much more to us, his chil - dren, he gives our dai - ly bread.
the seed - time and the har - vest, our life, our help, our food.
the gifts to you most pleas - ing are hum - ble, thank - ful hearts.

Text: Matthias Claudius, 1740–1815; tr. Jane Montgomery Campbell, 1817–1878
Music: Eugene Englert, ©

278. To Christ, the Prince of Peace

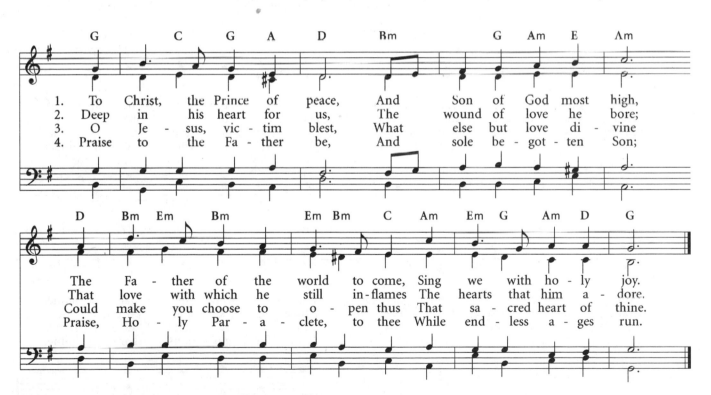

1. To Christ, the Prince of peace, And Son of God most high,
2. Deep in his heart for us, The wound of love he bore;
3. O Je - sus, vic - tim blest, What else but love di - vine
4. Praise to the Fa - ther be, And sole be - got - ten Son;

The Fa - ther of the world to come, Sing we with ho - ly joy.
That love with which he still in - flames The hearts that him a - dore.
Could make you choose to o - pen thus That sa - cred heart of thine.
Praise, Ho - ly Par - a - clete, to thee While end - less a - ges run.

Text: *Summi parentis filis*, Paris Breviary, 1736; tr. Edward Caswall, 1814–1876, alt.
Music: SINGENBERGER, 66 86, Otto A. Singenberger, 1944; arr. Richard W. Hillert, b. 1923
Music arrangement © 1978, J. S. Paluch, Inc.

279. Come, You Thankful People, Come

1. Come, you thank-ful peo-ple, come, Raise the song of har-vest home:
2. All the world is God's own field, Fruit un-to his praise to yield;
3. For the Lord our God shall come, And shall take his har-vest home;
4. E-ven so, Lord, quick-ly come To your fi-nal har-vest home;

All is safe-ly gath-ered in, Ere the win-ter storms be-gin;
Wheat and tares to-geth-er sown, Un-to joy or sor-row grown:
From his field shall in that day All of-fens-es purge a-way;
Gath-er all your peo-ple in, Free from sor-row, free from sin;

God, our Mak-er, does pro-vide For our wants to be sup-plied;
First the blade, and then the ear, Then the full corn shall ap-pear:
Give his an-gels charge at last In the fire the tares to cast,
There, for-ev-er pu-ri-fied, In your pres-ence to a-bide;

Come to God's own tem-ple, come, Raise the song of har-vest home.
Grant, O har-vest Lord, that we Whole-some grain and pure may be.
But the fruit-ful ears to store In his gar-ner ev-er-more.
Come, with all your an-gels, come, Raise the glo-rious har-vest home.

Text: Henry Alford, 1810–1871
Music: ST. GEORGE'S WINDSOR, 77 77 77 77, George Elvey, 1816–1893

280. We Gather Together

1. We gather together to ask the Lord's blessing; He chastens and hastens his will to make known; The wicked oppressing now cease from distressing, Sing praises to his name; he forgets not his own.

2. Beside us to guide us, our God with us joining, Ordaining, maintaining his kingdom divine; So from the beginning the fight we were winning: Thou, Lord, wast at our side, all glory be thine!

3. We all do extol thee, thou leader triumphant, And pray that thou still our defender will be; Let thy congregation escape tribulation: Thy name be ever praised! O Lord, make us free!

Text: Tr. Omer Westendorf, b. 1916, alt.
Music: KREMSER, 12 11 12 11, Dutch Traditional Melody; arr. Edward Kremser, 1838–1914

281. Now Thank We All Our God

1. Now thank we all our God, With heart, and hands, and voic - es,
2. O may this boun - teous God through all our life be near us!
3. All praise and thanks to God The Fa - ther now be giv - en,

Who won-drous things hath done, In whom his world re - joic - es:
With ev - er - joy - ful hearts And bless - ed peace to cheer us:
The Son, and him who reigns With them in high - est heav - en,

Who from our moth - er's arms Has blessed us on our way
And keep us in his grace, And guide us when per - plex'd,
The one e - ter - nal God, Whom heav'n and earth a - dore;

With count - less gifts of love, And still is ours to - day.
And free us from all ills In this world and the next.
For thus it was is now, And shall be, ev - er - more.

Text: Martin Rinkart, 1586–1649; tr. Catherine Winkworth, 1827–1878, alt.
Music: NUN DANKET, 67 67 66 66, Johann Crüger, 1598–1662; harm. William Henry Monk, 1823–1889, after Felix Mendelssohn-Bartholdy, 1809–1847.

282. GIVE THANKS TO GOD ON HIGH

1. Give thanks to God on high For saints of oth-er days, Whose hope it was to live and die In love's con-sum-ing blaze, For Christ and his king-dom, His glo-ry and his praise.

2. (Their) vi-sion long-ful-filled, Our prayer is still the same; Up-on their work of faith to build, Their word of truth pro-claim, For Christ and his king-dom, And for his ho-ly name.

3. (New) tasks to-day are ours Who serve a world in pain, New calls to chal-lenge all our pow'rs Of heart and hand and brain, For Christ and his king-dom, While life and breath re-main.

4. (Give) thanks to God on high For all the fu-ture sends, In praise of Christ to live and die Who calls his serv-ants friends, For Christ and his king-dom, Whose glo-ry nev-er ends!

Text: Timothy Dudley–Smith, b. 1926
Music: CEOLA, 66 86 66, Edward J. McKenna, b. 1939, ©

421

283. FATHER, WE THANK THEE WHO HAST PLANTED
284. BREAD OF THE WORLD, IN MERCY BROKEN

1. Fa - ther, we thank thee who hast plant - ed Thy ho - ly name with - in our hearts.
2. Watch o'er thy Church, O Lord, in mer - cy, Save it from e - vil, guard it still,

1. Bread of the world, in mer - cy bro - ken, Wine of the soul, in mer - cy shed,

Knowl - edge and faith and life im - mor - tal Je - sus thy Son to us im - parts.
Per - fect it in thy love, u - nite it, Cleansed and con - formed un - to thy will.

By whom the words of life were spo - ken, And in whose death our sins are dead:

Thou, Lord, didst make all for thy pleas - ure, Didst give us food for all our days.
As grain, once scat - tered on the hill - sides, Was in this bro - ken bread made one,

Look on the heart by sor - row bro - ken, Look on the tears by sin - ners shed;

Giv - ing in Christ the Bread e - ter - nal; Thine is the pow'r, be thine the praise.
So from all lands thy Church be gath - ered In - to thy king - dom by thy Son.

And be thy feast to us the to - ken That by thy grace our souls are fed.

No. 283—Text: Greek, c. 11, tr. F. Bland Tucker, 1895–1984, rev., ©
No. 284—Text: Reginald Heber, 1783–1826
Music: RENDEZ A DIEU, 98 98 98 98, Louis Bourgeois, c. 1510–1561, attr.

285. DRAW NEAR AND TAKE THE BODY OF YOUR LORD

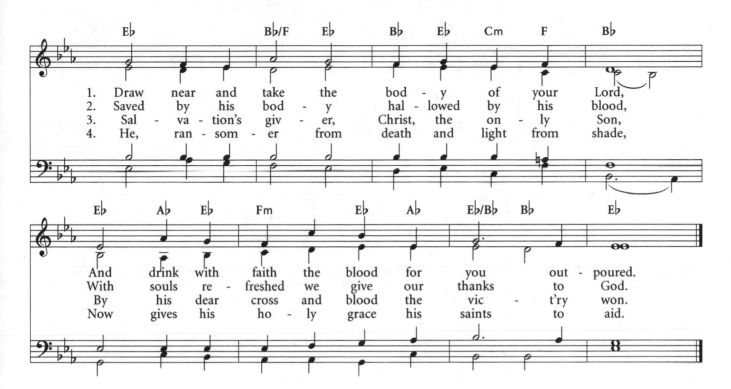

1. Draw near and take the bod-y of your Lord,
2. Saved by his bod-y hal-lowed by his blood,
3. Sal-va-tion's giv-er, Christ, the on-ly Son,
4. He, ran-som-er from death and light from shade,

And drink with faith the blood for you out-poured.
With souls re-freshed we give our thanks to God.
By his dear cross and blood the vic-t'ry won.
Now gives his ho-ly grace his saints to aid.

5. Let us approach
   with faithful hearts sincere,
   And take the pledges
   of salvation here.

6. The Lord in this world
   rules his saints, and shields,
   To all believers
   life eternal yields.

7. With heav'nly bread makes
   those who hunger whole,
   Gives living waters
   to the thirsting soul.

8. Before your presence, Lord,
   all people bow.
   In this your feast of love
   be with us now.

Text: Latin hymn, 7th cent.; tr. John M. Neale, 1818–1866, alt.
Music: COENA DOMINI, 10 10, Arthur S. Sullivan, 1842–1900

286. Gift of Finest Wheat

1. As when the shep-herd calls his sheep, They know and heed his voice,
2. With joy-ful lips we sing to you Our praise and grat-i-tude,
3. Is not the cup we bless and share The blood of Christ out-poured?
4. The mys-t'ry of your pres-ence, Lord, No mor-tal tongue can tell:
5. You give your-self to us, O Lord; Then self-less let us be,

So when you call your fam-'ly, Lord, We fol-low and re-joice.
That you should count us wor-thy, Lord, To share this heav'n-ly food.
Do not one cup, one loaf, de-clare Our one-ness in the Lord?
Whom all the world can-not con-tain Comes in our hearts to dwell.
To serve each oth-er in your name In truth and char-i-ty.

Text: Omer Westendorf, b. 1916
Music: EUCHARISTIC CONGRESS, 86 86 with Refrain, Robert E. Kreutz, b. 1922

287. COME, GATHER AT THE TABLE

1. Come, ga - ther at the ta - ble That Je - sus Christ has spread;
2. O come from farms and cit - ies, O come from toil and care;
3. Like flow - ers in a gar - den, We're dif - f'rent yet the same;

Come, drink the cup now of - fered, Come, eat the Ho - ly Bread.
In faith and hope now gath - er, This feast of love to share.
We long to be u - ni - ted In love to praise God's name.

O come and let us wor - ship. In Christ one Bod - y be:

"Do this in sa - cred mem - 'ry. In mem - o - ry of Me!"

Text: Jane Klimisch, O.S.B., © Sacred Heart Convent, Yankton, SD 57078
Music: AURELIA, 76 76 76 76, Samuel S. Wesley, 1810–1876

288. COME TO THE BANQUET

REFRAIN

This is the bread of life, This is the cup of joy; If you will eat from this ta - ble, Then you will nev - er die, then you will nev - er die.

VERSES

1. Come to the ban - quet of Je - sus; Come, eat the food that he gives;
2. Long in the past they ate man - na, Man - na that fell on the ground,
3. Christ showed the depth of his mer - cy, Christ showed the depth of his love,
4. I am the Bread from the heav - ens; My blood is of - fered for you;

Bread that will nour - ish the spir - it, Wine that will bright - en your soul.
Giv - ing them strength in the des - ert, Giv - ing great joy all a - round.
Giv - ing far bet - ter than man - na, Giv - ing us bread from a - bove.
Mine is a heart full of mer - cy, Mine are the words that are true.

Text: Willard F. Jabusch, b. 1930, ©
Music: Robert E. Kreutz, b. 1922, ©

289. Lord, Accept the Gifts We Offer

1. Lord, accept the gifts we offer At this Eucharistic feast.
2. May our souls be pure and spotless As the host of wheat so fine,
3. Take our gifts, almighty Father, Living God, eternal, true,

Bread and wine to be transformed now Through the work of Christ our priest.
May all stain of sin be crushed out, Like the grape that forms the wine,
Which we give through Christ, our Savior, Pleading here for us anew.

Take us, too, O Lord, transform us; be your grace in us increased.
As we, too, become partakers In this sacrifice divine.
Grant salvation to all present And our faith and love renew.

Text: Sr. Mary Teresine Hytrek, O.S.F., ©
Music: ST. THOMAS, 87 87 87, John F. Wade, 1711–1786; acc. Sr. Mary Teresine, O.S.F., ©

290. WHERE CHARITY AND LOVE PREVAIL

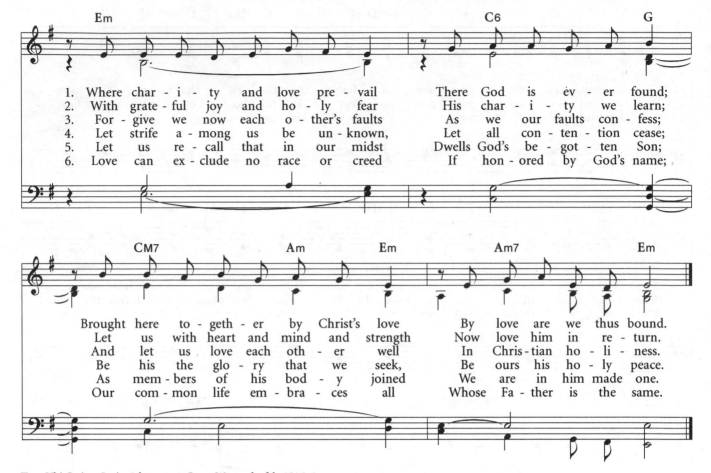

1. Where char-i-ty and love pre-vail There God is ev-er found;
2. With grate-ful joy and ho-ly fear His char-i-ty we learn;
3. For-give we now each o-ther's faults As we our faults con-fess;
4. Let strife a-mong us be un-known, Let all con-ten-tion cease;
5. Let us re-call that in our midst Dwells God's be-got-ten Son;
6. Love can ex-clude no race or creed If hon-ored by God's name;

Brought here to-geth-er by Christ's love By love are we thus bound.
Let us with heart and mind and strength Now love him in re-turn.
And let us love each oth-er well In Chris-tian ho-li-ness.
Be his the glo-ry that we seek, Be ours his ho-ly peace.
As mem-bers of his bod-y joined We are in him made one.
Our com-mon life em-bra-ces all Whose Fa-ther is the same.

Text: Ubi Caritas, Latin, 9th cent.; tr. Omer Westendorf, b. 1916, ©
Music: CHRISTIAN LOVE, 86 86, Paul Benoit, O.S.B., 1893–1979, ©

291. SEE US, LORD, ABOUT YOUR ALTAR

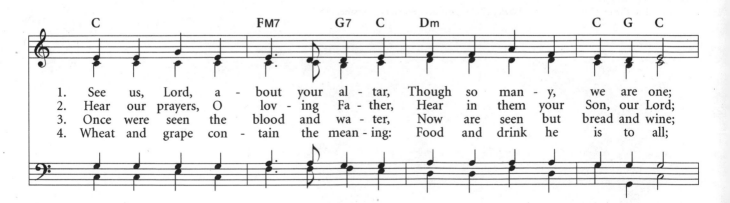

1. See us, Lord, a-bout your al-tar, Though so man-y, we are one;
2. Hear our prayers, O lov-ing Fa-ther, Hear in them your Son, our Lord;
3. Once were seen the blood and wa-ter, Now are seen but bread and wine;
4. Wheat and grape con-tain the mean-ing: Food and drink he is to all;

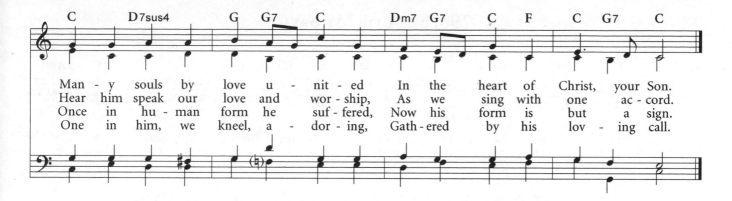

Man - y souls by love u - nit - ed In the heart of Christ, your Son.
Hear him speak our love and wor - ship, As we sing with one ac - cord.
Once in hu - man form he suf - fered, Now his form is but a sign.
One in him, we kneel, a - dor - ing, Gath - ered by his lov - ing call.

5. Hear us yet: so much is needful
   In our frail, disordered life;
   Stay with us and tend our weakness,
   Till that day of no more strife.

6. Members of his Mystic Body
   Now we know our prayer is heard,
   Heard by you because your children
   Have received the eternal Word.

Text: John Greally, b. 1934, alt., ©
Music: DRAKES BOUGHTON, 87 87, Edward William Elgar, 1857–1934, ©

292. O LORD, I AM NOT WORTHY

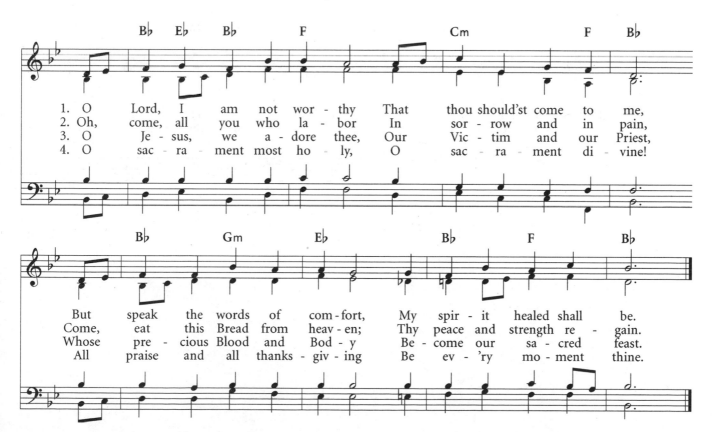

1. O Lord, I am not wor - thy That thou should'st come to me,
2. Oh, come, all you who la - bor In sor - row and in pain,
3. O Je - sus, we a - dore thee, Our Vic - tim and our Priest,
4. O sac - ra - ment most ho - ly, O sac - ra - ment di - vine!

But speak the words of com - fort, My spir - it healed shall be.
Come, eat this Bread from heav - en; Thy peace and strength re - gain.
Whose pre - cious Blood and Bod - y Be - come our sa - cred feast.
All praise and all thanks - giv - ing Be ev - 'ry mo - ment thine.

Text: Vv. 1 & 4, anon.; vv. 2 & 3, Irvin Udulutsch, O.F.M., Cap., ©
Music: NON DIGNUS (CLARIBEL), 76 76, *Burns* Traditional Melody

293. Soul of My Savior

1. Soul of my Sav-ior, sanc-ti-fy my breast; Bod-y of
2. Strength and pro-tec-tion may thy pas-sion be; O bless-ed
3. Guard and de-fend me from the foe ma-lign; In death's dread

Christ, be thou my sav-ing guest; Blood of my Sav-ior,
Je - sus, hear and an-swer me; Deep in thy wounds, Lord,
mo - ments make me on-ly thine; Call me and bid me

bathe me in thy tide, Wash me with wa-ter flow-ing from thy side.
hide and shel-ter me, So I shall nev-er, nev-er part from thee.
come to thee on high, Where I may praise thee with thy saints for aye.

Text: Pope John XXII, 1249–1334, attr.; tr. Edward Caswall, 1814–1878
Music: ANIMA CHRISTI, 10 10 10 10, William J. Maher, S.J., 1823–1877

294. Jesus, My Lord, My God, My All

1. Je - sus, my Lord, my God, my all, How can I love you as I ought?
2. Had I but Mar - y's sin - less heart, How I would love you, dear - est King!

And how re - vere this won - drous gift So far sur - pass - ing hope or thought?
O with what bursts of fer - vent praise Your good - ness, Je - sus, would I sing!

1.-2. O God of love, whom we a - dore, O make us love you

more and more; O make us love you more and more!

Text: Frederick William Faber, 1814–1863; adapt., ©
Music: SWEET SACRAMENT, 88 88 with Refrain, anon.; arr. Rev. Percy Jones, ©

295. HAIL OUR SAVIOR'S GLORIOUS BODY (ENGLISH)

1. Hail our Savior's glorious Body,
   Which his Virgin Mother bore;
   Hail the Blood which, shed for sinners,
   Did a broken world restore;
   Hail the sacrament most holy,
   Flesh and Blood of Christ adore!

2. To the Virgin, for our healing,
   His own Son the Father sends;
   From the Father's love proceeding
   Sower, seed and word descends;
   Wondrous life of Word incarnate
   With his greatest wonder ends.

3. On that paschal evening see him
   With the chosen twelve recline,
   To the old law still obedient
   In its feast of love divine;
   Love divine, the new law giving,
   Gives himself as bread and wine.

4. By his word the Word almighty
   Makes of bread his flesh indeed;
   Wine becomes his very life-blood;
   Faith God's living Word must heed!
   Faith alone may safely guide us
   Where the senses cannot lead!

5. Come, adore this wondrous presence;
   Bow to Christ, the source of grace!
   Here is kept the ancient promise
   Of God's earthly dwelling place!
   Sight is blind before God's glory,
   Faith alone may see his face!

6. Glory be to God the Father,
   Praise to his coequal Son,
   Adoration to the Spirit,
   Bond of love, in Godhead one!
   Blest be God by all creation
   Joyously while ages run! Amen.

Text: St. Thomas Aquinas, 1227–1274; tr. James D. Quinn, S.J., b. 1919, © 1969
Music: PANGE LINGUA GLORIOSI, 87 87 87, *Plainchant, Mode III;* acc. Eugene Lapierre, ©

296. Pange Lingua (Latin)

A - men.

1. Pange língua gloriósi
   Córporis mystérium,
   Sanguinísque pretiósi,
   Quem in mundi prétium
   Fructus ventris generósi
   Rex effúdit géntium.

2. Nobis datus, nobis natus
   Ex intácta Vírgine,
   Et in mundo conversátus,
   Sparso verbi sémine,
   Sui, moras incolátus
   Miro clausit órdine.

3. In suprémae nocte coenae,
   Recúmbens cum frátribus,
   Observáta lege plene
   Cibis in legálibus,
   Cibum turbae duodénae
   Se dat suis mánibus.

4. Verbum caro, panem verum
   Verbo carnem éfficit:
   Fitque sanguis Christi merum,
   Et si sensus déficit,
   Ad firmándum cor sincérum
   Sola fides súfficit.

5. Tantum ergo Sacraméntum
   Venerémur cérnui:
   Et antíquum documéntum
   Novo cedat rítui:
   Praestet fides suppleméntum
   Sénsuum deféctui.

6. Genitóri, Genitóque
   Laus et jubilátio,
   Salus, honor, virtus quoque
   Sit et benedíctio:
   Procedénti ab utróque
   Compar sit laudátio. Amen.

Text: St. Thomas Aquinas, 1227–1274; tr. James D. Quinn, S.J., b. 1919, © 1969
Music: PANGE LINGUA GLORIOSI, 87 87 87, *Plainchant, Mode III;* acc. Eugene Lapierre, ©

297. At That First Eucharist

1. At that first Eu - cha - rist be - fore you died, O Lord, you prayed that
2. For all your Church, O Lord, we in - ter - cede; O make our lack of
3. We pray for those who wan - der from the fold; O bring them back, Good
4. So, Lord, at length when sac - ra - ments shall cease, May we be one with

all be one in you; At this our Eu - cha - rist a - gain pre -
char - i - ty to cease; Draw us the near - er each to each, we
Shep - herd of the sheep, Back to the faith which saints be - lieved of
all your Church a - bove, One with your saints in one un - end - ing

side, And in our hearts your law of love re - new.
plead, By draw - ing all to you, O Prince of peace.
old, Back to the Church which still that faith does keep.
peace, One with your saints in one un - bound - ed love.

1.-4. Thus may we all one bread, one bod - y be, Through this blest sac - ra - ment of u - ni - ty.

Text: William Harry Turton, 1856–1938, alt.
Music: UNDE ET MEMORES, 10 10 10 10 with Refrain, William Henry Monk, 1823–1889, alt.

298. O Saving Victim
299. O Salutaris

1. O Sav-ing Vic-tim, o-p'ning wide, The gate of heav'n to us be-low!
2. To your great name be end-less praise, Im-mor-tal God-head, One in Three;
1. O sa-lu-tá-ris hó-sti-a, Quae cae-li pan-dis ó-sti-um:
2. U-ni tri-nó-que Dó-mi-no Sit sem-pi-ter-na gló-ri-a:

Our foes press on from ev-'ry side: Your aid sup-ply, your strength be-stow.
O grant us end-less length of days When our true na-tive land we see.
Bel-la pre-munt ho-stí-li-a, Da ro-bur fer au-xí-li-um.
Qui vi-tam si-ne tér-mi-no No-bis do-net in pá-tri-a.

Text: St. Thomas Aquinas, 1227–1274; tr. Edward Caswall, 1814–1878
Music: DUGUET, 88 88, Abbe Duguet, c. 1767

300. Tantum Ergo

1. Tan-tum er-go Sac-ra-mén-tum Ve-ne-ré-mur cér-nu-i:
2. Ge-ni-tó-ri Ge-ni-tó-que Laus et ju-bi-lá-ti-o,

Et an-tí-quam do-cu-mén-tum, No-vo ce-dat ri-tu-i:
Sa-lus, ho-nor, vir-tus quo-que Sit et be-ne-dí-cti-o:

Prae-stet fi-des sup-ple-mén-tum Sen-su-um de-féc-tu-i.
Pro-ce-dén-ti ab u-tro-que Com-par sit lau-dá-ti-o. A-men.

Text: St. Thomas Aquinas, 1227–1274
Music: *Plainchant, Mode III;* acc. Rev. Bartholomew Sayles, O.S.B., b. 1918, Sr. Cecile Gertkin, O.S.B., b. 1902, ©

301. On This Day of Sharing

1. On this day of shar-ing, Glad-ly do we come, / To the Lord's own ta - ble, Gath-ered here as one.
2. See the ta-ble lad-en, With the bread and wine, / Sign of Christ's own pres-ence, Pledge of love di - vine!
3. Food and drink sym-bol-ic, Of his life on earth: / Peace, good will to all earth, Prom-ised from his birth.
4. In the bread that's bro-ken, In the wine that's poured, / Be the name of Je - sus Ev - er-more a - dored!

Christ, our broth-er, make us one in thee, One in hope e - ter-nal, One in char-i - ty.

5. May our will be pleasing
To thy majesty;
Keep our love most faithful,
Lord, we ask of thee. *Refrain*

6. Daily may we serve you;
Worship you as God;
Follow as you lead us
In the way you trod. *Refrain*

7. Praise be to the Father,
Honor to the Son;
To the Holy Spirit,
Be the glory one! *Refrain*

Text: *Polish Hymnal;* tr. Br. Gerard Wojchowski, O.S.G., 1925–1995, ©
Music: BGDZIC POZDNOWIONA, 65 65 with Refrain, John Siedlecki, 1878

302. Lord and God, Devoutly You I Now Adore

1. Lord and God, de-vout - ly you I now a-dore, Hid-den un-der sym - bols,
2. Sight and touch and taste, Lord, are in you de-ceiv'd; By your Word a - lone, Lord,
3. All that you have taught me, I do firm-ly hold, Tru - er words than yours, Lord,
4. As I con-tem-plate you, sen-ses fail to see, But my heart and soul, Lord,

bread and wine no more;
can you be be - liev'd;
nev - er have been told.
with my faith a - gree.

1. - 4. Strength-en deep with - in me, faith and trust in you,

And with - in my heart, Lord, love for you re - new.

Text: Tr. Roger Schoenbechler, O.S.B.
Music: ADORE TE DEVOTE, Irregular

303. O Jesus, We Adore Thee

1. O Jesus, we a - dore thee, Who in thy love di - vine,
2. O Jesus, we a - dore thee, Our Vic - tim and our Priest,
3. O Jesus, we a - dore thee, Our Sav - ior and our King,
4. O Jesus, we a - dore thee, Come, live in us, we pray,
5. O come, all you who la - bor In sor - row and in pain;

Con - ceal thy might - y God - head In forms of bread and wine.
Whose pre - cious blood and bod - y Be - come our sa - cred feast.
And with the saints and an - gels A hum - ble hom - age bring.
That all our thoughts and ac - tions Be thine a - lone to - day.
Come, eat this bread from heav - en, Your peace and strength re - gain.

1.-5. O Sac - ra - ment most ho - ly, O Sac - ra - ment di - vine,

All praise and all thanks - giv - ing Be ev - 'ry mo - ment thine!

Text: Irvin Udulutsch, O.F.M., Cap., b. 1920, ©
Music: FULDA MELODY, 76 76 with Refrain, Fulda Melody; adapt. and arr. Roger Nachtwey, b. 1930, ©

304. AVE MARIA

A-ve Ma-rí - a, * gra-ti-a ple - na, Dó-mi-nus te-cum, be-ne-dí-cta tu

in mu-li-é-ri-bus, et be-ne-dí-ctus fru-ctus ven-tris tu-i, Je-sus.

San-cta Ma-rí - a, Ma-ter De - i, o-ra pro no - bis pec-ca-

tó-ri-bus, nunc et in ho - ra mor-tis no - strae. A-men.

Text: *Luke 1:26-37*
Music: AVE MARIA, Irregular, *Plainchant, Mode I;* acc. Rev. Bartholomew Sayles, O.S.B., b. 1918, Sr. Cecile Gertken, O.S.B., b. 1902, ©

305. Immaculate Mary

1. Im - mac - u - late Mar - y, your prais - es we sing.
2. In heav - en the bless - ed your glo - ry pro - claim,
3. We pray for the Church, our true moth - er on earth,

You reign now in splen - dor with Je - sus our King.
On earth now we your chil - dren in - voke your sweet name.
And beg you to watch o'er the land of our birth.

REFRAIN

A - ve, A - ve, A - ve, Ma - ri - a! A - ve, A - ve, Ma - ri - a!

Text: Anon.; tr. Irwin Udulutsch, O.F.M., Cap., b. 1920, ©
Music: LOURDES (MASSABIELLE), 65 65 with Refrain, Grenoble, 1882; acc. Irwin Udulutsch, O.F.M., Cap., b. 1920, alt., ©

306. THE GOD WHOM EARTH AND SEA AND SKY

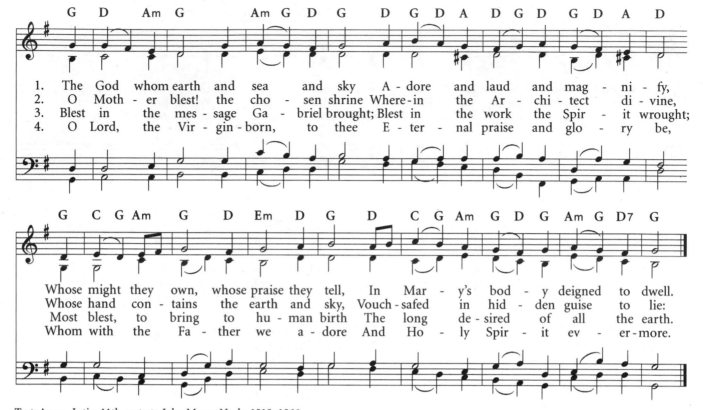

1. The God whom earth and sea and sky A-dore and laud and mag-ni-fy,
2. O Moth-er blest! the cho-sen shrine Where-in the Ar-chi-tect di-vine,
3. Blest in the mes-sage Ga-briel brought; Blest in the work the Spir-it wrought;
4. O Lord, the Vir-gin-born, to thee E-ter-nal praise and glo-ry be,

Whose might they own, whose praise they tell, In Mar-y's bod-y deigned to dwell.
Whose hand con-tains the earth and sky, Vouch-safed in hid-den guise to lie:
Most blest, to bring to hu-man birth The long de-sired of all the earth.
Whom with the Fa-ther we a-dore And Ho-ly Spir-it ev-er-more.

Text: Anon., Latin, 11th cent.; tr. John Mason Neale, 1818–1866
Music: WAREHAM, 88 88, Johann H. Schein, 1586–1630; harm. J. S. Bach, 1685–1750

307. HYMN TO THE SORROWFUL MOTHER

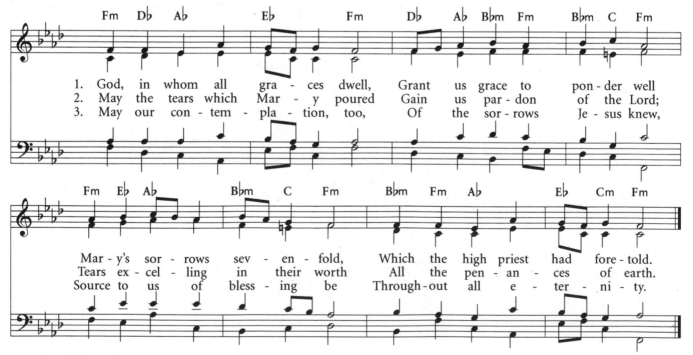

1. God, in whom all gra-ces dwell, Grant us grace to pon-der well
2. May the tears which Mar-y poured Gain us par-don of the Lord;
3. May our con-tem-pla-tion, too, Of the sor-rows Je-sus knew,

Mar-y's sor-rows sev-en-fold, Which the high priest had fore-told.
Tears ex-cel-ling in their worth All the pen-an-ces of earth.
Source to us of bless-ing be Through-out all e-ter-ni-ty.

Text: *Palunabella;* tr. Edward Caswall, 1814–1878, alt.
Music: NUN KOMM DER HEIDEN HEILAND, 77 77, *Plainchant,* adapt. Erfurt, 1524; acc. Seth Calvisius, 1594, adapt. Sr. Mary Teresine, O.S.F., ©

308. My Soul Gives Glory to the Lord

1. My soul gives glo - ry to the Lord; In God my Sav - ior I re - joice. My low - li - ness he did re - gard, Ex - alt - ing me by his own choice.
2. Now ev - 'ry one shall call me blest, For he has done great things for me. Of all great names his is the best, For it is ho - ly; strong is he.
3. His mer - cy goes to all who fear. From age to age and to all parts. His arm of strength to all is near; He scat - ters those who have proud hearts.
4. He casts the might - y from their thrones And rais - es those of low de - gree; He feeds the hun - gry as his own; The rich de - part in pov - er - ty.
5. He raised his serv - ant Is - ra - el, Re - mem - b'ring his e - ter - nal grace. As from of old he did fore - tell To A - bra - ham and all his race.
6. O Fa - ther, Son, and Spir - it blest In three - fold name you are a - dored; To you be ev - 'ry prayer ad - dressed, From age to age the on - ly Lord.

Text: *Luke 1:48-55*
Music: O WALY, WALY, 98 98, English Traditional Melody

443

309. HAIL, HOLY QUEEN ENTHRONED ABOVE

1. Hail, ho-ly Queen en-throned a-bove, O Ma-ri-a!
2. Our life, our sweet-ness here be-low, O Ma-ri-a!
3. As ex-iles all to you we cry, O Ma-ri-a!
4. Turn then, most gra-cious ad-vo-cate, O Ma-ri-a!

Hail, Queen of mer-cy and of love, O Ma-ri-a!
Our hope in sor-row and in woe, O Ma-ri-a!
Come, soothe with hope our mis-er-y, O Ma-ri-a!
Towards us your eyes com-pas-sion-ate, O Ma-ri-a!

REFRAIN

Tri-umph all ye Cher-u-bim, Sing with us ye Ser-a-phim,

Heav'n and earth re-sound the hymn: Sal-ve, Sal-ve, Sal-ve, Re-gi-na!

5. O gentle, loving, holy one, O Maria!
   Make us each day more like your Son, O Maria! Triumph ...

6. And when from death to life we've passed, O Maria!
   Show us your Son, our Lord, at last, O Maria! Triumph ...

Text: Hermanus Contractus, 1013–1054, attr.; vv. 1, 2, 5, and refrain tr. anon., c. 1884, alt., vv. 3, 4, 6 para. by editors of Collegeville Hymnal, ©
Music: SALVE REGINA COELITUM, 8 4 8 4 777 4 5

310. SING OF MARY

1. Sing of Mar - y, pure and low - ly, Vir - gin moth - er un - de - filed,
2. Sing of Je - sus, Son of Mar - y, In the home at Naz - a - reth,
3. Sing of Mar - y, sing of Je - sus, Ho - ly moth - er's ho - lier Son.
4. Joy - ful Moth - er, full of glad - ness, In your arms your Lord was borne.
5. Glo - ry be to God the Fa - ther, Glo - ry be to God the Son,

Sing of God's own Son most ho - ly, Who be - came her lit - tle child.
Toil and la - bor can - not wea - ry Love en - dur - ing un - to death.
From his throne in heav'n he sees us, There he calls us ev - 'ry one,
Mourn - ful Moth - er, full of sad - ness, All your heart with pain was torn.
Glo - ry be to God the Spir - it; Glo - ry to the Three in One.

Fair - est child of fair - est moth - er, God the Lord who came to earth,
Con - stant was the love he gave her, Though he went forth from her side,
Where he wel - comes home his moth - er To a place at his right hand,
Glo - ri - ous Moth - er, now re - ward - ed With a crown at Je - sus' hand,
From the heart of bless - ed Ma - ry, From all saints the song as - cends.

Word made flesh, our ver - y broth - er, Takes our na - ture by his birth.
Forth to preach, and heal, and suf - fer, Till on Cal - va - ry he died.
There his faith - ful ser - vants gath - er, There the bless - ed vic - tors stand.
Age to age your name re - cord - ed Shall be blest in ev - 'ry land.
And the Church the strain re - ech - oes Un - to earth's re - mot - est ends.

Text: Rev. Roland F. Palmer, S.S.J.E., 1891–1985, ©
Music: PLEADING SAVIOR (SALTASH), 87 87 87 87, acc. *Plymouth Collection*, New York, 1855

311. O Most Holy One
312. O Sanctissima

1. O most ho - ly one, O most low - ly one, Lov - ing Vir - gin, Ma -
2. Vir - gin ev - er fair, Moth - er, hear our prayer, Look up - on us, Ma -

1. O sanc - tís - si - ma, O pi - ís - si - ma, Dul - cis Vir - go, Ma -
2. Vir - go, ré - spi - ce, Ma - ter, á - spi - ce, Au - di nos, O Ma -

ri - a! Moth - er, Maid of fair - est love, La - dy, Queen of all a - bove,
ri - a! Bring to us your treas - ure, Grace be - yond all meas - ure;
rí - a! Ma - ter a - má - ta, In - te - me - rá - ta,
rí - a! Tu me - di - cí - nam Por - tas di - ví - nam,

REFRAIN

O - ra, o - ra pro no - bis!

Text: Anon.; tr. Charles W. Leland, C.S.B., ©
Music: SICILIAN MARINER'S, 10 7 10 7, Sicilian Traditional Melody, 18th cent.; acc. Healey Willian, 1880–1968

313. O Mary, Our Mother

1. O Mar-y, our moth-er, to you do we come; In all our af-
2. O Mar-y, our moth-er, be gra-cious to all; When bur-dened with
3. O Mar-y, our moth-er, so lov-ing, so mild; You love us as

flic-tions, your love is our home. Your heart is so gen-tle, so
sad-ness, to you do we call. In sor-row, in dark-ness, O
dear-ly as you loved your Child. In life let us ev-er be

lov-ing, so mild; You will not re-ject an-y sup-pli-ant child.
be at our side; For you are our moth-er, our com-fort and guide.
faith-ful and true, That death may but lead us to Je-sus and you.

Text: *Maria zu lieben;* Desmond A. Schmal, S.J., 1897–1958, alt.
Music: PADERBORN (MARIA ZU LIEBEN), 11 11 11 11, *Gesangbuch,* 1765

314. Daily, Daily Sing to Mary

1. Dai-ly, dai-ly sing to Mar-y, Sing with joy her prais-es due!
2. She is might-y in her plead-ing, Ten-der in her lov-ing care;
3. Sing my tongue, the Vir-gin's hon-ors, Who for us her mak-er bore,
4. All my sens-es, heart, af-fec-tions, Strive to sound her glo-ry forth.

All her feasts, her ac-tions hon-or, With the heart's de-vo-tion true.
Ev-er watch-ful, un-der-stand-ing, All our sor-rows she will share.
For the curse of old in-flict-ed, Peace and bless-ing to re-store.
Spread a-broad the sweet me-mo-rials Of the Vir-gin's price-less worth.

Lost in won-d'ring con-tem-pla-tion, Be her maj-es-ty con-fessed!
Ad-vo-cate and lov-ing Moth-er, Me-di-a-trix of all grace!
Sing in songs of praise un-end-ing, Sing the world's ma-jes-tic Queen;
Where the voice of mu-sic thrill-ing, Where the tongues of el-o-quence,

Call her Moth-er, call her Vir-gin, Hap-py Moth-er Vir-gin blest!
Heav-en's bless-ings she dis-pens-es On our sin-ful hu-man race.
Wea-ry not nor faint in tell-ing All the gifts that earth has seen.
That can ut-ter hymns be-fit-ting All her match-less ex-cel-lence?

5. All our joys do flow from Mary
All then join her praise to sing.
Trembling sing the Virgin Mother,
Mother of our Lord and King.
While we sing her awesome glory,
Far above our fancy's reach,
Let our hearts be quick to offer
Love the heart alone can teach.

Text: St. Bernard of Cluny, c. 1150, attr.; Henry Bittleston, 1818–1886; alt. Irvin Udulutsch, O.F.M., Cap., b. 1920, ©
Music: ALLE TAGE SING UND SAGE, 87 87 87 87, Traditional German Melody; acc. Sr. Mary Teresine, O.S.F., ©

315. AMERICA THE BEAUTIFUL

1. O beau-ti-ful for spa-cious skies, For am-ber waves of grain,
2. O beau-ti-ful for pil-grim feet, Whose stern, im-pas-sioned stress
3. O beau-ti-ful for he-roes proved In lib-er-at-ing strife,
4. O beau-ti-ful for pa-triot dream That sees be-yond the years

For pur-ple moun-tain maj-es-ties A-bove the fruit-ed plain!
A thor-ough-fare for free-dom beat A-cross the wil-der-ness!
Who more than self their coun-try loved, And mer-cy more than life!
Thine al-a-bas-ter cit-ies gleam, Un-dimmed by hu-man tears!

A-mer-i-ca! A-mer-i-ca! God shed his grace on thee,
A-mer-i-ca! A-mer-i-ca! God mend thine ev-'ry flaw,
A-mer-i-ca! A-mer-i-ca! May God thy gold re-fine,
A-mer-i-ca! A-mer-i-ca! God shed his grace on thee,

And crown thy good with broth-er-hood From sea to shin-ing sea.
Con-firm thy soul in self-con-trol, Thy lib-er-ty in law.
Till all suc-cess be no-ble-ness, And ev-'ry gain di-vine.
And crown thy good with broth-er-hood From sea to shin-ing sea.

Text: Katherine Lee Bates, 1859–1929
Music: MATERNA, 86 86 86 86, Samuel Augustus Ward, 1848–1903

449

316. BATTLE HYMN OF THE REPUBLIC

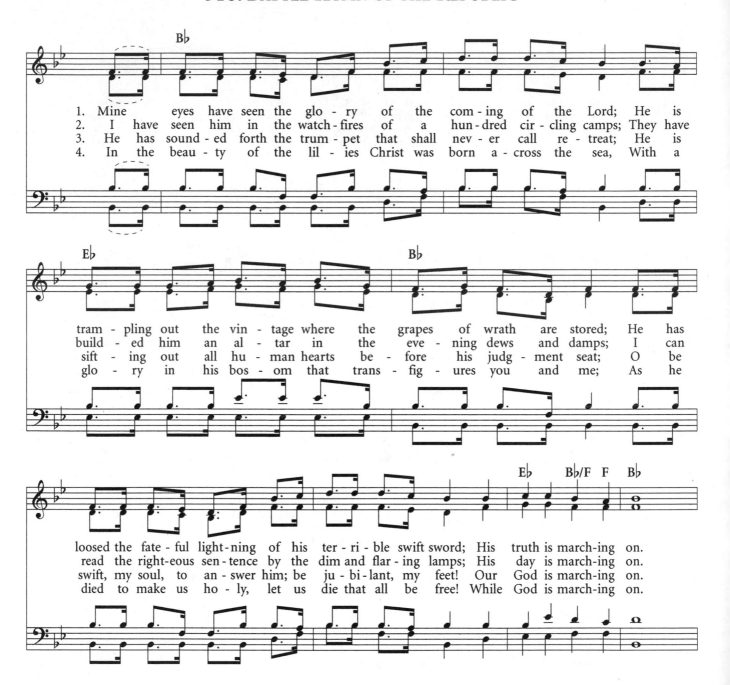

1. Mine   eyes have seen the glo - ry   of   the   com - ing   of   the   Lord;   He   is
2. I   have   seen   him   in   the watch - fires   of   a   hun - dred   cir - cling camps; They have
3. He   has   sound - ed   forth   the   trum - pet   that   shall   nev - er   call   re - treat;   He   is
4. In   the   beau - ty   of   the   lil - ies Christ   was   born   a - cross   the   sea,   With   a

tram - pling   out   the   vin - tage where   the   grapes   of   wrath   are   stored;   He   has
build - ed   him   an   al - tar   in   the   eve - ning   dews   and   damps;   I   can
sift - ing   out   all   hu - man hearts   be - fore   his   judg - ment   seat;   O   be
glo - ry   in   his   bos - om   that   trans - fig - ures   you   and   me;   As   he

loosed   the   fate - ful   light - ning   of   his   ter - ri - ble swift sword;   His   truth is march - ing   on.
read   the   right - eous sen - tence   by   the   dim   and   flar - ing   lamps;   His   day   is march - ing   on.
swift,   my   soul,   to   an - swer   him;   be   ju - bi - lant,   my   feet!   Our   God   is march - ing   on.
died   to   make   us   ho - ly,   let   us   die that all   be   free!   While   God   is march - ing   on.

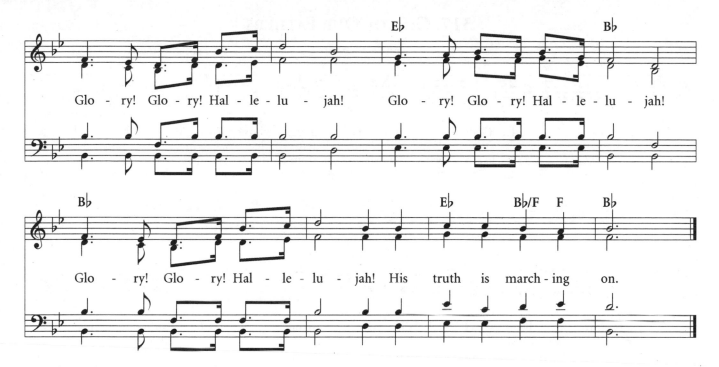

Glo - ry! Glo - ry! Hal - le - lu - jah! Glo - ry! Glo - ry! Hal - le - lu - jah!

Glo - ry! Glo - ry! Hal - le - lu - jah! His truth is march - ing on.

Text: Julia Ward Howe, 1819–1910
Music: BATTLE HYMN OF THE REPUBLIC, 15 15 15 6 with Refrain, John William Steffe, c. 1911, attr.

317. GOD OF OUR FATHERS

1. God of our fa - thers, whose al - might - y hand
2. Thy love di - vine hath led us in the past,
3. From war's a - larms, from dead - ly pes - ti - lence,
4. Re - fresh thy peo - ple on their toil - some way,

Leads forth in beau - ty all the star - ry band Of shin - ing worlds in
In this free land by thee our lot is cast; Be thou our rul - er,
Be thy strong arm our ev - er sure de - fense; Thy true re - li - gion
Lead us from night to nev - er - end - ing day; Fill all our lives with

splen - dor through the skies, Our grate - ful songs be - fore thy throne a - rise.
guard - ian, guide, and stay, Thy word our law, thy paths our cho - sen way.
in our hearts in - crease, Thy boun - teous good - ness nour - ish us in peace.
love and grace di - vine, And glo - ry, laud, and praise be ev - er thine.

Text: Daniel Crane Roberts, 1841–1907
Music: NATIONAL HYMN, 10 10 10 10, George William Warren, 1828–1902

452

318. AMERICA

1. My country, 'tis of thee, Sweet land of liberty, Of thee I
2. My native country, thee, Land of the noble free, Thy name I
3. Let music swell the breeze, And ring from all the trees Sweet freedom's
4. Our fathers' God to thee, Author of liberty, To thee we

sing; Land where my fathers died, Land of the pilgrims' pride,
love; I love thy rocks and rills, Thy woods and templed hills;
song: Let mortal tongues awake; Let all that breathe partake;
sing: Long may our land be bright With freedom's holy light;

From ev'ry mountainside Let freedom ring.
My heart with rapture thrills Like that above.
Let rocks their silence break, The sound prolong.
Protect us by thy might, Great God, our King.

Text: Samuel Francis Smith, 1808–1895
Music: AMERICA, 664 6664, anon.

453

319. Eternal Father, Strong to Save

1. E - ter - nal Fa - ther, strong to save, Whose arm has bound the rest - less wave, Who
2. O Christ, the Lord of hill and plain O'er which our traf - fic runs a - main By
3. O Spir - it, whom the Fa - ther sent To spread a - broad the fir - ma - ment; O
4. O Trin - i - ty of love and power, Our broth - ers shield in dan - ger's hour; From

bids the might - y o - cean deep Its own ap - point - ed lim - its keep: To
moun - tain pass or val - ley low; Wher - ev - er, Lord, your peo - ple go, Pro -
Wind of heav - en, by your might Save all who dare the ea - gle's flight, And
rock and tem - pest, fire and foe, Pro - tect them where - so - e'er they go; Thus

you we pray most ear - nest - ly For those in per - il on the sea.
tect them by your guard - ing hand From ev - ery per - il on the land.
keep them by your watch - ful care From ev - ery per - il in the air.
ev - er - more with thanks shall we Give praise from air and land and sea. A - men.

Text: William Whiting, 1825–1878, alt., sts. 1, 4; Robert Nelson Spencer, 1877–1961, sts. 2, 3
Music: MELITA, 88 88 88 88, John Bacchus Dykes, 1823–1876

INDEX OF FIRST LINES AND COMMON TITLES

INDEX OF SERVICE MUSIC

INDEX OF TUNE NAMES

ACKNOWLEDGMENTS

460

GREGORIAN CHANT PSALMODY

Simplified and Adapted to the Accentuation of the English Language
with Modal Accompaniments

Fr. Bartholomew Sayles, O.S.B., and Sr. Cecile Gertken, O.S.B.

*   This sign is used after the middle cadence.

\+   This sign after a word is used only in verses of extended length. It points out a drop (flex) in the voice to a lower pitch on the word accent. The flex when used appears only in the first half of a psalm or canticle verse. The majority of psalms do not use the flex note(s). In such cases the "measure" with the reciting tone followed by the flex note(s) is omitted.

＿   A line under a syllable points out the first note of the middle or final cadence.

( )   The extra note(s) in parentheses are used for words or combinations of words where the word accent at the flex or cadence is either second last or third last.

N.B.   The first "measure" or the two "pick-up" notes at the beginning of each tone are used <u>only</u> with the refrain or antiphon and also with each line of a canticle. These two notes are <u>not</u> used with the lines of the psalm. Each line of the psalm begins on the reciting tone.